TIME FOR KIDS ALMANAC 2003

with INFORMATION PLEASE®

Holly Hartman
Editor

Aaron Derr
Managing Editor

TIME FOR KIDS .COM

AOL keyword: TFK

FACT MONSTER™
from **Information Please®**

infoplease.com   factmonster.com

Unless otherwise noted, all information in this book
comes from FactMonster.com

TIME® FOR KIDS
ALMANAC 2003
with
INFORMATION PLEASE®

INFORMATION PLEASE

EDITOR: Holly Hartman
CONTRIBUTING EDITORS, SPORTS: Gerry Brown, John Gettings, Michael Morrison
CONTRIBUTOR: David P. Johnson, Jr.
FACT-CHECKING AND PROOFREADING: Ann-Marie Imbornoni
EDITORIAL ADVISER: Borgna Brunner
SENIOR VICE PRESIDENT, LEARNING NETWORK: Elizabeth Buckley Kubik

TIME FOR KIDS

MANAGING EDITOR: Claudia Wallis
PRESIDENT: Leanna Landsmann

PRESIDENT, TIME LEARNING VENTURES: Keith Garton
EDITOR: Aaron Derr
CONTRIBUTING EDITOR: Peter McGullam
PHOTOGRAPHY EDITOR: Sandy Perez
MAPS: Joe Lertola

ART DIRECTION AND DESIGN: Raúl Rodriguez and Rebecca Tachna for R studio T

TIME INC. HOME ENTERTAINMENT

PRESIDENT: Rob Gursha
VICE PRESIDENT, BRANDED BUSINESSES: David Arfine
EXECUTIVE DIRECTOR, MARKETING SERVICES: Carol Pittard
DIRECTOR, RETAIL & SPECIAL SALES: Tom Mifsud
DIRECTOR OF FINANCE: Tricia Griffin
MARKETING DIRECTOR: Kenneth Maehlum
ASSISTANT DIRECTOR: Ann Marie Ross
RETAIL MANAGER: Bozena Szwagulinski
PREPRESS MANAGER: Emily Rabin

SPECIAL THANKS TO: Suzanne DeBenedetto, Robert Dente, Gina Di Meglio, Peter Harper, Natalie McCrea, Jessica McGrath, Jonathan Polsky, Mary Jane Rigoroso, Steven Sandonato, Niki Whelan

Published by TIME For Kids Books
Time Inc.
1271 Avenue of the Americas
New York, New York 10020

First Edition

ISSN: 1534-5718
ISBN: 1-929049-52-8

"TIME For Kids" is a trademark of Time Inc. We welcome your comments and suggestions about TIME For Kids Books. Please write to us at:
TIME For Kids Books
Attention: Book Editors
PO Box 11016
Des Moines, IA 50336-1016

If you would like to order any of our hardcover Collector's Edition books, please call us at 1-800-327-6388 (Monday through Friday 7:00 a.m.-8:00 p.m. or Saturday 7:00 a.m.-6:00 p.m. Central Time).

Please visit our website at
www.TimeBookstore.com

Table of Contents

Charlotte's Web

E. B. White
Garth Williams

3

I'm on page 154.

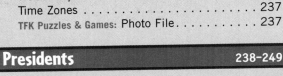

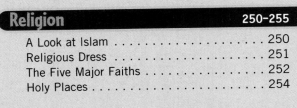

Austin ✪   Houston

America's Heroes

ON SEPTEMBER 11, 2001, walls at the Pentagon and the World Trade Center crumbled to the ground after the worst terrorist attacks in America's history. Such destruction, though, did not crush the spirit of the American people. Heroism was on display throughout the country. Here's a look at just a few of the people who performed selfless acts of courage and kindness from sea to shining sea.

Passengers of United Airlines Flight 93

Thomas Burnett Jr., 38, called his wife from United Airlines Flight 93 and told her to tell authorities that a hijacking was underway. Investigators think Burnett and other passengers may have stopped the plane from hitting its intended target—the White House or Camp David, the President's retreat. Instead, Flight 93 crashed into a Pennsylvania field. There were no survivors.

The People of the United States of America

Across the country, kids and adults held candlelight vigils to honor victims of the attacks. Millions of dollars were raised to help the victims' families. An entire nation came together out of respect for those whose lives were lost.

Policemen and Firefighters

New York City's 13,000 firefighters worked tirelessly to extinguish fires at the World Trade Center and to save lives. The New York City Police Department and the Port Authority Police Department both sent policemen to help people at the scene. Sadly, hundreds of firefighters and policemen were lost when the buildings collapsed.

9

The War Against Terror

Seventeen days after the terrorist attacks shocked America, the U.S. flexed its military muscle. Fighter planes roared into the air and bombed targets in Afghanistan. Operation Enduring Freedom was underway. The United States was striking back at terrorism.

President George W. Bush ordered the attacks after Afghanistan's rulers, the Taliban, refused to meet demands to hand over Osama bin Laden. Bin Laden was the main suspect in the attacks on the United States.

The U.S. attack focused on destroying terrorist training camps and Taliban command centers. The U.S. was successful in breaking apart bin Laden's network and forcing out the rulers who were protecting bin Laden and his fellow terrorists.

Although the United States met its goal of bringing down the Taliban, some American lives were lost in the process. And much of Afghanistan's capital, Kabul, was destroyed. "We are a peaceful nation, but the only way to pursue peace is to pursue those who threaten it," said President Bush.

The horror of September 11 united much of the world against terrorism. British troops were sent to the region to support Operation Enduring Freedom. "Sometimes, to safeguard peace, we have to fight," said British Prime Minister Tony Blair.

The Winter

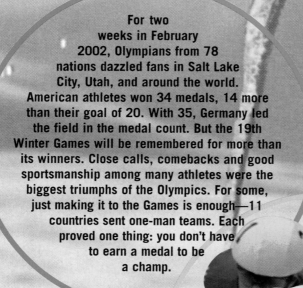

For two weeks in February 2002, Olympians from 78 nations dazzled fans in Salt Lake City, Utah, and around the world. American athletes won 34 medals, 14 more than their goal of 20. With 35, Germany led the field in the medal count. But the 19th Winter Games will be remembered for more than its winners. Close calls, comebacks and good sportsmanship among many athletes were the biggest triumphs of the Olympics. For some, just making it to the Games is enough—11 countries sent one-man teams. Each proved one thing: you don't have to earn a medal to be a champ.

Speed Skating: Apolo Anton Ohno won two medals, a gold and a silver. Ohno is so good at what he does, many expected him to win as many as four gold medals. But the 19-year-old wasn't at all disappointed with his performance. "If you give 100 percent, that's all you can do," he said.

Olympics

Aerials: Before the Games, Alisa Camplin had never won a major championship. But the Aussie underdog flipped her way to the top. She is the first Australian woman to win a gold medal in Winter Games history. After she won, she got a surprise: her mom and sister had flown in from Australia to watch her compete.

Bobsled: Jill Bakken and Vonetta Flowers sailed into Olympic history. Flowers is the first black athlete to win gold at a Winter Games. The former track star jumped into bobsledding after injuries dashed her hopes of competing in the Summer Olympics. Flowers is part of the first U.S. women's bobsled team to win gold!

Figure Skating: Sarah Hughes leaped from fourth place to first. The 16-year-old from Great Neck, New York, beat teammate Michelle Kwan, who fell during her program and slipped into third place. Irina Slutskaya of Russia won silver.

13

Enron

MR LAY

WE NEED ASSISTANCE NOW

It was the nation's seventh-largest company, employing 21,000 people in offices around the world. Its chief executive, **Kenneth Lay**, was among the most powerful American businessmen. How, then, did Enron suddenly go broke? How did it plunge so deeply into debt that it couldn't pay its bills and had to lay off more than 4,000 workers? Did it break the law by lying about its financial health?

Those were some of the questions asked by lawmakers in early 2002 in Washington, D.C. The FBI and at least 10 Congressional groups decided to investigate the giant Texas-based company.

Enron rose to power selling natural gas and electricity to consumers. But since its collapse, investigators have learned that Enron overstated its success. Partnerships with other companies were used to disguise losses and hide debt. Enron looked like a powerhouse, but it was a house of cards.

A NEW NATIONAL PARK

In 2000, President Bill Clinton approved a plan to create a new national park in Colorado. In 2002, a private conservation group called the Nature Conservancy helped move that plan along. The group agreed to purchase a 97,000-acre ranch and two 14,000-foot peaks in Southern Colorado for $31.28 million. The land lies next to Great Sand Dunes National Monument and Preserve, home of the tallest dunes in North America.

The Nature Conservancy will give the land to the federal government so that it can turn the 38,700-acre Great Sand Dunes and part of the ranch into the Great Sand Dunes National Park. The new park should open to the public by 2005.

Copy Cat!

She has big green eyes, perky pink ears and fluffy fur that just begs to be stroked. But "cc" (short for copy cat) is no ordinary kitten. Introduced by Texas scientists in February 2002, she is the world's first cloned cat, the product of a lab experiment.

Cloning is a high-tech way of breeding an animal that is an exact genetic copy of a parent. Scientists have already cloned mice, pigs, goats and sheep. Genetic Savings & Clone, the Texas company that paid for the research that produced cc, hopes to clone people's pets!

2000 mL

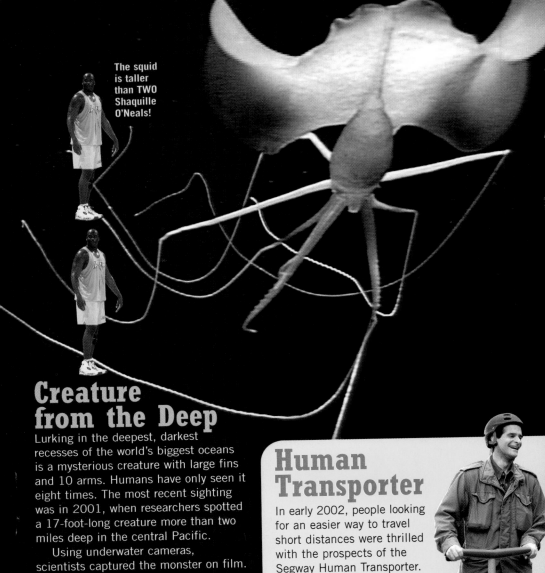

The squid is taller than TWO Shaquille O'Neals!

Creature from the Deep

Lurking in the deepest, darkest recesses of the world's biggest oceans is a mysterious creature with large fins and 10 arms. Humans have only seen it eight times. The most recent sighting was in 2001, when researchers spotted a 17-foot-long creature more than two miles deep in the central Pacific.

Using underwater cameras, scientists captured the monster on film. Now they are trying to determine exactly what it is. "I call it a mystery squid," says Michael Vecchione, who studies squids, octopuses and their relatives with the National Oceanic and Atmospheric Administration in Washington, D.C.

The creature, which ranges in length from 5 to 23 feet, is a new species of squid unlike any known species. Squids normally have eight arms plus two longer tentacles. The mystery squid has arms and tentacles that appear to be of about equal thickness and length. All 10 have "elbows" and at least some have suckers.

Human Transporter

In early 2002, people looking for an easier way to travel short distances were thrilled with the prospects of the Segway Human Transporter. Invented by millionaire Dean Kamen, the scooter is a two-wheeler that travels up to **17 miles an hour.** It weighs 65 to 80 pounds and costs up to $8,000. Kamen says it will change the way we travel. The Segway has no pedals, gears or motor. "It acts as an extension of your body," Kamen says. The Segway's sensors can tell which way its rider wants to go just by the way the rider leans. Riders can't fall off!

SKITTLES

Some cats go the distance for their owners. Take, for example, Skittles. Charmin Sampson lost the orange tabby in September 2001 while on a visit to Wisconsin. A heartbroken Sampson had to leave Wisconsin and return to her home in Minnesota without her pet. But on January 14, 2002, the cat came back. Skittles trekked 350 miles across two states! Aside from having raw paws, the cat was in purr-fect shape. Says Sampson: "It was a great present."

Minnesota

Wisconsin

The Concorde

Boom!

That's the sound a plane makes when it breaks the sound barrier at about 750 miles per hour. Finally, in 2002, Concorde jets were making that sound again. For the first time in more than 15 months, the world's fastest passenger jets were back in business. The planes had been grounded after a deadly crash in France on July 25, 2000. The Concorde is the only commercial jet that flies faster than the speed of sound. Both Air France and British Airways fly the supersonic jets.

Song & Screen

U2

U2 seems to have the luck of the Irish. Even before the 2002 Grammy Awards show, the Irish rock band already owned 10 Grammys. This year it received eight nominations—more than any other artist or group—and won four awards. When he isn't busy collecting awards and singing to sold-out stadiums, lead singer **Bono** meets with world leaders to persuade them to improve education, health care and opportunities for trade in poor African countries.

Bono, 41, is the founder of DATA (Debt, Aid, Trade for Africa). "He cares deeply about these issues and knows a lot about them," admits U.S. Treasury Secretary Paul O'Neill. Bono has always included political messages in the songs he writes, but that's no longer enough, he says: "I'm tired of dreaming. I'm into doing."

Alicia Keys

Alicia Keys, 21, is hitting all the right notes. She scored two 2002 American Music Awards for her debut album, *Songs in A Minor*, and went on to win five Grammy Awards. Keys began writing the music for *Songs* when she was only 14!

Keys credits her mom for her love of music, saying, "She told me I could quit anything, but I couldn't give up piano lessons." By age 9, the young musician was playing challenging classical pieces. She also graduated from high school at the top of her class. Keys says that music helped her deal with school pressures. And how does she handle the pressures of fame? "I'm still surrounded by people I love," she says.

Lil' Romeo

He likes to watch cartoons, shoot hoops and play with his dog. After all, says Lil' Romeo, "I'm a laid-back, regular kid." Well—not quite! The 12-year-old son of famous rapper Master P is traveling on his very own U.S. concert tour. Lil' Romeo is busy singing songs and promoting his hit CD *Lil' Romeo*.

The straight-A student writes many of his own tunes. He co-wrote *My Baby*. The song shot to the top of the charts, making Lil' Romeo the youngest solo artist ever to have a Number 1 single. Lil' Romeo says the best part of his job is "seeing the fans happy." He hopes to one day have yet another job: "I want to play basketball in the NBA."

Song&
Screen

Ice Age, Lilo and Stitch

Two groundbreaking animated movies did battle in 2002. The winner turned out to be movie audiences. Both *Ice Age* and *Lilo and Stitch* featured cutting-edge animation from the most modern computers available. *Ice Age* told the story of a group of prehistoric animals and their attempt to return a lost human child to its family. Disney's *Lilo and Stitch* was about a young Hawaiian girl who befriends an alien that doesn't know how to be friendly. *Ice Age* featured the voice of Ray Romano from TV's *Everybody Loves Raymond*. *Lilo and Stitch* featured classic songs from Elvis Presley. We can't decide which one we liked more!

What's the best thing about a hit movie? Chances are, you'll get to see a sequel sooner rather than later! And 2002 was a terrific year for "seconds," just in case the first movies weren't enough for you. Young actors Daryl Sabara and Alexa Vega returned in *Spy Kids 2: The Island of Lost Dreams*. Remember all those cool gadgets in the first *Spy Kids* movie? Well, on this island, none of those gadgets worked, and the brother-and-sister team had to come up with a new way to beat the bad guys. And who could forget *Harry Potter and the Chamber of Secrets*? Audiences certainly haven't forgotten about the young wizard, and they probably won't forget to show up for the third *Harry Potter* movie in 2003, either.

Movie Sequels

Maybe the only movie people were looking forward to in 2002 more than *Harry Potter* was the next *Star Wars* film. *Attack of the Clones*, a sequel to 1999's *The Phantom Menace*, once again blasted movie audiences to a galaxy far, far away. And even though it wasn't actually a sequel, *E.T.—The Extra Terrestrial 20th Anniversary Edition* felt twice as good as the original, with brand-new special effects.

23

Animals

From
TFK
magazine

By
Nicole
Iorio

Trainers, called mahouts, assist the elephants. But the design is up to each artist.

A Nose For the Arts

Talented Thai elephants find a new job

Watch out, Picasso. There are new artists on the scene. They're smart. They're strong. And they've got trunks full of talent!

Asian elephants have entered the arts, and some of their paintings already hang in museums. Elephants in Thailand are painting as a way of securing their own survival. Profits from their work support an elephant-conservation center.

For years, Thailand's elephants were used to carry heavy logs from rain forests. But when logging was banned in 1989 to preserve forests, hundreds of elephants lost their jobs and even their homes. The elephants could not be returned to their habitat because so many forests had been destroyed. Some were reduced to wandering the streets of Bangkok, Thailand's capital, begging for food!

Russian-born artists Vitaly Komar and Alex Melamid learned about the elephants' plight and decided to help. In 1998, they left their New York City homes for Thailand and set up the first elephant-art school in Lampang. Since then, the project has expanded to India and Bali. There are now about 100 elephant artists, and their paintings have sold for as much as $2,200!

Melamid says art lovers are drawn to the elephants' sweeping brushstrokes. Each elephant has his own painting style, but Melamid admits, "it's not about making breakthroughs in the art world. It's about helping these intelligent and sensitive creatures survive."

Where in the World Do Animals Live?

Animals live in the wild only where they can survive. Koala bears, for example, eat only the leaves of certain eucalyptus trees, so they must live in Australia, where these trees grow. All of the animals listed below can survive in the wild in only one place—and many of these animals are endangered.

NORTH AMERICA

Alligator, Arctic fox, Arctic tern, bald eagle, bison, California condor, California sea tern, musk ox, raven, snapping turtle, wild turkey

AFRICA

Aardvark, aardwolf, aye-aye, camel, chimpanzee, giraffe, green gecko, hippopotamus, hyena, indri, lion, ruffed lemur, spitting cobra, tsetse fly

AUSTRALIA AND NEW ZEALAND

Archie's frog, dingo, duck-billed platypus, kakapo, kiwi, koala, short-nosed rat kangaroo, short-tailed wallaby, Tasmanian devil

EUROPE

Reindeer, Scottish wildcat, wild goat

ASIA

Asiatic lion, giant panda, Komodo dragon, Przewalski's horse, snow leopard

SOUTH AMERICA

Alpaca, Darwin's finch, flightless cormorant, giant tortoise, llama, maned wolf, marine iguana, sloth, torrent duck, toucan, vicuña

ANTARCTICA

Adélie penguin, penguin, Ross seal, crabeater seal

What's the Difference Between Extinct and Endangered?

Extinct is forever. It means the entire species of animal has died out and can never return. Passenger pigeons are extinct. **Endangered** animals are in immediate danger of becoming extinct. The California condor is an endangered animal. Captive-breeding programs, preservation of habitat and reduction of toxins in the environment have kept some endangered animals and plants from becoming extinct.

See some of the Amazon's most amazing animals up close at www.timeforkids.com/amazon

Animals

Dolphins sleep at night.

Hummingbirds can hover in one spot.

Amazing ANIMAL FACTS

A **chameleon** can move its eyes in two different directions at the same time.

Dolphins sleep at night just below the surface of the water. They frequently rise to the surface for air.

A **cockroach** can live for up to a week without a head.

An **albatross** can sleep while flying. It can catch some shut-eye cruising at 25 miles an hour.

Amazon ants (red ants found in the western U.S.) steal the larvae of other ants to keep as slaves. The slave ants build homes for and feed the Amazon ants, who don't do anything but fight. They depend completely on their slaves for survival.

The hummingbird is the only bird that can hover and fly straight up, down or backward!

A **leech** is a worm that feeds on blood. It will pierce its victim's skin, fill itself with three to four times its own body weight in blood and will not feed again for months.

Lovebirds are small parakeets who live in pairs. Male and female lovebirds look alike, but most other male birds have brighter colors than the females.

Only female **mosquitoes** bite. Females need the protein from blood to produce their eggs.

A **slug** has four noses.

Despite its long neck, the **giraffe** has only seven neck bones—the same number as a person.

Sharks continually replace lost teeth. A shark may grow 24,000 teeth in a lifetime.

Classifying Animals

There are billions of different kinds of living things (organisms) on Earth. To help study them, biologists have created ways of naming and classifying them according to their similarities and differences.

The system most scientists use puts each living thing into seven groups, organized from most general to most specific. Therefore, each species belongs to a genus, each genus belongs to a family, each family belongs to an order, etc.

From largest to smallest, the groups are: ➡

Kingdom
Phylum
Class
Order
Family
Genus
Species

Kingdoms are huge groups, with millions of kinds of organisms in each. All animals are in one kingdom (called Kingdom Animalia); all plants are in another (Kingdom Plantae). It is generally agreed that there are five kingdoms: Animalia, Plantae, Fungi, Prokarya (bacteria) and Protoctista (organisms that don't fit into the four other kingdoms, including many microscopic creatures).

Species are the smallest groups. In the animal kingdom, a species consists of all the animals of a type who are able to breed and produce young of the same kind.

A Sample Classification:

TIP

To remember the order for classification, keep this silly sentence in mind: King Philip came over for good soup.

The Lion

Kingdom Animalia	includes all animals
Phylum Chordata	includes all vertebrate animals
Class Mammalia	includes all mammals
Order Carnivora	includes carnivorous, or meat-eating, mammals
Family Felidae	includes all cats
Genus Panthera	includes the great roaring cats: lions, tigers, jaguars and leopards
Species leo	lions!

Animals

Reptiles are cold-blooded.

Animal Groups

Almost all animals belong to one of two groups, **vertebrates** or **invertebrates**. Adult vertebrates have a spinal column, or backbone, running the length of the body; invertebrates do not. Vertebrates are often larger and have more complex bodies than invertebrates. However, there are many more invertebrates than vertebrates.

VERTEBRATES

Reptiles are cold-blooded and breathe with lungs. They have scales, and most lay eggs. Reptiles include turtles and tortoises, crocodiles and alligators, snakes and lizards.

Fish breathe through gills, and live in water; most are cold-blooded and lay eggs (although sharks give birth to live young).

Amphibians are cold-blooded and live both on land (breathing with lungs) and in water (breathing through gills) at different times. Three types of amphibians are frogs and toads, salamanders and caecilians. Caecilians are primitive amphibians that resemble earthworms. They are found in the tropics.

Frogs are amphibians.

Dinosaurs were reptiles, although some scientists believe that some dinosaurs were warm-blooded.

Birds are warm-blooded animals with feathers and wings. They lay eggs, and most birds can fly. Some, including penguins and ostriches, cannot fly.

Mammals are warm-blooded, and are nourished by their mothers' milk. Most are born live, but the platypus and echidna are hatched from eggs. Most mammals also have body hair.

Vervet monkeys are mammals.

INVERTEBRATES

Sponges are the most primitive of animal groups. They live in water, are sessile (do not move from place to place) and filter tiny organisms out of the water for food.

Echinoderms, including starfish, sea urchins and sea cucumbers, live in seawater and have external skeletons.

Worms come in many varieties and live in all sorts of habitats—from the bottom of the ocean to the inside of other animals. They include flatworms (flukes), roundworms (hookworms), segmented worms (earthworms) and rotifers (philodina).

Mollusks are soft-bodied animals, which often live in hard shells. They include snails, slugs, octopuses, squid, mussels, oysters, clams, scallops and cuttlefish.

Arthropods are the largest and most diverse of all animal groups. They have segmented bodies supported by a hard external skeleton (or exoskeleton). Arthropods include insects, arachnids (spiders and their relatives) and crustaceans (such as shrimp and lobster).

The octopus is a mollusk.

Coelenterates are also very primitive. Their mouths, which take in food and get rid of waste, are surrounded by stinging tentacles. Some coelenterates are jellyfish, corals and sea anemones.

Sea anemones do not have backbones.

Warm-blooded and Cold-blooded Animals

Warm-blooded animals regulate their own body temperatures; their bodies use energy to maintain a constant temperature. Cold-blooded animals depend on their surroundings to establish their body temperatures.

Snakes are cold-blooded.

Talk Like a Zoologist

Although these words sound scientific, they are commonly used to describe animal families or behavior.

- **Marsupials** are families of mammals, such as kangaroos and opossums, whose females carry their young in an external pouch.

- **Monotremes** are the rare mammals (the platypus and the echidna) that lay eggs.

- **Nocturnal** animals, such as owls, are active at night.

- **Diurnal** animals, such as squirrels, are awake during the day.

- **Pinnipeds** are aquatic mammals with flippers, such as seals and walruses.

- **Quadrupeds** are animals with four feet, such as cows.

- **Bipeds,** such as humans and gorillas, walk upright on two legs.

- **Primates** include humans and their closest relatives. They share flexible arms and legs, skilled fingers and relatively big brains.

- **Cetaceans** are ocean mammals, including whales and dolphins.

- **Rodents,** such as squirrels, have large front teeth for gnawing and cheek teeth for chewing.

- **Arachnids** are arthropods, such as spiders, scorpions, mites and ticks.

Kangaroos are marsupials.

Owls are nocturnal.

Gorillas are bipeds.

Spiders are arachnids.

Zoo Web Sites

Would you like to see amazing pictures or catch up on animal news? Through the American Zoo and Aquarium Association web site, you can visit hundreds of zoos and aquariums online!

go Check out www.aza.org

Animal Names: Male, Female and Young

ANIMAL	MALE	FEMALE	YOUNG
Bear	Boar	Sow	Cub
Cat	Tom	Queen	Kitten
Cattle	Bull	Cow	Calf
Chicken	Rooster	Hen	Chick
Deer	Buck	Doe	Fawn
Dog	Dog	Bitch	Pup
Duck	Drake	Duck	Duckling
Elephant	Bull	Cow	Calf
Fox	Dog	Vixen	Cub
Goose	Gander	Goose	Gosling
Horse	Stallion	Mare	Foal
Lion	Lion	Lioness	Cub
Pig	Boar	Sow	Piglet
Sheep	Ram	Ewe	Lamb
Swan	Cob	Pen	Cygnet

Animals

GAGGLES, CLUTTERS, PRIDES AND OTHER ANIMAL GROUP NAMES

Ants: colony
Bears: sleuth, sloth
Cats: clutter, clowder
Cattle: drove
Crows: murder
Ducks: brace, team
Elephants: herd
Elk: gang
Fish: school, shoal, draught
Foxes: leash, skulk
Geese: flock, gaggle, skein

Goats: trip
Gorillas: band
Hens: brood
Horses: pair, team
Hounds: cry, mute, pack
Kangaroos: troop
Kittens: kindle, litter
Lions: pride
Oxen: yoke
Oysters: bed
Parrots: company

Pigs: litter
Ponies: string
Rabbits: nest
Seals: pod
Sheep: drove, flock
Swans: bevy, wedge
Toads: knot
Turtles: bale

For more types of animal names, go WWW.FACT MONSTER.COM

Source: James G. Doherty, General Curator, The Wildlife Conservation Society

Besides skunks, who smells?

Skunks aren't the only creatures to use scent glands for defense. Some others are bedbugs, cockroaches, earwigs, foxes, mink, snakes and wolverines.

Dogs don't smell.

Do woodpeckers get headaches from all their hammering?

No, woodpeckers' heads are filled with pockets of air that cushion their head bones as they drill for food or bore the tunnels that lead to their nests.

What's the difference between teeth and tusks?

Nothing! Tusks are simply large teeth that protrude outside an animal's mouth.

What are scavengers?

Scavengers are animals that feed on dead or injured animals. They are not usually held in high esteem, but they have a job to do: they clean the earth of organic garbage. Vultures, bears and raccoons are among nature's scavengers.

What is camouflage?

Camouflage is coloring that matches or blends with an animal's surroundings and helps the animal to hide. The **Arctic fox**, green tree frog, penguin and polar bear are a few of the animals that use camouflage. Some animals, like the chameleon, can actually change the color of their skin to match their surroundings!

How do bats find their way around at night?

Bats navigate and track their prey with a special sense called echolocation. This is a very advanced form of hearing that allows them to "see" their surroundings by listening to the way sound reflects off objects in their environment. Bats' echolocation skills are so sharp that they can avoid an obstacle as narrow as a human hair.

THE BIG SLEEP

Hibernation and Aestivation

When weather conditions get tough, some animals pack up and head for better climates. Others dig in and wait for things to get better. To protect themselves, they may go into a state of inactivity called hibernation (in cold climates) or aestivation (in hot climates).

When an animal goes into a state of inactivity, body processes like breathing and heartbeat slow down greatly, allowing the animal to conserve energy and go without food or water for long periods of time.

TFK TOP 5 Sleepiest Animals

Joey the Koala was born in 2001 at a Cleveland, Ohio, zoo. He ventured out of his mom's pouch for the first time five months later—and fell asleep! Here are the animal kingdom's biggest sleepyheads:

1. Koala sleeps 22 hours a day

2. Sloth 20 hours

3. Armadillo & Opossum (tied) 19 hours

4. Lemur 16 hours

5. Hamster & Squirrel (tied) 14 hours

Source: Top 10 of Everything 2001, DK Publishing

Fish Facts

How many fish species are there?

An estimated 20,000 species exist. But there may be as many as 20,000 more.

What is the world's largest fish?

The largest fish is the whale shark, which grows to more than 50 feet in length and may weigh several tons.

What is the smallest fish?

The smallest fish is the tiny goby, an inhabitant of fresh-to-brackish-water lakes in Luzon, Philippines. It only grows to a half-inch at adulthood.

How long do fish live?

Some fish live just a few weeks or months (some of the small reef fishes); others live to 50 years or more (sturgeons). Scientists have learned that in temperate waters many species live 10 to 20 years.

Do some fish give birth to living young instead of laying eggs?

Yes, many do. These are called viviparous fishes. The sea perches of the Pacific Coast, for example, give birth to living young of considerable size. Several kinds of sharks produce living young.

Do fish breathe air?

Yes, but not directly into the lungs as mammals do. Actually, fish breathe oxygen, not air. As water passes over a system of extremely fine gill membranes, fish absorb the water's oxygen content.

Can fish swim backward?

A number can, but usually don't. Those that can are mostly members of one of the eel families.

The whale shark is the largest fish in the world.

Source: National Marine Fisheries Services' Northeast Fisheries Science Center

Calling All Animal Scientists

A person who specializes in the study of animals is called a zoologist. Zoologists who study certain kinds of animals have their own names.

Anthropologists study human beings.
Entomologists study insects.
Herpetologists study reptiles and amphibians.
Ichthyologists specialize in fish.
Malacologists study mollusks, like snails and clams.
Mammalogists specialize in mammals.
Nematologists study roundworms.
Ornithologists study birds.
Ethologists study animal behavior.

Animal Talk Around the World

Didn't you always suspect that animals spoke different languages? They do as far as their country's written word is concerned. So if your dog says "guf-guf" instead of "rrruf-ruf," maybe your dog is Russian! Here is a brief guide to international animal talk.

GUIDE TO INTERNATIONAL ANIMAL TALK

Animal	English	Russian	Japanese	French	German
Bird	Tweet-tweet	Squick	Qui-qui	Choon-choon	Piep-piep
Cat	Meow	Meau	Nyeow	Meow	Miau
Cow	Moo	Mu	Mo-mo	Meu-meu	Muh-muh
Dog	Rrruf-ruf	Guf-guf	Won-won	Whou-whou	Vow-vow
Duck	Quack-quack	Quack	Qua-qua	Coin-coin	Quack
Goat	Meh-meh	Beee	Mee-mee	Ma-ma	Eeh-eeh
Horse	Neigh-neigh	Eohoho	He-heeh	Hee-hee-hee	Meh-meh
Owl	Whoo	Ooooo	Hoo-hoo	Oo-oo	Wooo-wooo
Pig	Oink-oink	Qrr-qrrr	Boo	Groan-groan	Grunz
Rooster	Cocka-doodle-do	Kukuriki	Kokekock-ko	Cocorico	Kikeriki

Qua-qua

Coin-coin

What languages are these two little ducks speaking?

The World's Favorite Pets

- Household pets are common in America, Europe, Australia and Asia.

- In China and Hong Kong, cats are thought to bring good luck and are kept in shops as well as homes.

- The Japanese keep birds and crickets as pets.

- In Arab countries, dogs are considered unclean. Contact with a dog must be followed by a ritual washing.

- Many Italians also have little use for dogs but find cats charming and companionable. Thousands of stray cats live in the Forum, the Colosseum and other historic landmarks in Rome.

- The Inuit of northern Canada adopt bear cubs, foxes, birds and baby seals.

- Animals are rarely kept as pets in Africa.

- Half of all the households in England have a pet.

Pets in the U.S.

You can find a pet in about 60% of U.S. homes! Almost 4 in 10 U.S. homes include at least one dog. Just over 3 in 10 include at least one cat. In addition, millions of Americans share their homes with fish, "pocket pets" like guinea pigs and hamsters, reptiles and other animal companions.

For more on pets,
go www.FACT MONSTER.COM

My name is Lady!

Most Popular Pet Names

Did you know your furry friend was destined to be a "Max" the moment you looked into his soulful eyes? You're not alone. The American Society for the Prevention of Cruelty to Animals (A.S.P.C.A.) has done a veterinarian survey, reviewing hundreds of thousands of pet names to find out which ones are most popular in the U.S. today.

Here's a look at the top ten:

1. Max
2. Sam
3. Lady
4. Bear
5. Smokey
6. Shadow
7. Kitty
8. Molly
9. Buddy
10. Brandy

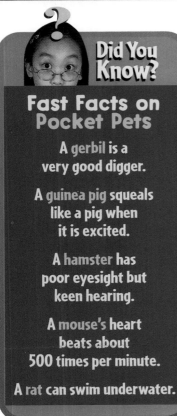

Did You Know?

Fast Facts on Pocket Pets

A gerbil is a very good digger.

A guinea pig squeals like a pig when it is excited.

A hamster has poor eyesight but keen hearing.

A mouse's heart beats about 500 times per minute.

A rat can swim underwater.

TFK Mystery Person

In the 1880s, this French scientist developed a vaccination for rabies, a disease that affects the nervous system of animals. To this day, dogs still get their rabies vaccinations every year.

Who is he?

The Color Wheel

A color wheel shows how colors are related.

YELLOW-ORANGE · YELLOW · YELLOW-GREEN
ORANGE · GREEN
RED-ORANGE · BLUE-GREEN
RED · BLUE
RED-VIOLET · BLUE-VIOLET
VIOLET

Red, **yellow** and **blue** are the primary colors. Primary colors are the most basic colors. You can't make them by mixing any other colors.

Orange, **green** and **violet** are the secondary colors. A secondary color is made by mixing two primary colors. For instance, if you mix red and yellow, you get orange. That is why orange is between red and yellow on the color wheel.

What goes between primary and secondary colors? Intermediate, or tertiary, colors are made by mixing a primary color and a secondary color. **Red-orange**, **yellow-orange** and **yellow-green** are some intermediate colors.

All those colors from just red, yellow and blue— that's awesome!

Values

The lightness or darkness of a color is called its **value**. You can find the values of a color by making its tints and shades.
- **Tints** are light values that are made by mixing a color with white. Pink is a tint of red.
- **Shades** are dark values that are made by mixing a color with black. Maroon is a shade of red.

Try It Yourself!

Making a color wheel is a good way to understand how colors work. Start with red, yellow and blue paint. Then, mix the secondary and intermediate colors. Finally, you can make tints and shades by mixing black and white with the colors you've made.

For more on colors, go » www.FACT MONSTER.com

The World of Art

A mosaic is a picture or design made by gluing together small stones, pieces of glass or other hard materials. In ancient times, grand homes sometimes had mosaic floors.

From prehistoric cave paintings to graffiti art today, painting has always been a part of human life. Some of the world's best-known artists, such as Michelangelo and Picasso, were painters.

Photography was invented almost 200 years ago. We see photographs every day in newspapers and magazines, on billboards and buses and in museums and galleries.

For thousands of years, people all over the world have made masks to use in rituals, work, theater and just for fun. Have you ever made a mask from a paper bag?

Drawing is everywhere—in newspapers, books, posters and more. It is an art by itself, but it is also the starting point for other arts, such as painting or sculpture.

In prehistoric times, people wore jewelry even before they wore clothing. Jewelry has been created using everything from berries to gold.

People have made sculpture from materials such as clay, marble, ice, wood and bronze. Some artists today create sculptures that move with the wind.

There are as many uses for baskets as there are ways to make them. Archaeologists have found 7,000-year-old farming baskets in Egypt.

People have been weaving since the Stone Age. Tapestries and rugs in every color have brought warmth and beauty to walls and floors.

As technology changes, the tools artists use change, too. New media includes video, performance, computer imagery and installation (where an entire room may be made into a work of art).

Figure, a 1939 painting by Pablo Picasso.

In this new-media work by Nam June Paik, 166 monitor screens become a turtle.

Grandma Moses was known for her sweet, snowy scenes, like this one.

Art

Major Types of Painting

How many of these types of paintings have you tried? Some paintings combine types. For example, a portrait might also include details of a still life.

A **landscape** is an outdoor scene. An artist can paint land, water, clouds, air and sunlight.

A **portrait** is an image of a person or animal. Besides showing what someone looks like, a portrait often captures a mood or personality.

A **real life** scene captures life in action. It could show anyplace where living goes on.

A **religious work of art** shares a religious message.

A **still life** shows objects. It reveals an artist's skill in painting shapes, light and shadow.

STYLE

Some paintings seem to show exactly what an artist saw, while others focus on exploring shapes or expressing feelings. One artist might paint a landscape with realistic details, such as craggy rocks and green blades of grass. Another might paint the same landscape in swirling shapes and colors that capture how the air and sunlight felt.

TFK Puzzles & Games

You Ought to Be in Plaster!

An artist has made sculptures of the six kids in this picture. Draw a line from each real kid in the group to the sculpture that looks like him or her.

A Real Stunner

In May 1990, Vincent van Gogh's *Portrait of Dr. Gachet* sold at auction for a record $82.5 million.

Some Art Museums Online

Art Institute of Chicago
www.artic.edu/aic

Fine Arts Museums of San Francisco
www.thinker.org

Kimbell Art Museum
www.kimbellart.org

The Metropolitan Museum of Art
www.metmuseum.org/collections/index.asp

Museum of Fine Arts, Boston
www.mfa.org

Smithsonian Institution
www.si.edu

TFK Mystery Person

This part-Spanish, part-French painter and sculptor is one of the most famous artists of all time. He worked for 80 years, and his influence can still be seen everywhere in modern art.

Who is he?

Books

What to Read While You're Waiting for the Next Harry Potter

Harry Potter wasn't the first young hero to discover he had magical powers, or the first to join a battle of good vs. evil. Check out these classics for more fantasy and suspense. And there's more—each is part of a series!

The Dark Is Rising
by Susan Cooper
On his eleventh birthday, a boy discovers that he has ancient powers.

The Golden Compass
by Phillip Pullman
A young adventurer is drawn into the terrifying secrets of an alternate world.

Half Magic
by Edward Eager
What looks like an old coin turns out to be a quirky magic talisman.

The Hobbit
by J. R. R. Tolkien
A hobbit must leave his cozy home for a wild and unpredictable journey.

The House with a Clock in Its Walls
by John Bellairs
A shy orphan learns that his uncle's mansion hides a deadly secret.

Redwall
by Brian Jacques
Can the peaceful mice of Redwall unite when a wicked rat invades?

The Voyage of the Dawn Treader
by C.S. Lewis
Three children enter a magic painting and join the quest of a legendary king.

Wren to the Rescue
by Sherwood Smith
Magic and imagination help a feisty girl to rescue a kidnapped princess.

Wild Magic
by Tamora Pierce
An orphan's gift for talking with animals may help her save a kingdom.

A Wizard of Earthsea
by Ursula K. LeGuin
A young boy is chosen to enroll at a school for wizards.

Can a half-magic wish turn you half-invisible?

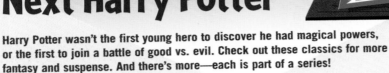

TFK Spotlight

Inspiration from a Wizard

Harry Potter cast a spell on Ben Buchanan, 12, and helped turn him into a published author! Ben has dyslexia, a learning disorder that makes it hard for him to read and write. But that didn't stop him from eagerly reading all four of J. K. Rowling's books. When he was in the fifth grade, Ben even made a Harry Potter board game, which won a creativity award in a school contest. Ben decided to write about his experience. He shares the story of his triumph over dyslexia in *My Year with Harry Potter* (Lantern Books). He also co-wrote *Journey to Gameland* (Lantern), which tells kids and adults how to create a board game.

Ben says writing the books was "pretty hard and exhausting, but well worth it." He hopes his words will help other kids realize "a learning disability doesn't have to keep you down."

TFK Puzzles & Games

Harry at Hogwarts

How well do you know the famous wizarding school?

1. Moaning Myrtle lives in
   a. a staircase
   b. the kitchen
   c. a bathroom

2. Which class has had a different teacher each year?
   a. Transfiguration
   b. Divination
   c. Defense Against the Dark Arts

3. The violent tree on the grounds is known as
   a. the whomping willow
   b. the battering beech
   c. the obstreperous oak

4. Who is the house ghost at Ravenclaw?
   a. The Fat Friar
   b. The Grey Lady
   c. Nearly Headless Nick

5. What is the house symbol for Gryffindor?
   a. lion
   b. badger
   c. falcon

6. What color robes does Hufflepuff wear at Quidditch?
   a. green
   b. yellow
   c. blue

Books

go ▸ For more Harry Potter fun, go to www.FACT MONSTER.com

2002 Children's Book Award Winners

The Caldecott Medal
The Three Little Pigs
by David Wiesner

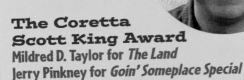

The Newbery Medal
A Single Shard
by Linda Sue Park

The Coretta Scott King Award
Mildred D. Taylor for *The Land*
Jerry Pinkney for *Goin' Someplace Special*

NOT JUST FOR TOTS

These classic picture books are enjoyed by readers of all ages.

D'Aulaire's Greek Myths
by Ingri and Edgar Parin D'Aulaire

Eloise
by Kay Thompson and Hilary Knight

Martha Calling
by Susan Meddaugh

Polkabats and Octopus Slacks
by Calef Brown

The Shrinking of Treehorn
by Florence Parry Heide and Edward Gorey

The Stinky Cheese Man and Other Fairly Stupid Tales
by Jon Scieszka and Lane Smith

Great Poetry Books

The Adventures of Isabel
by Ogden Nash

Where the Sidewalk Ends
by Shel Silverstein

Brats
by X.J. Kennedy

The Dream Keeper and Other Poems
by Langston Hughes

Insectlopedia
by Douglas Florian

Love That Dog
by Sharon Creech

My Life, My Love, My Lasagne
by Steven Herrick

The Paper Doorway
by Dean Koontz

Roald Dahl's Revolting Rhymes
by Roald Dahl

Something Big Has Been Here
by Jack Prelutsky

"Charlotte" might be the name of a spider, but *Charlotte's Web* is also about a pig and a little girl and the farm on which they live. It's the best-selling paperback children's book of all time! Here's a list of the titles that have been chasing Charlotte for years:

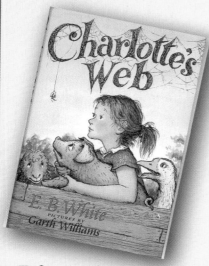

1 Charlotte's Web (1974)
by E. B. White,
9.9 million copies sold

2 The Outsiders (1968)
by S. E. Hinton, **9.7 million**

3 Tales of a Fourth Grade Nothing (1976)
by Judy Blume, **7.1 million**

4 Love You Forever (1986)
by Robert Munsch, **7.0 million**

5 Where the Red Fern Grows (1973)
by Wilson Rawls, **6.8 million**

Source: Publishers Weekly (through the end of 2001)

Awesome
Animal Books

Since the days of Aesop's fables, animal stories have brought readers closer to the animal kingdom while pointing up truths about the human world.

Arabel's Raven by Joan Aiken
Always hungry and often cranky, Arabel's pet raven Mortimer brings endless trouble.

Babe the Gallant Pig by Dick King-Smith
Yes, it's that Babe—the movie star—as he first appeared, in this wacky British novel.

Capyboppy by Bill Peet
In this true story, a giant rodent takes over a family's home—and pool.

Charlotte's Web by E. B. White
What would happen if a clever spider could weave not only webs, but words?

The Cricket in Times Square by George Selden
Street-smart Tucker Mouse and Harry Cat befriend a musical country cricket.

Fantastic Mr. Fox by Roald Dahl
Mr. Fox creates an underground world with splendid feasts.

Julie of the Wolves by Jean Craighead George
On a lengthy solo journey, an Eskimo girl is accepted by a pack of wolves.

Misty of Chincoteague by Marguerite Henry
This classic portrays real events on Chincoteague Island, where wild horses swim.

Mrs. Frisby and the Rats of NIMH by Robert C. O'Brien
A field mouse encounters a colony of lab rats with humanlike intelligence.

The Wind in the Willows by Kenneth Grahame
Mole leaves hibernation for adventures with brave Rat, shy Badger and impossible Toad.

Books

Meet Mysterious Author
Lemony Snicket

Warning labels are not normally found on the covers of books, but there's nothing normal about the books of **Lemony Snicket**. "If you have just picked up this book, then it's not too late to put it back down," warns a note on the back of *The Ersatz Elevator*, the sixth in Snicket's *A Series of Unfortunate Events*. "There is nothing to be found in these pages but misery, despair and discomfort."

Despite such warnings, kids keep snapping up Snicket's tragic tales. Two appeared on the New York *Times* list of the Top 10 best-selling children's books (behind the four Harry Potter volumes). The series chronicles the ups and downs (well, really just the downs) of the Baudelaire orphans: Violet, a 14-year-old inventor; Klaus, who's 12 and seems to have read every book in the library; and Sunny, a baby with four very sharp teeth. The three are pursued by their dreadful, distant (but not distant enough) cousin Count Olaf, who is after their fortune.

What has inspired Snicket to tell these terrible tales? "I feel compelled simply because their story has never been told correctly," he says. "I made a solemn vow to fill that void."

Reference Books:
You Could Look It Up

Atlas
A book of maps with or without text
Example: *Rand McNally Atlas of the Earth's Resources*

Biographical Index
A book of information about people who are well known in a particular field
Example: *Who's Who*

Dictionary
Definitions, spellings and pronunciations of words, arranged in alphabetical order
Example: *The American Heritage Dictionary*

Encyclopedia
Information on just about every subject arranged in alphabetical order
Example: *Encyclopædia Britannica*

Guidebook
Information and directions, often for travelers
Example: *Eyewitness Travel Guide to Japan*

Thesaurus
Synonyms, or near synonyms, for words as well as related terms
Example: *Roget's Thesaurus*

Yearbook/Almanac
Current information on a wide range of topics ➡

Mystery Initials

Ever wonder what the two R's stand for in J. R. R. Tolkien? Want to know J. K. Rowling's middle name? Read on to solve those mysteries—and get on a first-name basis with other favorite children's authors.

- **J. M. Barrie**
Known for: *Peter Pan*
Full name: James Matthew Barrie

- **L. Frank Baum**
Known for: *The Wonderful Wizard of Oz*
Full name: Lyman Frank Baum

- **E. L. Konigsburg**
Known for: *From the Mixed-Up Files of Mrs. Basil E. Frankweiler*
Full name: Elaine Loeb Konigsburg

- **C. S. Lewis**
Known for: *The Lion, the Witch and the Wardrobe*
Full name: Clive Staples Lewis

- **A. A. Milne**
Known for: *Winnie the Pooh*
Full name: Alan Alexander Milne

- **L. M. Montgomery**
Known for: *Anne of Green Gables*
Full name: Lucy Maud Montgomery

- **E. Nesbit**
Known for: *Five Children and It*
Full name: Edith Nesbit

- **J. K. Rowling** (at left)
Known for: *Harry Potter* series
Full name: Joanne Kathleen Rowling

- **R. L. Stine**
Known for: *Goosebumps* series
Full name: Robert Lawrence Stine

- **J. R. R. Tolkien**
Known for: *The Hobbit*
Full name: John Ronald Reuel Tolkien

- **P. L. Travers**
Known for: *Mary Poppins*
Full name: Pamela Lyndon Travers

- **E. B. White**
Known for: *Charlotte's Web*
Full name: Elwyn Brooks White

Mystery Solvers

Who wouldn't love to track down clues and uncover secrets? Here are some mystery solvers to meet.

Nancy Drew, in *Nancy's Mysterious Letter* by Carolyn Keene

The Hardy Boys, in *House on the Cliff* by Franklin W. Dixon

Encyclopedia Brown, in *Encyclopedia Brown: Boy Detective* by Donald J. Sobol

Sherlock Holmes, in *The Hound of the Baskervilles* by Arthur Conan Doyle

The Three Investigators, in *The Secret of Terror Castle* by Robert Arthur

TFK Mystery Person

Long before J. K. Rowling even dreamed up Harry Potter, this British author described a world of wizards and magic. In 1937, he wrote *The Hobbit*, the first book in a series about a mythical place called Middle Earth. His books take readers to a land where humans, elves, dwarves, trolls, hobbits and other creatures live.

Who is he?

Books

Builders make a wall of ice for Canada's new Ice Hotel.

Winter Wonderland

By Kathryn Hoffman

Guests at the Ice Hotel come into the cold

People are paying as much as $186 a night to sleep in the snow! In 2001, North America's first Ice Hotel opened its doors to 19 brave—and bundled—guests. "It's like going back to nature," said Jean-Cristophe Jourde, one of the hotel's first visitors. The gung-ho group slept on beds of ice, nestled under fur blankets and in sleeping bags made for very cold temperatures.

Modeled after an ice hotel in Sweden, this hotel in Quebec, Canada, is made of 250 tons of ice and nearly 5,000 tons of snow. It has a movie theater, two art galleries and ice chandeliers hanging from the ceilings! The building has electricity and running water for the fully equipped heated bathrooms. (The toilets are not made of ice!) Workers built the hotel in about four weeks. Now local artists are helping with the final touches—carving sculptures and furniture out of ice blocks.

"My first reaction was to touch everything," says Helene Barbeau, who works for the hotel. "It almost doesn't seem real." There is even a fireplace made of ice at the main entrance. Do guests sit there to warm themselves? "You have to bring your imagination," Barbeau says. Or a very warm coat: it's about 26°F inside the building. Outside, it's usually around -3°F.

World Records

- **Tallest tower:** the Canadian National Tower, in Toronto, Canada—1,815 feet high

- **Longest bridge:** the Akasi Kaikyo bridge in Hyogo, Japan, with a main span* of 6,529 feet

- **Longest canal:** the St. Lawrence Seaway, between the U.S. and Canada—2,400 feet long

- **Longest railroad tunnel:** the Seikan tunnel in Tsugaru Strait, Japan— 33.5 miles long

- **Longest subway system:** the London Underground, with 244 miles of track

*The main span of a bridge is the longest distance between two supports.

TFK TOP 5 Tallest Buildings in the World

Location	How Tall
1. Petronas Towers 1 & 2, in Kuala Lumpur, Malaysia	1,483 feet
2. Sears Tower, in Chicago, Illinois	1,450 feet
3. Jin Mao Building, in Shanghai, China	1,381 feet
4. Citic Plaza, in Guangzhou, China	1,283 feet
5. Shun Hing Square, in Shenzhen, China	1,260 feet

Famous Structures

● **The pyramids and the Great Sphinx of Giza,** near Cairo, are some of the wonders of ancient Egyptian architecture.

● **The Parthenon of Greece,** built on the Acropolis in Athens, was the chief temple to the goddess Athena. It is believed to have been completed by 438 B.C.

● **The Colosseum of Rome,** the largest and most famous of the Roman amphitheaters, was opened for use in A.D. 80.

● **The Pantheon** at Rome was begun in 27 B.C. It has served for 20 centuries as a place of worship.

● **The Tower of London** is a group of buildings covering 13 acres. The central White Tower was begun in 1078.

● **The Vatican** is a group of buildings in Rome that includes the residence of the Pope. The Basilica of St. Peter, the largest church in the Christian world, was begun in 1450.

The Great Sphinx and pyramids are wonders of the ancient world.

Many gladiator fights took place in the Colosseum.

● **The Eiffel Tower** in Paris was built in 1889. It is 984 feet high (1,056 feet including the television tower).

● The white marble **Taj Mahal** (built 1632-1650) at Agra, India, was built by Shah Jahan as a tomb for his wife.

● The **12th-century temples at Angkor Wat** in Cambodia are surrounded by a moat and have walls decorated with sculpture.

● The **Great Wall of China** (begun 228 B.C.), designed as a defense against nomadic tribes, is so big and long that it can be seen from the moon!

● The **Statue of Liberty** sits on her own island in New York Harbor. In 1886 the French gave the 152-foot-high, steel-reinforced copper Lady Liberty to the U.S.

● San Francisco's **Golden Gate Bridge,** completed in 1937, is one of the most recognizable structures in the U.S.

● The massive standing stones of **Stonehenge** are located in the south of England. Begun some 5,000 years ago, their purpose remains a mystery.

For more about famous structures around the world,
go ⊫ www.FACT MONSTER.COM

The Seven Wonders
of the Ancient World

Since ancient times, people have put together many "**seven wonders**" lists. Below are the seven wonders that are most widely agreed upon as being in the original list.

1. Pyramids of Egypt
A group of three pyramids located at Giza, Egypt, were built around 2680 B.C. Of all the Ancient Wonders, only the pyramids are still standing.

2. Hanging Gardens of  **Babylon** These terraced gardens, located in what is now Iraq, were supposedly built by Nebuchadnezzar around 600 B.C. to please his queen.

3. Statue of Zeus (Jupiter) at Olympia The sculptor Phidias (fifth century B.C.) built this 40-foot-high statue of gold and ivory. It was located in Olympia, Greece.

4. Temple of Artemis (Diana) at Ephesus This beautiful marble structure was begun about 350 B.C. in honor of the goddess Artemis. It was located in Ephesus, Turkey.

5. Mausoleum at Halicarnassus This huge above-ground tomb was erected in Bodrum, Turkey, by Queen Artemisia in memory of her husband, who died in 353 B.C.

6. Colossus at Rhodes This bronze statue of Helios (Apollo), about 105 feet high, was the work of the sculptor Chares. Rhodes is a Greek island in the Aegean Sea.

7. Pharos of Alexandria The Pharos (lighthouse) of Alexandria was built during the third century B.C. off the coast of Egypt. It stood about 450 feet high.

A Future Wonder?

A structure known as the Bionic Tower has been proposed for Shanghai, China. If built, the Bionic Tower will be the tallest building in the world—and one of the most amazing.

The 300-story, 3,700-foot-high building would provide homes for 100,000 people. It would also include hotels, offices, movie theaters and hospitals. The enormous structure would rest on a series of foundations that would spread, like tree roots, more than 600 feet underground. A lake would be built around the base to absorb earthquake vibrations.

The Twin Towers

The **Twin Towers** of the World Trade Center were more than just buildings. Brash, glitzy and grand, they were symbols of New York.

Construction of the towers began in 1965 and was completed in 1973. Standing 1,368 feet and 1,362 feet tall, they were the world's tallest buildings until the Sears Tower in Chicago opened a month later. (However, the north tower sported a 360-foot television mast that technically made it even taller.)

The Twin Towers became the most popular postcard image in the world. Some three dozen movies were made at the towers, including the 1976 remake of *King Kong*.

Each tower had 110 floors, and each floor was roughly 50,000 square feet. Shopping malls beneath the towers housed restaurants, chapels, stores and banks. The six basements included two New York subway stations as well as trains to New Jersey.

One of the world's most glamorous business addresses, the complex had its own zip code—10048. Some 50,000 people worked in the buildings, while another 200,000 passed through each day. From the top floor observation deck, visitors could see for 45 miles on a clear day. From the ground, the towers were visible for 20 miles.

The Twin Towers during construction.

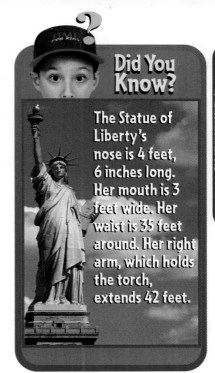

Did You Know?

The Statue of Liberty's nose is 4 feet, 6 inches long. Her mouth is 3 feet wide. Her waist is 35 feet around. Her right arm, which holds the torch, extends 42 feet.

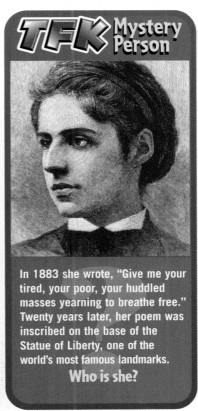

TFK Mystery Person

In 1883 she wrote, "Give me your tired, your poor, your huddled masses yearning to breathe free." Twenty years later, her poem was inscribed on the base of the Statue of Liberty, one of the world's most famous landmarks.

Who is she?

Calendars

Measuring Years

The calendar most Americans use is called the Gregorian calendar. In an ordinary year this calendar has 365 days, which is about the amount of time it takes Earth to make one trip around the sun.

Earth's journey actually takes slightly more than a year. It takes about 365 days, 5 hours, 48 minutes and 46 seconds. Every fourth year these extra hours, minutes and seconds are added up to make another day. When this happens, the year has 366 days and is called a leap year.

Groups of Years
- Olympiad: 4 years
- Decade: 10 years
- Score: 20 years
- Century: 100 years
- Millennium: 1,000 years

Seasons

In the Northern Hemisphere, the year is divided into four seasons. **Each season begins at a solstice or an equinox.**

It's Different Down South

In the Southern Hemisphere, the dates (and the seasons) are reversed. The summer solstice (still the longest day of the year) falls around December 21, and the winter solstice is around June 21. So when it's summer in North America, it's winter in South America (and vice versa).

SPRING

● The spring equinox brings the start of spring, around March 21. At the equinox, day and night are of about equal length.

SUMMER

● The summer solstice, which happens around June 21, has the longest daylight time. It's also the first day of summer.

Months

Months are based roughly on the cycles of the moon. A lunar (moon) month is 29½ days, or the time from one new moon to the next.

But 12 lunar months add up to just 354 days—11 days fewer than in our calendar year. To even things out, these days are added to months during the year. As a result, most months have 30 or 31 days.

To figure out how many days are in a month, **remember:** "30 days have September, April, June and November. All the rest have 31, except February, which has 28."

The Names of the Months

January was named after **Janus**, protector of the gateway to heaven.

February was named after **Februalia**, a time period when sacrifices were made to atone for sins.

March was named after **Mars**, the god of war, signifying that fighting interrupted by the winter could be resumed.

April is from **aperire**, Latin for "to open" (buds).

May was named after **Maia**, the goddess of growth of plants.

June is from **Junius**, Latin for the goddess Juno.

July was named after **Julius Caesar**.

August was named after **Augustus**, the first Roman Emperor.

September is from **septem**, Latin for seven.

October is from **octo**, Latin for eight.

November is from **novem**, Latin for nine.

December is from **decem**, Latin for ten.

FALL

● Fall begins at the fall equinox, around September 21. Day and night are of about equal length.

WINTER

● The winter solstice, around December 21, has the shortest daylight time and officially kicks off winter.

I can't believe that when it's summer in the U.S., it's winter in Australia.

The Jewish Calendar

The Jewish calendar is counted from 3761 B.C. Nisan is considered the first month, although the new year begins with Rosh Hashanah, on the first of Tishri, which is the seventh month. **The year 2003 is the Jewish year 5763-5764.** In 2003, the Jewish New Year begins on September 27.

Months	Number of days
NISAN	30
IYAR	29
SIVAN	30
TAMMUZ	29
AV	30
ELUL	29
TISHRI	30
HESHVAN	29 or 30
KISLEV	29 or 30
TEVET	29
SHEVAT	30
ADAR	29 or 30
ADAR SHENI*	29

*(additional month in leap year only)

The Islamic Calendar

The Islamic calendar is based on a lunar year of 354 days. Each month begins about two days after the new moon. The Islamic calendar is counted from A.D. 622. **The year 2003 is the Islamic year 1423-1424.** In 2003, the Islamic New Year begins on March 5.

Months	Number of days
MUHARRAM	29 or 30
SAFAR	29 or 30
RABI I	29 or 30
RABI II	29 or 30
JUMADA I	29 or 30
JUMADA II	29 or 30
RAJAB	29 or 30
SHA'BAN	29 or 30
RAMADAN	29 or 30
SHAWWAL	29 or 30
DHU'L-QA'DAH	29 or 30
DHU'L-HIJJAH	29 or 30

Hindu (Indian National) Calendar

The Indian National calendar was introduced in 1957 in a push for all of India to use the same calendar. However, some older calendars are still used. Indian National years are counted from A.D. 78. **The year 2003 is the Indian National year 1924-1925.** In 2003, the Hindu New Year begins on March 22.

Months	Number of days
CAITRA	30 or 31
VAISAKHA	31
JYAISTHA	31
ASADHA	31
SRAVANA	31
BHADRA	31
ASVINA	30
KARTIKA	30
AGRAHAYANA	30
PAUSA	30
MAGHA	30
PHALGUNA	30

The Chinese Calendar

The Chinese year is divided into 12 months of 29 or 30 days. Each year is named after one of 12 animals. The Chinese New Year is celebrated at the second new moon after the winter solstice and falls between January 21 and February 19 on the western calendar. In the year 2003, the Chinese year 4701 begins. It will be the **Year of the Goat**.

Fill in the years below, then answer the questions.

1. The year 2003 is named for which animal?

   — — — —

2. People born in 1991 are said to be

   — — — — — — — —

3. 2004 will be the year of the

   — — — — — —

BONUS: WHEN IS THE NEXT YEAR OF THE DRAGON?

RAT	OX	TIGER	RABBIT	DRAGON	SNAKE	HORSE	GOAT	MONKEY	ROOSTER	DOG	PIG
popular	dependable	brave	nice	energetic	wise	cheerful	artistic	smart	hard-working	loyal	good students
1960	1961	1962	1963	1964	1965	1966	1967	1968	1969	1970	1971
1972	1973			1976	1977	1978		1980			1983
1984				1988		1990	1991				1995
	1997	1998		2000	2001	2002					2007

Birthstones

Month	Stone
JANUARY	GARNET
FEBRUARY	AMETHYST
MARCH	AQUAMARINE OR BLOODSTONE
APRIL	DIAMOND
MAY	EMERALD
JUNE	PEARL, ALEXANDRITE OR MOONSTONE
JULY	RUBY OR STAR RUBY
AUGUST	PERIDOT OR SARDONYX
SEPTEMBER	SAPPHIRE OR STAR SAPPHIRE
OCTOBER	OPAL OR TOURMALINE
NOVEMBER	TOPAZ OR CITRINE
DECEMBER	TURQUOISE, LAPIS LAZULI, BLUE ZIRCON OR BLUE TOPAZ

Source: Jewelry Industry Council

go ▸ How old are you in seconds? In music videos? Find out at *www.timeforkids.com/age*

The Zodiac

Twelve constellations, together called "**the Zodiac**," form a circle around Earth. As Earth revolves around the sun, a different part of the sky becomes visible, and each month a different one of these 12 constellations can be seen above the horizon.

The word *Zodiac* means "circle of figures" or "circle of life."

Aries
The Ram
March 21 •
April 19

Pisces
The Fish
Feb. 20 •
March 20

Taurus
The Bull
April 20 •
May 20

Aquarius
The Water Bearer
Jan. 20 •
Feb. 19

Gemini
The Twins
May 21 •
June 20

Capricorn
The Sea Goat
Dec. 22 •
Jan. 19

Cancer
The Crab
June 21 •
July 22

Sagittarius
The Archer
Nov. 22 •
Dec. 21

Leo
The Lion
July 23 •
Aug. 22

Scorpio
The Scorpion
Oct. 23 •
Nov. 21

Virgo
The Virgin
Aug. 23 •
Sept. 22

Libra
The Scales
Sept. 23 •
Oct. 22

Days

A day is measured by how long it takes Earth to rotate (turn) once, which is 24 hours.

The names of the days are based on seven celestial bodies—the sun, the moon, Mars, Mercury, Jupiter, Venus and Saturn. The ancient Romans believed these bodies revolved around Earth and influenced its events.

Europe used the Roman names. But some languages, including English, used Germanic versions of the names of four of the Roman gods: Tiw, the god of war, replaced Mars; Woden, the god of wisdom, replaced Mercury; Thor, the god of thunder, replaced Jupiter; and Frigg, the goddess of love, replaced Venus.

The Names of the Days of the Week

Latin	Old English	English	German	French	Italian	Spanish
Dies Solis	Sun's Day	Sunday	Sonntag	dimanche	domenica	domingo
Dies Lunae	Moon's Day	Monday	Montag	lundi	lunedì	lunes
Dies Martis	Tiw's Day	Tuesday	Dienstag	mardi	martedì	martes
Dies Mercurii	Woden's Day	Wednesday	Mittwoch	mercredi	mercoledì	miércoles
Dies Jovis	Thor's Day	Thursday	Donnerstag	jeudi	giovedì	jueves
Dies Veneris	Frigg's Day	Friday	Freitag	vendredi	venerdì	viernes
Dies Saturni	Seterne's Day	Saturday	Samstag	samedi	sabato	sábado

Calendars

SATURN
Saturday

SUN
Sunday

MOON
Monday

VENUS
Friday

Days of the Week and Heavenly Bodies

MARS
Tuesday

JUPITER
Thursday

MERCURY
Wednesday

TFK Mystery Person

The month of August gets its name from this Roman Emperor. He was also known as Octavian, Gaius Octavius and Gaius Julius Caesar Octavianus. He was adopted by Julius Caesar and went on to change nearly every aspect of Roman life.
Who is he?

Game History, Bit by Bit

1972 **Magnavox's Odyssey**
The first home video-game system: black and white, just one game

1977 **Atari 2600**
First big multi-game system. Hits: Donkey Kong, Space Invaders

1985 **Nintendo Entertainment System**
Boosted the sagging game industry and made Mario a star 8 bits

1989 **Nintendo Game Boy**
The handheld player that made popular games like Tetris portable 8 bits

Sega Genesis
With better graphics than the 8-bit players, it made Sonic one hot hedgehog 16 bits

1995 **Sony PlayStation**
Even better graphics, with games like Crash Bandicoot and Madden NFL on CDs instead of cartridges 32 bits

1996 **Nintendo 64**
A hot player, with cutting-edge graphics that put characters like Mario and Pikachu in 3-D worlds 64 bits

1999 **Sega Dreamcast**
A superfast computer chip took 3-D games to the next level. First of its kind to have online games and a built-in modem 128 bits

2000 **PlayStation 2**
Sony's second PlayStation is smaller, faster and can even play DVD movies and CD audio discs. An 8-MB memory card transfers data up to 250 times faster than the card used with PlayStation 1.
128 bits

2001 **Nintendo Game Boy Advance**
More powerful than the wildly popular Game Boy Color, Nintendo's newest handheld system features a wider screen, better graphics and room for four-player match-ups 32 bits

Nintendo GAMECUBE
Nintendo's boxy new console dazzles with impressive graphics and amazing speed. Critics also like its easy-to-use controller, funky look and (comparatively) reasonable price tag. 128 bits

Microsoft Xbox
The most power-packed of the new home videogame consoles. Features: a lightning-fast Pentium III processor, tons of memory, DVD compatibility and ports for dial-up or broadband modems 128 bits

The Dawn of an Electronic Era

The computer age began when **ENIAC** (Electronic Numerical Integrator and Calculator) was completed in 1945. The first multipurpose computer, ENIAC set speed records with an amazing 5,000 additions per second. Computers have come a long way since—a laptop today can do 500,000,000 additions per second.

That's not the only difference. ENIAC weighed more than 30 tons, filled an 1,800-square-foot room and included 6,000 manual switches. It used so much electricity that it sometimes caused power shortages in its home city of Philadelphia. By contrast, a notebook PC today might weigh in at about 3 pounds.

Bugging Out

The term "bug" has been used for problems in machinery since electricity was invented. But the first computer bug was actually a moth! In 1945, a computer being tested at Harvard University stalled when a moth got caught inside. The engineers taped the moth into their computer log with the note, "First actual case of bug being found."

Did You Know?

You may know that "booting" your computer means starting it up. But did you know the word comes from "pulling yourself up by your bootstraps"? That's an expression that means taking charge of yourself, which is what a computer seems to do when it starts up!

Computer Milestones

Year	Milestone
1975	The MITS Altair, a PC-building kit, hits stores
1978	Floppy disks replace older data cassettes
1981	IBM introduces a complete desktop PC
1983	TIME magazine names the PC "Man of the Year"
1984	The user-friendly Apple Macintosh goes on sale
1992	The Apple PowerBook and IBM ThinkPad debut

TIME
MACHINE OF THE YEAR
The Computer Moves In

Computers & the Internet

What's a Domain?

Did you ever wonder what those funny endings are in Internet addresses—like "dot com"? They're part of the domain. The domain is the name of a network or computer that is linked to the Internet. You can find the domain in an e-mail address after the @ sign. The e-mail address for the First Lady, for example, is first.lady@whitehouse.gov. You can see that "whitehouse.gov" is the domain. The ending of a domain tells you what type it is.

.com = commercial
.gov = government
.org = organization
.edu = educational institution

What Else Do They Call It?

The Internet goes by many names. Here are some of the most popular. You can make up your own terms, too!

> Cyberspace
> Global Electronic Communication Network
> Hyperspace
> Information Superhighway
> Infobahn
> The Net
> Virtual Library

TFK TOP 5
Countries Using the Internet

People online*

1. U.S. --------> 174.6 million
2. Japan --------------> 46.6
3. Germany ------------> 31.3
4. United Kingdom ---> 24.7
5. Canada -------------> 17.1

*January 2002

Source: Nielsen/Netratings

Who REALLY Invented the Internet?

In 1999, Vice President Al Gore told a reporter, "During my service in the United States Congress, I took the initiative in creating the Internet." Afterward, comedians and politicians teased Gore about his claim. Although Gore supported laws that helped develop the Internet, it took many researchers and computer programmers to create it.

The Internet was started in the late 1960s and developed in the 1970s to allow government and university researchers to share information. It wasn't until the late 1980s that the Internet began to be used widely. The Internet is not controlled by any single group or organization. Today, the Internet offers an amazing variety of information and activities. Most people say that e-mail is their top reason for using the Internet.

 Find out about playing it safe online at *www.timeforkids.com/safeweb*

Smiley City

Sometimes when you're sending an e-mail to a friend, you want to use more than just words. That is the perfect time to include a smiley. **Smileys**, also called emoticons, can show your feelings about a person or subject, or just add a touch of fun.

:-)	smiling
;-)	winking
:-(	frowning
:'-(	crying
:-P	tongue sticking out
:-D	ha ha
:-O	oh no!
:-\	doubtful
d:-)	wearing a cap
8-)	wearing glasses
:-*	here's a kiss
(::()::)	band-aid
=^..^=	cat
><)))">	fish
@-->--	rose
^^^^^:-	snake

Smiley Faces

Can you figure out who these famous faces are?

1. ~8-) _____

2. (:V) _____

3. :-.) _____

Because GMTA

In e-mail and online chat rooms, people often try to type as fast as they can. Using acronyms or abbreviations helps them keep up their speed. Here's a quick taste of the language sometimes known as "**e-mailese**" or "**chatroomsy**."

ACE: am confused, explain
BIF: before I forget
BRB: be right back
DTS: don't think so
FWIW: for what it's worth
FYEO: for your eyes only
GMTA: great minds think alike
GTG: got to go
HAW: homework a-waiting
ICCL: I couldn't care less
IMHO: in my humble opinion
KWIM: know what I mean?
LOL: laughing out loud
MMBS: mail me back soon
MMD: made my day
PXT: please explain that
TTFN: ta ta for now

TFK Mystery Person

Not only did this technology whiz start a successful computer company, he also founded a movie studio called Pixar. You might not know that the same guy behind *A Bug's Life*, *Toy Story* and *Monsters, Inc.* is also in charge of Macintosh computers! **Who is he?**

Computers & the Internet

Dance

From earliest times people have used dance for a variety of purposes—to entertain, to celebrate, to convey beliefs and feelings, and just for the sheer fun of it.

Almost every culture in the world has used dance as a means of expression. Argentina, for example, is the home of the sultry ballroom dance called the **tango**, which evokes a passionate mood.

Traditional African dances often form part of religious ceremonies or mark important events. **Square dances**, which developed in colonial America, became an opportunity for farmers to gather socially with their often far-flung neighbors.

Dance is both a part of everyday life and an art performed on stage in front of an audience. Some of the most common forms of dance performance are **ballet**, **modern dance** and **Broadway musical dance**.

Types of Dance

Some Popular Dance Crazes

Boogie-woogie
Cakewalk
Cha-cha
Fandango
Fox-trot
Frug
Funky chicken
Hustle
Jitterbug
Jive
Lindy hop
Macarena
Rumba
Shimmy
Twist

Ballet was first created in 16th-century Italy. Each position and step in ballet is carefully worked out. Many ballets convey a feeling of delicate beauty and lightness—ballet dancers' graceful motions seem airy and effortless, and much of the movement is focused upward, as if the dancers are reaching for the stars. Toe (or pointe) shoes allow ballerinas to dance on their toes and make them appear to defy gravity.

Modern dance, created in the 20th century, was a rejection of the traditions of ballet. It went against what was viewed as ballet's rigid steps, limited emotional expression and dainty sense of beauty. Modern dance steps often seem informal, and modern dancers don't mind if a step looks rough as long as it expresses the truth.

Flamenco is a fiery, emotional dance that originated in Spain and is characterized by hand clapping and fast, rhythmic foot stamping.

The **waltz** is a romantic ballroom dance in which the couple revolves in circles to a beat of three. The Viennese waltz is the most famous.

Native American dance
is often ceremonial or religious, calling on the spirits for help in farming or hunting, or giving thanks for rain or victory in war.

Hip-hop was developed by teenagers in New York City's South Bronx in the 1970s. It brings together driving rhythm, athletic moves and urban style.

Whirling dervishes
are members of a mystical Islamic group from Turkey who express their religious devotion through a spinning dance that puts them in a trance-like state.

Russian folk dance,
full of energy and very acrobatic, features dancers kicking up their boots and sailing through the air.

The **cancan** is a daring dance invented in Paris, France, in the 1890s. Women kicked their heels up in the air, revealing their black-stockinged legs—something that was considered scandalous.

TFK Mystery Person

This New York City-born entertainer is both an accomplished tap dancer and a movie star. Movies such as *White Nights* and *The Cotton Club* showcased his dancing ability. But most importantly, he's one of the most famous tap dancers in America!
Who is he?

Dinosaurs

From TFK magazine

Dinosaur Feathers!

By Martha Pickerill

The best proof yet of dinosaurs' link to birds

FARMERS IN NORTHEASTERN CHINA found the fossil of a duck-size dromaeosaur (*dro*-me-uh-sawr) on their land last year. Little did they know that the fossil might settle a hot scientific debate: are birds the closest relatives of dinosaurs?

The remains of the young dromaeosaur, revealed by the team of Chinese and American paleontologists who studied them, are the clearest link ever between birds and dinosaurs. The specimen boasts the best-preserved body covering of several birdlike dinosaur fossils found in recent years. It shows at least three different kinds of feathers, from head to tail.

"This fossil is the strongest evidence yet that dinosaurs were the ancestors of birds," said Richard Prum, an ornithologist (bird specialist) from the University of Kansas Natural History Museum. "It has things that are undeniably feathers, and it is clearly a small, vicious theropod similar to the velociraptors that chased the kids around the kitchen in *Jurassic Park*."

Dromaeosaurs didn't fly: they had no wings! So why did they have feathers? Scientists are still exploring that question. Some say dinosaurs developed primitive feathers for warmth, to attract mates or distract predators. Over millions of years, feathers developed from tiny tufts of fluff into their modern structure, which helps birds fly.

"When this thing was alive, it looked like a Persian cat with feathers instead of hair," says Mark Norell of the American Museum of Natural History. "There's a huge amount of evidence that these were feathered, at least when they were young. Even baby tyrannosaurs probably looked like this one."

Short feather patterns appear all over the fossil's body, except for the lower legs. Its arms had longer feathers.

go For more dinosaur stories, dig into

How Are Dinosaurs Classified?

The word **dinosaur** comes from *Dinosauria*, which means "terrible lizards." Dinosaurs belong to a group of reptiles called *Archosauria* (ruling reptiles). They are classified into **two orders**, based on the shape of their pelvises (hip areas).

Dinosaurs

Saurischian (lizard hipped)

All Saurischian dinosaurs had lizardlike pelvises. In a lizard pelvis, an arch in the front points forward, which makes the animal's rear end very stable. Saurischians  included both carnivores and herbivores. Neither chewed their food much. Saurischian carnivores swallowed meat in chunks, and Saurischian herbivores swallowed plant material in a wad called a bolus.

Saurischians included *Allosaurus* (different lizard), *Apatosaurus* (deceptive lizard), formerly called *Brontosaurus*, and *Tyrannosaurus* (tyrant lizard).

Ornithischian (bird hipped)

All Ornithischian dinosaurs had pelvises similar to those of modern birds. In a bird pelvis, an arch in the front points backward, which allows room for a longer digestive tract that makes digestion easier. Ornithischians were herbivores. They chewed their food well. Most of them had cheeks, just as a cow or a human does, which would  help them to chew their food neatly.

Ornithischians included *Iguanodon* (iguana tooth), *Stegosaurus* (plated lizard) and *Triceratops* (three-horned face).

When Did Dinosaurs Live?

Dinosaurs lived throughout the **Mesozoic Era**, which began 245 million years ago and lasted for 180 million years. It is sometimes called the "Age of Reptiles." The era is divided into three periods.

TRIASSIC	JURASSIC	CRETACEOUS
245 to 208 millions of years ago	208 to 146 millions of years ago	146 to 65 millions of years ago
Rise of small, lightly built dinosaurs	Dinosaurs rule	Great variety of dinosaurs
Flying reptiles, frogs, turtles, crocodiles appear	Giant herbivores, like *Diplodocus*, emerge	Large carnivores, like *T. rex*, emerge
First mammals evolve	First appearance of birds	At end of this period, dinosaurs become extinct

DINO

HALL OF FAME

Seismosaurus

LARGEST DINOSAUR

Seismosaurus (seismic lizard)

Cretaceous Period

Found: New Mexico

Although larger creatures may yet be found, for now *Seismosaurus* would probably win the largest dino award. It measured about 120 feet (36 meters) from head to tail and about 18 feet (5.5 meters) high. It had a whiplike tail and four short, stout legs.

SMALLEST DINOSAUR

Compsognathus (pretty jaw)

Jurassic Period

Found: Germany, France and Portugal

The smallest known dinosaur was about the size of a chicken and weighed around 6.5 pounds (3 kg). It had a long tail, moved quickly on two skinny legs and ate meat.

Compsognathus

LONGEST NECK

Mamenchisaurus
(Mamenchin lizard)

Jurassic Period

Found: China

The neck of *Mamenchisaurus* was an amazing 46 feet (14 meters) long. This herbivore probably used its long neck to reach into forests where its 12-ton body couldn't fit. But hold that medal: the recently discovered *Sauroposeidon* may have had an even longer neck.

FASTEST

Ornithomimus (bird mimic)

Cretaceous Period

Found: Western U.S., Mongolia

Resembling an ostrich, this dinosaur was estimated to run at a speed of 40 to 50 miles per hour (64 to 80 km). It was 6 to 8 feet (1.8 to 2.4 meters) tall and had two long legs, a long tail and a beak.

SMARTEST

Troodon (wounding tooth)

Cretaceous Period

Found: North America and Asia

Troodon had the largest brain-to-body ratio of all known dinosaurs. It is believed to have been as intelligent as modern-day birds. A meat-eater, it was about 6 feet (1.75 meters) tall and ran quickly on two narrow legs.

Stegosaurus

DUMBEST

Stegosaurus (plated lizard)

Jurassic Period

Found: U.S., Europe, India, China and Africa

The *Stegosaurus* had a brain the size of a walnut. If brain-to-body ratio indicates intelligence (or lack of!), this three-ton herbivore wasn't a mental giant.

EARLIEST DINOSAUR

Eoraptor lunensis (dawn thief)

Triassic Period

Found: Argentina

The earliest known dinosaur was *Eoraptor*. This small carnivore walked on two feet some 227 million years ago.

FIRST DISCOVERED

Iguanodon (iguana tooth)

Triassic Period

Found: North America, Europe and Asia

In 1822 an Englishwoman, Mary Mantell, found some large teeth and bones that were determined to be unlike any known reptile. The fossil creature was named *Iguanodon* because its teeth looked like those of the modern iguana.

BEST DEFENSE

Ankylosaurus (bent/crooked lizard)

Cretaceous Period

Found: Montana, U.S., and Alberta, Canada

Ankylosaurus was the most heavily armored of all dinosaurs, with bony plates, studs and spikes lining its entire back. It even had spikes on its eyelids! Its tail had a thick knob of bone at the end, which was probably used as a club.

MOST FAMOUS

Tyrannosaurus rex (tyrant lizard)

Tyrannosaurus rex

Cretaceous Period

Found: North America and Asia

Tyrannosaurus certainly ran the show during the Cretaceous Period. As the world's best-known dinosaur, this regal beast still rules in the popular imagination.

DINO
Fact & Fiction

When did the dinosaurs first appear on Earth?

The oldest-known dinosaur fossils were found in Argentina and Brazil. They are about 230 million years old. The most primitive of these, *Eoraptor*, was a small, meat-eating dinosaur. Because *Eoraptor*'s skeleton shows some advanced skeletal features, older dinosaurs may yet be found.

What colors were dinosaurs?

Paleontologists think that some dinosaurs had protective colors, such as pale undersides to reduce shadows, or irregular color patterns ("camouflage") to make them less visible in vegetation. Dinosaurs that had armor, such as the *Stegosaurus*, may not have needed protective colors but may have been brightly colored as a warning to predators. Most dinosaurs probably were as brightly colored as modern lizards, snakes or birds.

Did people and dinosaurs live at the same time?

No! After the dinosaurs died out, nearly 65 million years passed before people appeared on Earth. However, small mammals were alive at the time of the dinosaurs. Many scientists who study dinosaurs now think that birds are direct descendants of one line of carnivorous dinosaurs, and some say that birds represent modern living dinosaurs.

When did dinosaurs become extinct?

Dinosaurs became extinct about 65 million years ago (at the end of the Cretaceous Period), after living on Earth for about 165 million years. The dinosaurs' long period of dominance makes them unqualified successes in the history of life on Earth.

Where did dinosaurs live?

Paleontologists, scientists who study fossils, now have evidence that dinosaurs lived on all of the continents. At the beginning of the age of dinosaurs, the continents we now know were arranged together as a single supercontinent called Pangaea. During the 165 million years that dinosaurs lived on Earth, this supercontinent slowly broke apart. Its pieces then gradually spread across the globe.

Why did dinosaurs become extinct?

There are dozens of theories. Throughout the Mesozoic Era, individual dinosaur species were evolving and becoming extinct for various reasons. The massive extinction at the end of the Cretaceous Period exterminated the last of the dinosaurs. There is now evidence that a meteorite impact was at least the partial cause for this extinction. Other factors may include volcanic gases, climatic cooling, sea-level change, low reproduction rates, poison gases from a comet or changes in Earth's orbit or magnetic field.

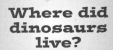

Source: The United States Geological Survey

CAREFUL
Feeding This Baby

I n 1998, scientists discovered the most complete young *T. rex.* The baby, a male, was probably one-quarter the size of its parents and was still young enough that its spine was not fully developed. Like other youngsters, it had long, gangly legs. But even as a baby it had the bone-crushing jaws of an adult. This suggests that even though a Kid Rex would not have been strong enough to tackle large prey, it ate an adult diet supplied by its parents. This 66-million-year-old baby, nicknamed "Tinker," died with half a duck-billed dinosaur in his belly.

With a skeleton that could be 90% complete, researchers hope to gain new understanding of the *T. rex* life cycle. Paleontologists believe that this fossil opens a window into the childhood of the world's favorite dinosaur. It wasn't an easy childhood—this youngster appears to have been chewed by a larger dinosaur.

"Tinker"

Weight: 1,350 pounds (612 kg)

Length: 21 feet (6.5 m)

Age: lived 66 million years ago

Found: South Dakota

Nothing but the Tooth

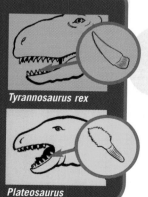

Meat-eating **carnivores**, such as *Tyrannosaurus rex*, have sharp, pointy teeth that can tear apart animal flesh. In contrast, **herbivores**, such as *Plateosaurus*, have dull, flat teeth— excellent tools for grabbing and grinding plants.

Tyrannosaurus rex

Plateosaurus

TFK Mystery Person

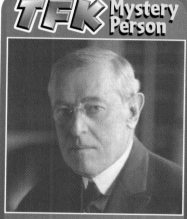

The 28th President of the United States is best known for his decision to get America involved in World War I. But you might not know that he also created the Dinosaur National Monument to protect an area in Utah and Colorado that is full of dinosaur bones.

Who is he?

United in Grief

In Iowa, people join hands during a memorial service for victims of the attacks in New York City and Washington, D.C.

America vows to remember the brave

On the morning of September 11, 2001, the Twin Towers of New York City's World Trade Center touched the crisp blue sky. But now the Twin Towers are gone from the New York skyline. And part of the Pentagon building, which is located near Washington, D.C., is severely damaged.

The terrorist attacks on the World Trade Center and on the Pentagon were meant to knock down all that Americans believe in. But in the midst of devastation, it became clear that the spirit of Americans remained unbroken.

Government officials estimated that at least 3,000 people died in the attacks. That's more than the number who died in the Japanese attack on Pearl Harbor in 1941.

President George W. Bush, New York City Mayor Rudolph Giuliani and other leaders sprang into action. Bush appeared on television, hoping to reassure a frightened nation. "None of us will ever forget this day," he said. "Yet we go forward to defend freedom and all that is good in our world." Giuliani walked through the streets of a shaken city, ordering people to evacuate lower Manhattan.

In New York City and Washington, D.C., people gathered in churches and public squares to honor the victims of the attacks. First Lady Laura Bush visited victims of the Pentagon attack. Later, she reached out to schoolchildren, saying, "I want to reassure you that many people love and care about you and are looking out for your safety."

By Kathryn R. Hoffman

Some of the biggest disasters are not natural at all but are human accidents. Here are some that made history.

A *Titanic* Disaster
April 15, 1912

They called it "unsinkable." But on its maiden voyage, the British luxury steamship *Titanic* collided with a massive iceberg southeast of Newfoundland. The ship began to fill with icy water. Less than three hours later, the 883-foot-long *Titanic* turned on end and then slipped into the ocean. More than 1,500 people died.

The bow of the *Titanic*, on the ocean floor near Newfoundland

The Fall of the *Hindenburg*
May 6, 1937

The German airship *Hindenburg* burst into flames 200 feet over its intended landing spot at New Jersey's Lakehurst Naval Air Station. Thirty-five people on board the flight were killed, along with one crewman on the ground. The majestic ship turned into a ball of flames on the ground in only 34 seconds.

The *Challenger* Explosion January 28, 1986

The *Challenger* space shuttle exploded 73 seconds after liftoff, killing all seven aboard— six NASA astronauts and Christa McAuliffe, a schoolteacher who was to be the first civilian in space. A booster leak had ignited the fuel, causing the explosion. Millions who had tuned in to watch the launch on television saw the tragedy unfold.

Nuclear Disaster at Chernobyl April 26, 1986

In the worst nuclear disaster in history, a reactor blew at a nuclear power plant in Chernobyl, Ukraine. The explosion released eight tons of radioactive material over part of the Soviet Union, eastern Europe, Scandinavia and later western Europe. Total casualties are unknown, but estimates run into the thousands.

The *Exxon Valdez* Oil Spill March 24, 1989

The *Exxon Valdez* oil tanker hit an undersea reef and tore open, spilling 11.2 million gallons of crude oil into Alaska's Prince William Sound. The worst oil spill in U.S. history, it killed millions of birds, fish and other wildlife. Cleanup efforts began late and ended up costing billions of dollars.

Earthquakes and Tidal WAVES

An earthquake is a trembling movement of Earth's crust. The movement causes vibrations to pass through and around Earth in waves, just as ripples are created when a pebble is dropped into water. Volcanic eruptions, landslides and explosions can also cause earthquakes.

A tidal wave is a very high sea wave that follows an earthquake or volcanic eruption. *Tsunami* is the Japanese word for a tidal wave caused by an undersea earthquake.

WORST EARTHQUAKE *IN* HISTORY

- **Where: Near East & Mediterranean Sea**
- **When: 1201**
- **This quake took an estimated 1 million lives.**

A MONSTER WAVE WALLOPS JAPAN

- **Where: Honshu, Japan**
- **When: 1933**
- **A deadly tsunami killed 3,000 people on the island of Honshu. The tidal wave, caused by an earthquake, sank 8,000 ships and destroyed 9,000 homes.**

WHAT CAUSES A QUAKE?

Earth's crust is not a solid globe like a ball. It is made up of pieces that slowly shift. A fault is a weak line below the surface, where two pieces of the crust meet. An earthquake happens when any two pieces suddenly move in opposite directions. A quake begins at a point called the focus. Vibrations traveling outward from the focus are called seismic waves. The areas closest to the focus are hit hardest.

TFK TOP 5
Largest Recorded Earthquakes

Since 1900, earthquakes have usually been measured on a scale that records vibrations in the ground. The lowest number is 1 and the highest is typically around 9 or 10.

Location, Date	Measurement
1. Chile, 1960	9.5
2. Prince William Sound, Alaska, 1964	9.2
3. Andreanof Islands, Alaska 1957	9.1
4. Kamchatka Peninsula, Russia 1952	9.0
5. Ecuador, 1906	8.8

Every year, there are about 18 major earthquakes and 2 million minor ones. This one hit Turkey in 2002.

Source: National Earthquake Information Center, U.S. Geological Survey

What Makes a VOLCANO Blow Its Top?

A volcanic eruption occurs when molten rock, ash and steam pour through a vent in Earth's crust. Volcanoes can be active (erupting), dormant (not erupting at the present time) or extinct (no longer able to erupt). Some volcanoes explode. Others are slow-flowing fountains of lava, which is hot fluid rock. Here are two of the most famous eruptions.

MOUNT VESUVIUS
Italy A.D. 79
The eruption of Mount Vesuvius buried the towns of Pompeii and Herculaneum under 20 feet of ash and lava, killing thousands of people. The ash that buried the town and the people also preserved them. The work of uncovering the ancient cities began in 1748 and continues to this day.

KRAKATAU
Indonesia 1883
The greatest explosion in modern times occurred when Krakatau erupted. The roar of the explosion was heard over one-thirteenth of the surface of Earth. The eruption wiped out 163 villages, killing 36,380 people.

Did You Know?

Both Vesuvius and Krakatau are still active volcanoes. Vesuvius has erupted many times over the years, including three times in the 20th century—1906, 1929 and 1944. And activity at Krakatau has been recorded as recently as March 2001.

This kitty was rescued during a 1993 flood in Des Moines, Iowa.

DEVASTATING FLOODS

A flood happens when a body of water rises and overflows onto dry land. Floods are most often caused by heavy rain, melting ice and snow or a combination of these.

- **Where:** Pennsylvania
- **When:** 1889
- The Johnstown Flood is one of the worst disasters in U.S. history. After a rainstorm, a dam 74 miles upriver from Johnstown broke. One out of 10 people in the path of the flood died—2,000 people were killed in less than an hour.

- **Where:** Italy
- **When:** 1966
- After heavy rain, the Arno River overflowed, flooding the streets of Florence. Art in the city's famous museums was damaged. In two days, more than 100 people died, and the city was covered with half a million tons of mud, silt and sewage.

Destructive Avalanches

An avalanche is any quick movement of snow, ice, mud or rock down a mountain or slope. Avalanches can reach speeds of more than 200 miles per hour! An avalanche might be triggered by earthquake, human disturbance or extreme rain.

- **Where:** Washington State
- **When:** 1910
- The worst snowslide in U.S. history occurred in the Cascade Mountains in Wellington, Washington, when 118 people were trapped in a snowbound train. An avalanche then swept them to their deaths in a gorge 150 feet below the tracks.

- **Where:** Peru
- **When:** 1962
- Tons of ice and snow slid down Huascarán Peak in the Andes Mountains, killing nearly 4,000 people. It is considered the world's worst avalanche.

Every year the U.S. government spends tens of billions of dollars helping to clean up after floods, hurricanes, earthquakes and other natural disasters.

BLIZZARD BLITZ

A blizzard is a winter storm with high winds, low temperatures and driving snow. According to the U.S. Weather Bureau's official definition, the winds must exceed 35 miles (56 km) per hour and the temperature must drop to 20°F (-7°C) or lower.

The worst winter storm in U.S. history
- **Where:** United States
- **When:** 1888
- The Blizzard of 1888 surprised the northeastern United States with as much as five feet of snow in some areas. Two hundred boats sank and more than 400 people died due to very powerful winds and cold temperatures.

DROUGHTS and Famines

Droughts are long periods of insufficient rain that can ruin crops and deplete water supplies. Droughts may lead to famines—extreme food shortages that cause people to die of starvation.
- **Where:** Egypt
- **When:** 1200-1202
- The Egyptians relied on the annual flooding of the Nile River for growing crops. After a shortage of rain, however, the Nile didn't rise. People were unable to grow food and began to starve to death. As many as 110,000 people died as a result of the famine.

- **Where:** Northern China
- **When:** 1959-1961
- The world's deadliest famine killed about 30 million people in China. News of the famine was not revealed to the rest of the world until 1981, some 20 years later.

For more on disasters of all kinds, go www.FACTMONSTER.COM

TFK Mystery Person

Colorado's first female Attorney General is now the Secretary of the U.S. Department of the Interior. Part of her job is to manage the U.S. Geological Survey, which studies earthquakes, floods, volcanoes and other natural disasters. One of her achievements was cleaning up toxic-waste sites in Colorado.

Who is she?

Environment

Meltdown!

The world is feeling the heat of global warming. Will the U.S. help stop it?

These Adélie penguins in Antarctica are really on thin ice. Global warming is causing ice floes like this one to melt.

By Ritu Upadhyay

Glaciers and polar ice are melting. Coral reefs are dying as the seas get too warm. Lakes and rivers in colder climates are freezing later and thawing earlier, disrupting the life cycles of native plants and animals. What is causing this breakdown in nature?

A report issued by the United Nations' Intergovernmental Panel on Climate Changes (IPCC) in 2001 says the world has warmed up. Average temperatures climbed more than 1°F over the past century, and the 1990s were the hottest decade on record. By 2100, the IPCC predicts, the average temperature on Earth will be between 2.5°F and 10.4°F hotter than it is today.

A degree or two may sound like a tiny change, but the consequences can be terrible. As glaciers and polar ice melt, low-lying coastal areas such as southern Louisiana and Florida; Venice, Italy; and parts of India and Egypt could be flooded. Higher temperatures could cause drought and violent storms around the world.

Most climate experts now believe that the current warming is caused in part by humans. Every time we burn gasoline for our cars or coal to generate electricity in power plants, carbon dioxide (CO_2) and other gases are released into the atmosphere. They form a hazy blanket around the earth. Now the blanket is too thick. Too much heat is getting trapped close to Earth's surface.

The U.S. is a major CO_2 polluter. Although our country is home to 4% of the world's population, it produces 25% of greenhouse gases. Politicians are having trouble deciding on a solution. One thing's for sure—if they don't come up with one soon, things could get worse.

Other Environmental Dangers

The **greenhouse effect** is the term used to describe the warming of the atmosphere that happens when certain gases let in sunlight and prevent heat from escaping. This is similar to the way the glass in a greenhouse works.

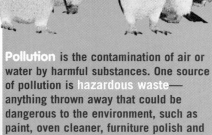

Pollution is the contamination of air or water by harmful substances. One source of pollution is hazardous waste— anything thrown away that could be dangerous to the environment, such as paint, oven cleaner, furniture polish and pesticide. These materials can seep into water supplies and contaminate them.

Another source of pollution is acid rain, which occurs when rainwater is contaminated with pollutants such as sulfur dioxide and nitrogen oxide. These gases come from fuels being burned at high temperatures and from car exhausts. When acid rain falls, it can damage wildlife.

The **ozone layer**, a thin sheet of an invisible gas called ozone, surrounds Earth about 15 miles above its surface. Ozone protects us from the sun's harmful rays. In recent years, scientists have learned that the amount of ozone in the atmosphere is decreasing, probably due to man-made gases called chlorofluoro-carbons (CFCs) and certain chemicals. As the ozone level decreases, we are in greater danger of damage by the sun.

What Can We Do?

Americans lead the world in carbon dioxide (CO_2) pollution. Here are some simple ways you and your family can cut back:

1 DON'T BE FUELISH Walk or ride a bike instead of having a grownup drive you places. Average annual CO_2 reduction: 20 lbs. for each gallon of gas saved

2 PITCH IN Reduce paper waste at your school or home. Help set up community recycling programs. Average annual CO_2 reduction: 4 lbs. per pound of paper recycled

3 HOME IMPROVEMENT Help plant trees next to your house. They absorb CO_2 from the air and give off oxygen. Average annual CO_2 reduction: about 5,000 lbs.

4 GET IT JUST RIGHT Don't overheat or overcool rooms. Set the thermostat lower in winter and higher in summer. Average annual CO_2 reduction: about 500 lbs. for each 2°F change

5 PUT IN SOME PADDING Your family can insulate walls and ceilings to help the inside temperature remain constant. Average annual CO_2 reduction: as much as 2,000 lbs.

Environment

Major Biomes of the World

Have you visited any biomes lately? A biome is a large community of plants and animals that is supported by a certain type of climate.

Arctic Tundra

Where: The Arctic tundra is a cold, treeless area of low, swampy plains in the far north around the Arctic Ocean.

Special features: This is Earth's coldest biome. The Arctic tundra's frozen subsoil, called permafrost, makes it impossible for trees to grow.

What lives there? Animals that live in this biome include polar bears, arctic foxes, caribou and grey wolves. Plants that you might find include small shrubs and the lichen that covers the tundra's many rocks.

Coniferous Forest

Where: The coniferous-forest biome is south of the Arctic tundra. It stretches from Alaska across North America and across Eurasia.

Special features: These forests consist mainly of cone-bearing trees such as spruce, hemlock and fir. The soil is not very fertile, because there are no leaves to decompose and enrich it.

What lives there? Some animals that thrive in this biome are ermine, moose, red foxes, snowshoe rabbits and great horned owls.

Deciduous Forest

Where: This biome is in the mild temperate zone of the Northern Hemisphere. Major regions are found in eastern North America, Europe and eastern Asia.

Special features: Deciduous trees lose their leaves in fall. The natural decaying of the fallen leaves enriches the soil and supports all kinds of plant and animal life.

What lives there? Oak, beech, ash and maple trees are typical, and many types of insect and animal life abound. In the U.S., the deciduous forest is a home for many animals including deer, American gray squirrels, rabbits, raccoons, woodpeckers and cardinals.

Desert

Where: About one-fifth of Earth's land surface is desert. Deserts are found on every continent except Europe. There are two kinds: hot and dry (such as the Sahara) and cold and dry (such as Antarctica).

Special features: The lack of water and the intense heat or cold make this biome unfriendly for most life forms.

What lives there? Most of the plants you'll see in the hot desert are types of cactuses. A few animals—mainly reptiles, such as snakes and lizards, and amphibians, such as frogs and toads—are adapted to the hot desert. Another famous hot-desert animal is the camel. The emperor penguins are well-known animals living at the edge of the Antarctic desert.

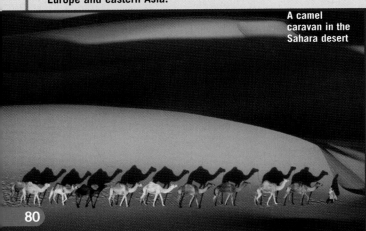

A camel caravan in the Sahara desert

Grasslands

Where: Grasslands are known throughout the world by different names. In the U.S. they are called prairies.

Special features: Grasslands are places with hot, dry climates that are perfect for growing food. This inland biome is made of vast areas of grassy field. It receives so little rain that very few trees can grow.

What lives there? The U.S. prairies are used to graze cattle and to raise cereal crops. There is little variety of animal life. Today, common grassland animals include the prairie dog and the mule deer in North America, the giraffe and the zebra in Africa and the lion in Africa and Asia.

Mountains

Where: Mountains exist on all the continents. Many of the world's mountains lie in two great belts. The Circum-Pacific chain runs from the west coast of the Americas through New Zealand and Australia, and through the Philippines to Japan. The Alpine-Himalayan system stretches from the Pyrenees in Spain and France through the Alps, and on to the Himalayas before ending in Indonesia.

Trekkers in the Himalayan mountains use hearty mountain yaks.

Special features: A mountain biome is very cold and windy. The higher the mountain, the colder and windier the environment. There is also less oxygen at high elevations.

What lives there? Mountain animals that have adapted to the cold, the lack of oxygen and the rugged landscape include the mountain goat, sheep and puma. Lower elevations are commonly covered by forests, while very high elevations are usually treeless.

Rain Forests

Where: Tropical rain forests are found in Asia, Africa, South America, Central America and on many of the Pacific islands. Almost half are in Brazil.

Special features: Tropical rain forests receive at least 70 inches of rain each year and have more species of plants and animals than any other biome. The thick vegetation absorbs moisture, which then evaporates and falls as rain.

A rain forest grows in three levels. The canopy, or tallest level, has trees between 100 and 200 feet tall. The second level, or understory, contains a mix of small trees, vines and palms as well as shrubs and ferns. The third and lowest level is the forest floor, where herbs, mosses and fungi grow.

What lives there? The combination of heat and moisture makes the tropical rain forest the perfect environment for more than 15 million plants and animals. Some of the animals of the tropical rain forest are the anteater, jaguar, lemur, orangutan, macaw, sloth and toucan. Among the many plant species are bamboo, banana trees and rubber trees.

Earth's Biosphere

Earth is composed of four different spheres:

The **biosphere** is the "layer of life" that includes all the planet's living organisms, both plants and animals. It includes ocean creatures, jungle plants and YOU!

The **atmosphere** is the envelope of gases that surrounds Earth. It includes the air we breathe and the clouds in the sky. Gases from the atmosphere are found as far as 600 miles from our planet.

The **hydrosphere** contains all the water on Earth. Oceans, rivers and lakes fill parts of the lithosphere. Earth's water can be solid (ice), liquid (water) or gaseous (water vapor, which can condense to become clouds and precipitation).

The **lithosphere** contains all Earth's rocks and minerals. It includes the ground we walk on as well as the layers inside the Earth—from the semi-solid rock beneath the soil to Earth's hot, iron core.

Environmental Terms

The biosphere's amazing variety of plant and animal species is called biodiversity. Scientists believe that there may be up to 30 million different species living on Earth.

An ecosystem is a community of plants and animals in an environment that supplies them with the raw materials they need, such as nutrients and water. An ecosystem may be as small as a puddle or as large as a forest.

Did You Know?

Garbologists are scientists who study, measure and weigh the things people throw away. They want to discover better ways to deal with garbage.

Remember the **Three R's** of the **Environment**

Reduce Reducing waste is the best way to help the environment.

Reuse Instead of throwing things away, find ways to use them again!

Recycle Recycled items are new products made out of the materials from old ones.

 Become an environmental hero at *www.timeforkids.com/heroes*

TFK TOP 5
CO₂ Producing Countries

Country	Billions of tons of CO_2 emissions since 1950
1. USA	**186.1**
2. European Union	**127.8**
3. Russia	**68.4**
4. China	**57.6**
5. Japan	**31.2**

Source: World Resources 2000-2001

Environmental Web Sites

Greenpeace
www.greenpeaceusa.org
Works to preserve Earth and solve environmental problems

National Audubon Society
www.audubon.org
Helps people learn about land, water and other natural resources

National Wildlife Federation
www.nwf.org
Works to protect nature and wildlife

Rainforest Alliance
www.rainforest-alliance.org
Works to save tropical rain forests worldwide

The Sierra Club
www.sierraclub.org
Works to preserve national parks and wilderness areas

Energy and the Earth

Energy is the power we use for transportation, for heat and light in our homes and for the manufacture of all kinds of products.

- Most of the energy we use comes from fossil fuels, such as coal and petroleum. These natural resources are not renewable. Once these natural resources are used up, they are gone forever. The process of gathering these fuels can be harmful to the biomes (such as the tropical rain forests and the Arctic tundra) from which they come.

- During production, fossil fuels are put through a process called combustion in order to produce energy. Combustion releases pollution, such as carbon monoxide and sulfur dioxide, which may contribute to acid rain and global warming.

The environmental impact of fossil fuels has led many people to look for other sources of energy. There are a number of ways that renewable energy from the sun, the wind and water can be used for everyday needs. Some people use solar panels on their homes to convert sunlight into electricity. Others use the power of the wind to generate energy.

TFK Mystery Person

This former New Jersey Governor is now the administrator of the Environmental Protection Agency. The mission of the EPA is to protect the environment and human health.

Who is she?

Environment

83

From **TFK** magazine

Dressed for Success

Uniforms are a growing trend in U.S. schools. Are they a smart idea?

n the first day of class in public schools throughout Philadelphia, Pennsylvania, in fall 2001, everyone wore identical navy blue skirts and white shirts. Even the principal wore the same outfit.

At the William Cramp School in Philadelphia, Principal Adrienne Carpenter wears the same uniform as her students.

That's because each of Philadelphia's 265 public schools has a mandatory uniform policy. Each school can pick its own style of uniform. Students must wear that uniform every school day.

In 1996, President Bill Clinton encouraged the use of school uniforms as part of an education program that sought to improve safety and discipline. Since then, a growing number of school systems in the U.S. have donned stricter dress codes and uniform policies. In 21 states and the District of Columbia, schools and districts have the authority to tell their students what to wear.

Six of the nation's largest school districts now have uniform policies. Philadelphia joins New York City; Los Angeles, California; Chicago, Illinois; Miami, Florida; and Houston, Texas. They hope that the use of uniforms and dress codes will increase student safety and enhance learning.

School officials in Long Beach, California, say that since uniforms became a requirement in 1994, the number of suspensions and fights has dropped dramatically. Also, the average attendance has reached an all-time high.

Still, many kids don't want to be told what to wear. And some parents and teachers believe that kids should be able to express themselves as individuals. Where do you stand on the uniform debate? Are you for them or against them?

By Kathryn R. Hoffman

Fancy Feet

- Sandals originated in warm climates where the soles of the feet needed protection but the top of the foot needed to be cool.

- In the Middle East heels were added to shoes to lift the foot from the burning sand.

- In Europe in the 16th and 17th centuries heels on shoes were often colored red.

- Shoes all over the world were identical for both feet until the 19th century, when left- and right-footed shoes were first made in Philadelphia.

- The ancient Romans wore platform shoes to keep their feet out of mud and water. Platform shoes were revived in the 1930s and again in the 1970s and 1990s.

- Sneakers were invented in the U.S. in 1917. They were called Keds.

UNDERPANTS IN HISTORY

- Ancient people used loincloths, cloth wrappings that were ancestors of today's underpants. King Tutankhamen had 150 of these in his tomb.

- As the 20th century began, most Americans wore union suits or "all-in-ones"—undergarments that combined pants and a top.

- In the 1930s, Americans traded their union suits for separates. Boxers and briefs swept a nation, and the word "underpants" entered dictionaries.

- The 1930s saw another major change of underwear: easy elastic waists replaced button, snap and tie closures.

- Colorful Underoos® hit stores in 1978. The fun underwear secretly transformed thousands of kids into Batman and Wonder Woman.

- *The Adventures of Captain Underpants* flew onto bookstore shelves in 1997. This comic superhero saves the world wearing undies and a cape.

TFK TOP 5
School Uniform Colors

1. Navy **58%**
2. Khaki **23%**
3. Black **8%**
4. Grey **4%**
5. Hunter Green **2%**

Fashion

CLOTHES ENCOUNTERS

100 Years of U.S. Fashion

1900s

- corsets for tiny waists
- tight collars
- lots of lace
- long, lightweight "duster" coats
- upswept hair
- narrow shoes for both men and women
- straw "boater" hats for men
- feathered hats for women

1910s

- bathing costumes
- lace-up boots
- decorated stockings
- narrow "hobble" skirts
- trenchcoats
- beaded handbags
- Middle Eastern patterns
- V-neck sweaters

1920s

- drop-waist "flapper" dresses
- cloches (close-fitting hats) for women
- baggy flannel trousers for men
- long, wide coats
- costume jewelry
- T-strap shoes
- sheer stockings
- bobbed hair

1930s

- hats worn at an angle
- patterned sweaters
- one-piece wool bathing suits
- long, flowing gowns
- sandals
- fox-fur collars
- wide overcoats for men
- rectangular wristwatches

1940s

- matching skirts and sweaters
- fur muffs
- rolled-up blue jeans
- narrow "drainpipe" trousers
- the "pompadour" hairstyle
- sleek evening dresses
- cork-soled "wedgie" shoes
- baggy pull-on sweaters
- Hawaiian shirts for men

1950s

- white T-shirts
- motorcycle jackets
- pedal pushers (Capris)
- Bermuda shorts
- poodle skirts
- saddle shoes
- full skirts with petticoats
- strapless evening gowns

1960s

- bell bottoms
- miniskirts
- T-shirts with messages
- pale lipstick and dark eyeliner
- longer hair for men and women
- white vinyl "go-go" boots
- peace signs
- paisley and Indian prints

1970s

- Western boots
- lots of lip gloss and blush
- T-shirts with logos
- denim, denim, denim
- legwarmers
- pantsuits
- earth tones
- leotards with wrap-around skirts

1980s

- big hair with lots of mousse
- fingerless lace gloves
- frills on collars and hems
- bright vests and shirts for men
- "power suits" with big shoulder pads
- long fake-pearl necklaces
- tunics over leggings
- Levi's 501s

1990s

- bare midriffs
- designer athletic shoes
- puffy jackets
- chain wallets
- baggy pants
- small eyeglasses
- hooded sweatshirts
- mehndi (henna tattoos)

2000s

- cornrows
- brand T-shirts
- khaki pants
- flip-flops

TFK Mystery Person

Many consider her the most important fashion designer of the 20th century. In the 1930s, she introduced sweater sets, pleated skirts and fake pearl necklaces. Her signature perfume remains a top seller.

Who is she?

How many trendsetters pictured here can you name?

Answers on page 340

Fashion

Geography

Salto Angel is the world's tallest waterfall.

LARGEST CONTINENT:
Asia, 17,212,041 square miles
(44,579,160 sq km)

SMALLEST CONTINENT:
Australia, 2,967,966 square miles
(7,687,027 sq km)

HIGHEST MOUNTAIN:
Mount Everest, Himalayan Mountains,
Nepal/Tibet, 29,035 feet (8,850 m) above
sea level

LOWEST POINT ON LAND:
The Dead Sea, Israel/Jordan, 1,349 feet
(411 m) below sea level

HIGHEST UNDERWATER PEAK:
Mount Pico of the Azores Islands,
7,711 feet (2,350 m) above sea
surface, 20,000 feet (6,096 m)
below sea surface to sea floor

DEEPEST UNDERWATER TRENCH:
Mariana Trench, 200 miles (322 km)
southwest of Guam in the Pacific Ocean,
36,198 feet (11,033 m) below
the ocean surface

HIGHEST LAKE:
The highest navigable lake is
Lake Titicaca in Peru, 12,506 feet
(3,812 m) above sea level

LOWEST LAKE:
The Dead Sea, Israel/Jordan, 1,349 feet
(411 m) below sea level

LARGEST LAKE:
Caspian Sea, 152,239 square miles
(394,299 sq km)

LARGEST FRESHWATER LAKE:
Lake Superior, U.S./Canada,
31,820 square miles (82,414 sq km)

DEEPEST LAKE:
Lake Baikal, Russia, 5,315
feet deep (1,620 m)

DEEPEST OCEAN:
Pacific Ocean, average depth, 13,215 feet
(4,028 m); deepest point, 36,198 feet
(11,033 m)

LARGEST OCEAN:
Pacific Ocean, 64,000,000 square miles
(165,760,000 sq km)

Lake Titicaca is in the Andes Mountains of South America.

SMALLEST OCEAN:
Arctic Ocean, 5,440,200 square miles (14,090,000 sq km)

LARGEST GULF:
Gulf of Mexico, 580,000 square miles (1,502,200 sq km)

LARGEST BAY:
The Bay of Bengal, 839,000 square miles (2,173,010 sq km)

LARGEST ISLAND:
Greenland, 839,999 square miles (2,175,600 sq km)

LARGEST PENINSULA:
Arabia, 1,250,000 square miles (3,237,500 sq km)

LARGEST ARCHIPELAGO
(string of islands):
Indonesia, 3,500-mile (5,632-km) stretch of 13,000 islands

LARGEST GORGE:
Grand Canyon, Colorado River, Arizona, U.S., 277 miles (446 km) long, up to 18 miles (29 km) wide, 1 mile (1.6 km) deep

LONGEST MOUNTAIN RANGE:
The Andes of South America, more than 5,000 miles (8,000 km)

LONGEST RIVER:
The Nile, Africa, 4,145 miles (6,670 km)

SHORTEST RIVER:
The Roe, Montana, U.S., 201 feet (61 m)

LARGEST LAGOON:
Lagoa dos Patos, Brazil, 158 miles (254 km) long, 4,110 square miles (10,645 sq km)

HIGHEST WATERFALL:
Angel (Salto Angel), Venezuela, 3,212 feet (979 m) high

The Nile flows north through Africa.

The SEVEN Continents

CONTINENT	APPROX. AREA	HIGHEST POINT	LOWEST POINT
Africa	11,608,156 square miles (30,065,107 sq km)	Mount Kilimanjaro, Tanzania, 19,340 feet (5,895 m)	Lake Assal, Djibouti, 512 feet (156 m) below sea level
Antarctica	5,100,021 square miles (13,209,047 sq km)	Vinson Massif, 16,066 feet (4,897 m)	Ice covered 8,327 feet (2,538 m) below sea level
Asia (includes the Middle East)	17,212,041 square miles (44,579,160 sq km)	Mount Everest, Tibet/Nepal, 29,035 feet (8,850 m)	Dead Sea, Israel/Jordan, 1,349 feet (411 m) below sea level
Australia (includes Oceania)	2,967,966 square miles (7,687,027 sq km)	Mount Kosciusko, Australia, 7,316 feet (2,228 m)	Lake Eyre, Australia, 52 feet (16 m) below sea level
Europe	3,837,082 square miles (9,938,037 sq km)	Mount Elbrus, Russia/Georgia, 18,510 feet (5,642 m)	Caspian Sea, Russia/Kazakhstan, 92 feet (28 m) below sea level
North America	9,365,290 square miles (24,256,087 sq km)	Mount McKinley, Alaska, U.S., 20,320 feet (6,194 m)	Death Valley, California, U.S., 282 feet (86 m) below sea level
South America (includes Central America and the Caribbean)	6,879,952 square miles (17,819,065 sq km)	Mount Aconcagua, Argentina, 22,834 feet (6,960 m)	Valdes Peninsula, Argentina, 131 feet (40 m) below sea level

The FOUR Oceans

OCEAN	AREA	AVERAGE DEPTH
Pacific Ocean	64,000,000 square miles (165,760,000 sq km)	13,215 feet (4,028 m)
Atlantic Ocean	31,815,000 square miles (82,400,000 sq km)	12,880 feet (3,926 m)
Indian Ocean	25,300,000 square miles (65,526,700 sq km)	13,002 feet (3,963 m)
Arctic Ocean	5,440,200 square miles (14,090,000 sq km)	3,953 feet (1,205 m)

EXTREME Points of the U.S.

Extreme	Latitude	Longitude	Distance*
Northernmost point: Point Barrow, Alaska	71°23' N	156°29' W	2,507 miles (4,034 km)
Easternmost point: West Quoddy Head, Maine	44°49' N	66°57' W	1,788 miles (2,997 km)
Southernmost point: Ka Lae (South Cape), Hawaii	18°55' N	155°41' W	3,463 miles (5,573 km)
Westernmost point: Cape Wrangell, Alaska (Attu Island)	52°55' N	172°27' E	3,625 miles (5,833 km)

*From the geographic center of the U.S. in Castle Rock, South Dakota

Other Notable HIGHS, LOWS and In-Betweens of the U.S.

Highest point: Mount McKinley, Alaska	20,320 feet (6,198 m)
Lowest point: Death Valley, California	282 feet (86 m) below sea level
Average elevation:	2,500 feet (763 m)
Points farthest apart (50 states): Log Point, Elliot Key, Florida, and Kure Island, Hawaii	5,859 miles (9,429 km)
Geographic center, including Alaska and Hawaii: in Butte County, South Dakota (near Castle Rock)	44°58' N latitude, 103°46' W longitude
Geographic center, not including Alaska and Hawaii: in Smith County, Kansas (near Lebanon)	39°50' N latitude, 98°35' W longitude
Boundaries:	
Between Alaska and Canada	1,538 miles (2,475 km)
Between U.S. (not including Alaska) and Canada	3,987 miles (6,416 km)
Between U.S. and Mexico	1,933 miles (3,111 km)

Source: U.S. Geological Survey

The Lines on a Map

The equator divides Earth into two halves, or **hemispheres**. The Northern Hemisphere is the half of Earth between the North Pole and the equator. The Southern Hemisphere is the half of Earth between the South Pole and the equator.

Earth can also be divided into the Eastern Hemisphere and the Western Hemisphere. The Western Hemisphere includes North and South America, their islands and the surrounding waters. The Eastern Hemisphere includes Asia, Africa, Australia and Europe.

Latitude measures distance from the equator. Latitude is measured in degrees and shown on a map by lines that run east and west.

Longitude measures distance from the prime meridian, an imaginary line on a map that runs through Greenwich, England. Longitude is measured in degrees and shown on a map by lines that run north and south.

Together, the lines of latitude and the lines of longitude form a grid on which it is possible to locate any place on Earth.

The **Tropic of Cancer** is a line of latitude that is one-quarter of the way from the equator to the North Pole. During the summer solstice, the sun is directly overhead this line.

The **Tropic of Capricorn** is a line of latitude that is one-quarter of the way from the equator to the South Pole. During the winter solstice, the sun is directly overhead this line.

ARCTIC CIRCLE

LINE OF LONGITUDE

TROPIC OF CANCER

LINE OF LATITUDE

EQUATOR

TROPIC OF CAPRICORN

ANTARCTIC CIRCLE

Three-quarters of the way between the equator and the North Pole lies the **Arctic Circle**. Above this imaginary line is the Arctic region. It is known as the Land of the Midnight Sun because in summer the sun never sets.

The **Antarctic Circle** lies three-quarters of the way between the equator and the South Pole.

TFK Puzzles & Games — Animal Safari!

Almost one-tenth of Kenya is parkland! Every year, thousands of tourists visit its 59 national parks and reserves. The parks are home to 844 types of birds and 359 mammal species. We have shown a few on the map. Follow the steps below to go on safari in Kenya.

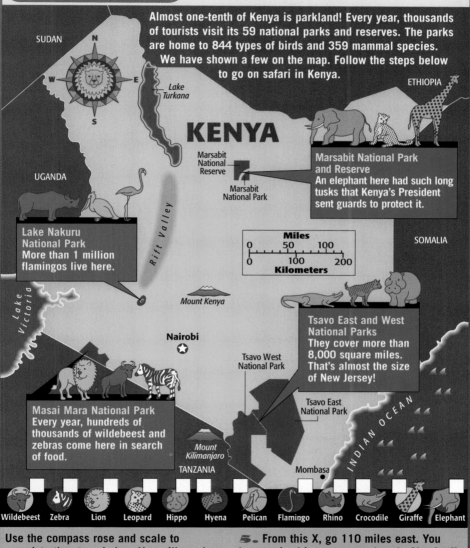

SUDAN

N
W E
S

Lake Turkana

ETHIOPIA

KENYA

Marsabit National Reserve

Marsabit National Park and Reserve
An elephant here had such long tusks that Kenya's President sent guards to protect it.

Marsabit National Park

UGANDA

Rift Valley

Lake Nakuru National Park
More than 1 million flamingos live here.

SOMALIA

Miles
0   50   100
0   100   200
Kilometers

Lake Victoria

Mount Kenya

Tsavo East and West National Parks
They cover more than 8,000 square miles. That's almost the size of New Jersey!

Nairobi ★

Tsavo West National Park

Tsavo East National Park

INDIAN OCEAN

Masai Mara National Park
Every year, hundreds of thousands of wildebeest and zebras come here in search of food.

Mount Kilimanjaro

TANZANIA

Mombasa

Wildebeest · Zebra · Lion · Leopard · Hippo · Hyena · Pelican · Flamingo · Rhino · Crocodile · Giraffe · Elephant

Use the compass rose and scale to complete the steps below. You will need a ruler to measure distance.

1. Start in Nairobi, Kenya's capital.
2. Go 60 miles north. Draw an X.
3. From this X, go 50 miles west. You are now in your first park. Check off the animals you see here on the list above.
4. From this park, go 160 miles north. When you reach the spot, draw an X again.

5. From this X, go 110 miles east. You have arrived in your second park. Check off the animals you see on the list.
6. From this second park, go 150 miles south. Draw an X. This is the end of your trip!
7. What famous landmark is 20 miles west of this last stop? _____.

Bonus The animal you saw whose name starts with "L" is a _____.

IMPORTANT EXPLORERS

985 Eric the Red (Viking) settled in Greenland

1000 Leif Ericsson (Viking) explored Labrador and Newfoundland in Canada

1272 Marco Polo (Italian) explored China

1325-1349 Ibn Batuta (Arab) explored Africa, Middle East, Europe, parts of Asia

1488 Bartolomeu Dias (Portuguese) rounded South Africa's Cape of Good Hope

1492 Christopher Columbus (Italian) arrived in the West Indies

1498 Vasco da Gama (Portuguese) explored the coast of India

1513 Ponce de León (Spanish) reached Florida

1519-1521 Hernando Cortés (Spanish) conquered Mexico

1519-1522 The expedition led by Ferdinand Magellan (Portuguese) circled the globe

1532-1533 Francisco Pizarro (Spanish) conquered Peru

1535-1536 Jacques Cartier (French) sailed up Canada's St. Lawrence River

1539-1542 Hernando de Soto (Spanish) explored the southeastern U.S.

1607 John Smith (English) settled Jamestown, Virginia

1609-1610 Henry Hudson (English) explored the river, strait and bay that bear his name

1769 James Cook (English) explored New Zealand

1804-1806 Meriwether Lewis and William Clark (U.S.) explored the northwest U.S.

1855 David Livingstone (Scottish) reached Victoria Falls in East Africa

1909 Robert E. Peary (U.S.) reached the North Pole

MYTHS ABOUT EXPLORERS

Most people think . . .

. . . Columbus discovered America.

In fact, in the year 1000 the Vikings, led by Leif Ericsson, were the first Europeans to land on the coast of North America. Columbus landed in the West Indies in 1492. And, of course, native people were living in North America when Ericsson arrived.

. . . Magellan was the first to sail around the world.

In fact, he was dead before the voyage was over. Magellan sailed from Spain in 1519 with five ships and was killed in a fight with the natives of Macatan Island in the Pacific Ocean in 1521. In 1522, one of his ships completed the journey.

. . . Charles Lindbergh was the first to fly across the Atlantic Ocean.

In fact, "Lucky Lindy" became the first to fly solo (alone) across the Atlantic in 1927. The first nonstop flight across the Atlantic was made by Alcock and Brown, two British aviators, in 1919.

Not All Earth's Wonders Have Been Explored

More than 200 waterfalls were recently discovered in **America's Yellowstone National Park.** Explorers Paul Rubinstein, Mike Stevens and Lee H. Whittlesey published their findings in *The Guide to Yellowstone Waterfalls and Their Discovery.*

Yellowstone became a national park in 1872. While the rest of the West was being explored and settled, Yellowstone remained a wilderness—and it still is. Its vast 2.2 million acres include dense forests, steep canyons and abundant wildlife. Deep snows keep the park's few roads closed for much of the year.

These modern explorers faced many dangers in their 20 years of hunting waterfalls. They had near misses with deadly snowstorms, boiling geysers and charging bears. Two of them were struck by lightning. But their "thrilling and rewarding" discoveries made it all worthwhile. And they're not done exploring! They believe that many of Yellowstone's wonders have yet to be found.

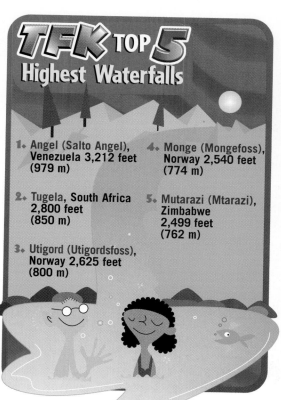

TFK TOP 5 Highest Waterfalls

1. **Angel (Salto Angel), Venezuela 3,212 feet (979 m)**

2. **Tugela, South Africa 2,800 feet (850 m)**

3. **Utigord (Utigordsfoss), Norway 2,625 feet (800 m)**

4. **Monge (Mongefoss), Norway 2,540 feet (774 m)**

5. **Mutarazi (Mtarazi), Zimbabwe 2,499 feet (762 m)**

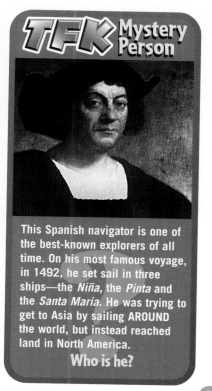

TFK Mystery Person

This Spanish navigator is one of the best-known explorers of all time. On his most famous voyage, in 1492, he set sail in three ships—the *Niña*, the *Pinta* and the *Santa Maria*. He was trying to get to Asia by sailing **AROUND** the world, but instead reached land in North America.

Who is he?

Government

The Constitution

★ ★ ★ ★ ★ ★

In 1787 leaders of the states gathered to write the Constitution—a set of principles that told how the new nation would be governed. The Constitution went into effect in 1789.

The Constitution begins with a famous section called the preamble. The preamble says that the U.S. government was created by the people and for the benefit of the people:

We the people of the United States, in order to form a more perfect Union, establish justice, insure domestic tranquility, provide for the common defense, promote the general welfare, and secure the blessings of liberty to ourselves and our posterity, do ordain and establish this Constitution for the United States of America.

The leaders of the states wanted a strong and fair national government. But they also wanted to protect individual freedoms and prevent the government from abusing its power. They believed they could do this by having three separate branches of government: the Executive, the Legislative and the Judicial. This separation is described in the first three articles, or sections, of the Constitution.

The Constitution was originally made up of seven articles.

ARTICLE I Creates the Legislative Branch—the House of Representatives and the Senate—and describes its powers and responsibilities.

ARTICLE II Creates the Executive Branch, which is led by the President, and describes its powers and responsibilities.

ARTICLE III Creates the Judicial Branch, which is led by the Supreme Court, and describes its powers and responsibilities.

ARTICLE IV Describes the rights and powers of the states.

ARTICLE V Explains how amendments (changes or additions) can be made to the Constitution.

ARTICLE VI Says the Constitution is "the supreme law of the land."

ARTICLE VII Tells how the Constitution would be ratified (approved and made official) by the states.

The Bill of Rights

As Article V shows, it was expected from the beginning that amendments, or changes or additions, would be made to the Constitution. There are now **27 amendments**.

The first ten amendments are known as the Bill of Rights. They list individual freedoms promised by the new government. The Bill of Rights was approved in 1791.

AMENDMENT I Guarantees freedom of religion, speech and the press.

AMENDMENT II Guarantees the right of the people to have firearms.

AMENDMENT III Says that soldiers may not stay in a house without the owner's agreement.

AMENDMENT IV Says that the government cannot search people and their homes without a strong reason.

AMENDMENT V Says that every person has the right to a trial, and to having his or her rights protected while waiting for a trial. Also, private property cannot be taken without payment.

AMENDMENT VI Says that every person shall have the right to "a speedy and public trial."

AMENDMENT VII Guarantees the right to a trial in various types of legal cases.

AMENDMENT VIII Outlaws all "cruel and unusual punishment."

AMENDMENT IX Says that people have rights in addition to those listed in the Constitution.

AMENDMENT X Says that the powers that the Constitution does not give to the national government belong to the states and to the people.

Other Notable Amendments

Amendment XIII (approved 1865) Declares slavery illegal.

Amendment XV (approved 1870) Says the right to vote cannot be denied because of race.

Amendment XVI (approved 1913) Gives Congress the power to tax incomes.

Amendment XIX (approved 1920) Grants women the right to vote.

Suffragists—women who fought for the right to vote—held marches in Washington (inset).

Amendment XXII (approved 1951) Says that a President may serve no more than two four-year terms.

Amendment XXIV (approved 1964) Forbids poll taxes—money paid for the right to vote—in national elections.

Amendment XXVI (approved 1971) Lowers the voting age to 18.

go For the complete Constitution, including all the amendments, www.FACT MONSTER.COM

Government

The
Legislative Branch

The **Legislative Branch** is made up of the two houses of Congress—the **Senate** and the **House of Representatives**. The most important duty of the Legislative Branch is to make laws. Laws are written, discussed and voted on in Congress.

There are **100 Senators** in the Senate, two from each state. Senators are elected by their states and serve six-year terms. The Vice President of the U.S. is considered the head of the Senate, but does not vote in the Senate unless there is a tie.

There are **435 Representatives** in the House of Representatives. The number of Representatives each state gets is based on its population. For example, California has many more Representatives than Montana. Representatives are elected by their states and serve two-year terms. The Speaker of the House, elected by the Representatives, is considered the head of the House.

President George W. Bush signs three proclamations as Vice President Dick Cheney and congressional leaders looR on.

A joint session of Congress on Capitol Hill

Find and contact your own congresspeople at
go www.timeforkids.com/congress

The
Executive Branch

The President is the head of the Executive Branch, which makes laws official. The President is elected by the entire country and serves a four-year term. The President approves and carries out laws passed by the Legislative Branch. He appoints or removes Cabinet members

THE PRESIDENT

THE VICE PRESIDENT

and officials. He negotiates treaties, and acts as head of state and Commander-in-Chief of the armed forces.

The Executive Branch also includes the **Vice President** and other officials, such as members of the **Cabinet**. The Cabinet is made up of the heads of the 14 major departments of the government.

The Cabinet gives advice to the President about important matters.

THE CABINET

Secretary of Agriculture	Secretary of Commerce	Secretary of Defense	Secretary of Education	Secretary of Energy

Ann Veneman   Donald Evans   Donald Rumsfeld   Rod Paige   Spencer Abraham

Secretary of Health and Human Services	Secretary of Housing and Urban Development	Secretary of the Interior	Attorney General	Secretary of Labor

Tommy Thompson   Melquiades Martinez   Gale Norton   John Ashcroft   Elaine Chao

Secretary of State	Secretary of Transportation	Secretary of the Treasury	Secretary of Veterans' Affairs

Colin Powell   Norman Mineta   Paul O'Neill   Anthony Principi

Government

The
Judicial Branch

The **Judicial Branch** oversees the court system of the U.S. Through court cases, the Judicial Branch explains the meaning of the Constitution and laws passed by Congress. **The Supreme Court** is the head of the Judicial Branch. Unlike a criminal court, the Supreme Court rules whether something is constitutional or unconstitutional—whether or not it is permitted under the Constitution.

On the Supreme Court there are **nine Justices**, or judges: eight associate justices and one Chief Justice. The judges are nominated by the President and approved by the Senate. They have no term limits. The Supreme Court is the highest court in the land. Its decisions are final, and no other court can overrule those decisions. Decisions of the Supreme Court set precedents— new ways of interpreting the law.

Chief Justice William Rehnquist, center, and the eight associate Justices

Significant Supreme Court Decisions

1803 *Marbury v. Madison*
The first time a law passed by Congress was declared unconstitutional

1857 *Dred Scott v. Sanford*
Declared that a slave was not a citizen, and that Congress could not outlaw slavery in U.S. territories

1896 *Plessy v. Ferguson*
Said that racial segregation was legal

1954 *Brown v. Board of Education*
Made racial segregation in schools illegal

TFK Puzzles & Games — What's My Branch?

Draw a line from each person to the branch of government where he or she works.

PRESIDENT **GEORGE W. BUSH**

SENATOR **EDWARD M. KENNEDY**

REPRESENTATIVE **NYDIA VELÁZQUEZ**

VICE PRESIDENT **RICHARD B. CHENEY**

JUSTICE **RUTH BADER GINSBURG**

SECRETARY OF STATE **COLIN POWELL**

LEGISLATIVE

EXECUTIVE

JUDICIAL

State Government

All the states follow the laws of the Federal Government. But each state also has its own government and can make its own laws, as long as they do not conflict with federal laws. Like the Federal Government, each state government has three branches: Legislative, Executive and Judicial. The Governor heads the state Executive Branch.

Powers of the Government

Federal Government	State Government	Federal and State Government
★ Print money	★ Issue licenses	In addition to their unique powers, both the Federal Government and state governments have the power to:
★ Regulate interstate (between states) and international trade	★ Regulate intrastate (within the state) businesses	
★ Make treaties and conduct foreign policy	★ Conduct elections	★ Collect taxes
★ Declare war	★ Establish local governments	★ Build roads
★ Provide an army and navy	★ Ratify amendments to the Constitution	★ Borrow money
★ Establish post offices	★ Take measures for public health and safety	★ Establish courts
★ Make laws necessary and proper to carry out these powers	★ May exert powers the Constitution does not delegate to the Federal Government or prohibit the states from using	★ Make and enforce laws
		★ Charter banks and corporations
		★ Spend money for the good of the people
		★ Take private property for public use, with fair payment

Source: The U.S. Government Printing Office

Checks and Balances

The system of checks and balances is an important part of the Constitution. With checks and balances, each of the three branches of government can limit the powers of the others. This way, no one branch becomes too powerful. Each branch "checks" the power of the other branches to make sure that the power is balanced among them. How does this system of checks and balances work?

The process of how laws are made (see the following page) is a good example of checks and balances in action. First, the **Legislative Branch** introduces and votes on a bill. The bill then goes to the **Executive Branch**, where the President decides whether he thinks the bill is good for the country. If so, he signs the bill, and it becomes a law.

If the President does not believe the bill is good for the country, he does not sign it. This is called a veto. But the Legislative Branch gets another chance. With enough votes, the Legislative Branch can override the Executive Branch's veto, and the bill becomes a law.

Once a law is in place, the people of the country can test it through the court system, which is under the control of the **Judicial Branch**. If someone believes a law is unfair, a lawsuit can be filed. Lawyers then make arguments for and against the case, and a judge decides which side has presented the most convincing arguments. The side that loses can choose to appeal to a higher court, and the case may eventually reach the highest court of all, the Supreme Court.

If the Legislative Branch does not agree with the way in which the Judicial Branch has interpreted the law, it can introduce a new piece of legislation, and the process starts all over again.

How a Bill Becomes a Law

★ ★ ★ ★ ★ ★

1 A member of Congress introduces a bill.

When a Senator or Representative introduces a bill, it is sent to the clerk of the Senate or House, who gives it a number and title. Next, the bill goes to the appropriate committee.

2 Committees review and vote on the bill.

Committees specialize in different areas, such as foreign relations or agriculture, and are made up of small groups of Senators or Representatives.

The committee may reject the bill and "table" it, meaning it is never discussed again. Or it may hold hearings to listen to facts and opinions, make changes in the bill and cast votes. If most committee members vote in favor of the bill, it is sent back to the Senate and the House for debate.

3 The Senate and the House debate and vote on the bill.

Separately, the Senate and the House debate the bill, offer amendments and cast votes. If the bill is defeated in either the Senate or the House, the bill dies.

Sometimes, the House and the Senate pass the same bill, but with different amendments. In these cases, the bill goes to a conference committee made up of members of both houses of Congress. The conference committee works out differences between the two versions of the bill.

Then the bill goes before all of Congress for a vote. If a majority of both the Senate and the House votes for the bill, it goes to the President for approval.

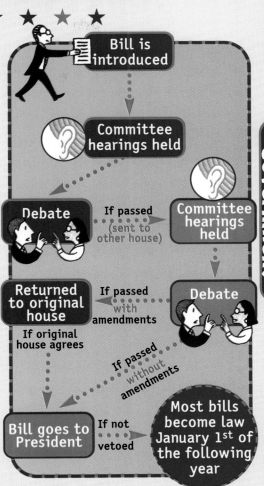

Bill is introduced

Committee hearings held

Debate — If passed (sent to other house)

Committee hearings held

Returned to original house — If passed with amendments

Debate

If original house agrees

If passed without amendments

Bill goes to President — If not vetoed

Most bills become law January 1st of the following year

4 The President signs the bill—or not.

If the President approves the bill and signs it, the bill becomes a law. However, if the President disapproves, he can veto the bill by refusing to sign it.

Congress can try to overrule a veto. If both the Senate and the House pass the bill by a two-thirds majority, the President's veto is overruled and the bill becomes a law.

How the President Gets Elected

STEP BY STEP on the Campaign Trail

1 Candidate announces plan to run for office.

This announcement launches the candidate's official campaign. Speeches, debates and baby-kissing begin.

2 Candidate campaigns to win delegate support.

The first stage of a presidential campaign is the nomination campaign. At this time the candidate is competing with other candidates in the same party, hoping to get the party's nomination. The candidate works to win delegates—representatives who pledge to support the candidate's nomination at the national party convention—and to persuade potential voters in general.

3 Caucuses and primary elections take place in the states.

Caucuses and primaries are ways for the general public to take part in nominating presidential candidates.

At a caucus, local party members gather to nominate a candidate. A caucus is a lively event at which party leaders and activists debate issues and consider candidates. The rules governing caucus procedures vary by party and by state.

A primary is more like a general election. Voters go to the polls to cast their votes for a presidential candidate (or delegates who will represent that candidate at the party convention).

Primary elections are the main way for voters to choose a nominee.

4 Nominee for President is announced at national party convention.

There are two primary political parties in the U.S.—the Democratic Party and the Republican Party. The main goal of a national party convention is to unify party members. Thousands of delegates gather to rally support for the party's ideas and to formally nominate party candidates for President and Vice President.

After the convention, the second stage of the presidential campaign begins: the election campaign. In this stage, candidates from different parties compete against each other as they try to get elected President.

5 Citizens cast their votes.

Presidential elections are held every four years on the Tuesday after the first Monday of November.

Many Americans think that when they cast their ballot, they are voting for their chosen candidate. Actually, they are selecting groups of electors in the Electoral College.

George W. Bush on the campaign trail in 2000

6 The Electoral College casts its votes.

Some of the Founding Fathers wanted Congress to elect the President. Others wanted the President to be elected by popular vote. The Electoral College represents a compromise between these ideas.

Every state has a number of electors equal to its number of Senators and Representatives. In addition, there are three electors for the District of Columbia. In the 2000 election there were 538 electors. Laws vary by state, but electors are usually chosen by popular vote. An elector may not be a Senator, Representative or other person holding a U.S. office.

In most cases, the electoral votes from a particular state go to the candidate who leads the popular vote in that state. (Only Maine and Nebraska divide electoral votes among candidates.) This "winner takes all"

system can produce surprising results; in the elections of 1824, 1876, 1888 and 2000, the candidate who had the greatest popular vote did not win the greatest Electoral College vote, and so lost the presidency.

On the first Monday after the second Wednesday in December, the electors cast their ballots. At least 270 electoral votes are required to elect a President. If this majority is not reached, the House of Representatives chooses the President.

7 The President is inaugurated.

On January 20, the President enters office in a ceremony know as the inauguration and takes the presidential oath: "I do solemnly swear (or affirm) that I will faithfully execute the office of President of the United States, and will to the best of my ability, preserve, protect, and defend the Constitution of the United States."

 Run for office with TFK's Campaign Games
www.timeforkids.com/campaign

Party Animals

The **Democratic donkey** was first associated with Democrat Andrew Jackson's 1828 presidential campaign. His opponents called him a jackass (a donkey), and Jackson decided to use the image of the strong-willed animal on his campaign posters. Later, cartoonist Thomas Nast used the Democratic donkey in newspaper cartoons and made the symbol famous.

Nast invented another famous symbol—the **Republican elephant**. After the Republicans lost the White House to the Democrats in 1877, Nast drew a cartoon of an elephant walking into a trap set by a donkey. He chose the elephant to represent the Republicans because elephants are intelligent but easily controlled.

Democrats today say the donkey is smart and brave, while Republicans say the elephant is strong and dignified.

Who can vote?

Anyone who is
1. 18 years of age
2. a citizen of the U.S.

and meets the residency requirements of his or her state.

Who can be a Senator?

Anyone who is
1. at least 30 years old
2. a citizen of the U.S. for at least 9 years
3. a resident of the state where he or she is elected.

Who can be a Representative?

Anyone who is
1. at least 25 years old
2. a citizen of the U.S. for at least 7 years
3. a resident of the state where he or she is elected.

Who can be President?

Anyone who is
1. a natural-born citizen of the U.S.
2. at least 35 years of age
3. a resident of the U.S. for at least 14 years.

★★ ELECTION HEADLINES ★★

Ronald Reagan

Candidate with the highest popular vote: Ronald Reagan (1984)—54,455,075

Candidate with the highest electoral vote: Reagan (1984)—525

Candidates who carried the most states: Richard M. Nixon (1972) and Reagan (1984)—49

Candidates who won the Electoral College but lost the popular vote: Hayes (1876), Benjamin Harrison (1888) and George W. Bush (2000)

Candidate who became President but lost BOTH the Electoral College AND the popular vote: John Quincy Adams (1824), who was elected by the House of Representatives

The Presidential Succession

Who would take over if the President died, resigned or was removed from office? The list of who's next in line is known as **presidential succession.**

- ★ The Vice President
- ★ Speaker of the House
- ★ President pro tempore of the Senate
- ★ Secretary of State
- ★ Secretary of the Treasury
- ★ Secretary of Defense
- ★ Attorney General
- ★ Secretary of the Interior
- ★ Secretary of Agriculture
- ★ Secretary of Commerce
- ★ Secretary of Labor
- ★ Secretary of Health and Human Services
- ★ Secretary of Housing and Urban Development
- ★ Secretary of Transportation
- ★ Secretary of Energy
- ★ Secretary of Education
- ★ Secretary of Veterans' Affairs

Two members of the current Cabinet cannot become President because they were not born in the U.S. Can you name them?

TFK Mystery Person

This important American leader was a second cousin of President John Adams. He strongly opposed Britain's control of the U.S. colonies, even when many other Americans disagreed with him. He later signed the Declaration of Independence and went on to become Governor of Massachusetts.

Who is he?

Your Body

If you could peek inside your own body, what would you see? Hundreds of bones, miles of blood vessels and trillions of cells, all of which are constantly working together.

Skin

MAIN JOB: To protect your internal organs from drying up and to prevent harmful bacteria from getting inside your body
HOW MUCH: The average person has about six pounds of skin.

Main layers:
- **Epidermis:** Outer layer of skin cells, hair, nails and sweat glands
- **Dermis:** Inner layer of living tissue, containing nerves and blood vessels

Bones

DID YOU KNOW? The largest bone in the body is the femur, or thighbone. In a six-foot-tall person, it is 20 inches long. The smallest is the stirrup bone, in the ear. It is .1 inch long.
MAIN JOB: To give shape and support to your body
HOW MANY: At birth you had more than 300 bones in your body. As an adult you'll have 206, because some bones fuse together.

Kinds of Bones
- **Long** bones are thin; they are found in your legs, arms and fingers.
- **Short** bones are wide and chunky; they are found in your feet and wrists.
- **Flat** bones are flat and smooth, like your ribs and shoulder blades.
- **Irregular** bones, like the bones in your inner ear and the vertebrae in your spine, come in many different shapes.

Joints

DID YOU KNOW? Bones don't bend. It is the joint that allows two bones next to each other to move.
MAIN JOB: To allow bones to move in different directions

Ligaments

MAIN JOB: To hold joints together. These bands of tough tissue are strong and flexible.

Muscles

MAIN JOB: To make body movement possible
HOW MANY: Your body has more than 650 muscles.

Kinds of Muscles
- **Skeletal** muscles help the body move. You have about 400 skeletal muscles.
- **Smooth** muscles are located inside organs, such as the stomach and intestines.
- **Cardiac** muscle is found only in the heart.

Tendons

MAIN JOB: To hold your muscles to your bones
DID YOU KNOW? Tendons look like rubber bands.

Viscera

This term refers to the organs that fill your body's chest and abdominal cavity.
MAIN JOB: To provide your body with food and oxygen and to remove waste
HOW MANY: The viscera include the

trachea (windpipe), lungs, liver, kidneys, gallbladder, spleen, stomach, large intestine, small intestine and bladder.

Glands

MAIN JOB: To manufacture substances that help your body to function

Kinds of Glands

- **Endocrine** glands make hormones, which tell the different parts of your body when to work.
  - **Oil glands** keep your skin from drying out.
  - **Salivary** glands make saliva, which helps to digest carbohydrates in your mouth and aids in swallowing.
  - **Sweat** glands make perspiration, which regulates your body temperature.

Cells

DID YOU KNOW? There are 26 billion cells in a newborn baby and 50 trillion cells in an adult.

MAIN JOB: To perform the many jobs necessary to staying alive, such as moving oxygen around your body, taking care of the fuel supply and waste removal.

Some Different Cells

- **Bone** cells help build your skeleton by producing the fibers and minerals from which bone is made.
  - **Fat** cells contain fat, which is burned to create energy.
  - **Muscle** cells are organized into muscles, which move body parts.
- **Nerve** cells pass nerve messages around your body.
- **Red** blood cells carry oxygen around your body.
- **White** blood cells fight disease.

 Test your health IQ! Play Trivia Fever at **www.timeforkids.com/health**

Your Body's Systems

Circulatory System

The circulatory system transports blood throughout the body. The heart pumps the blood and the **arteries** and **veins** transport it. Blood is carried away from the heart by arteries. The biggest artery, called the **aorta**, branches from the left side of the heart into smaller **arteries**, which then branch into even smaller vessels that travel all over the body. When blood enters the smallest of these vessels, which are called **capillaries**, it gives nutrients and oxygen to cells and takes in carbon dioxide, water and waste. The blood then returns to the heart through **veins**. Veins carry waste products away from cells and bring blood back to the heart, which pumps it to the lungs to pick up oxygen and eliminate waste carbon dioxide.

Digestive System

The digestive system breaks down food into protein, vitamins, minerals, carbohydrates and fats, which the body needs for energy, growth and repair. After food is chewed and swallowed, it goes down a tube called the **esophagus** and enters the **stomach**, where it is broken down by powerful acids. From the stomach the food travels into the **small intestine**, where it is broken down into nutrients. The food that the body doesn't need or can't digest is turned into waste and eliminated from the body through the **large intestine**.

Endocrine System

The endocrine system is made up of glands that produce **hormones**, the body's long-distance messengers. Hormones are chemicals that control body functions, such as metabolism and growth. The **glands**, which include the pituitary gland, thyroid gland, adrenal glands, pancreas, ovaries and testes, release hormones into the bloodstream, which then transports the hormones to organs and tissues throughout the body.

Immune System

The immune system is our body's defense system against infections and diseases. It works to respond to dangerous organisms (such as viruses or bacteria) and substances that may enter the body. There are **three** types of response systems in the immune system.

- The **anatomic response** physically prevents dangerous substances from entering your body. The anatomic system includes the mucous membranes and the skin.
- The **inflammatory system** eliminates the invaders from your body. Sneezing and fever are examples of the inflammatory system at work.
- The **immune response** is made up of white blood cells, which fight infection by gobbling up toxins, bacteria and other threats.

Muscular System

The muscular system is made up of tissues that work with the skeletal system to control movement of the body. Some muscles—like the ones in your arms and legs—are **voluntary**, meaning that you decide when to move them. Other muscles, like the ones in your stomach, heart and intestines, are **involuntary**. This means they're controlled by the nervous system and hormones—you often don't even realize they're at work.

Nervous System

The nervous system is made up of the brain, the spinal cord and nerves. The nervous system sends and receives nerve impulses that tell your muscles and organs what to do. There are three parts of your nervous system that work together.

- **The central nervous system consists of the brain and spinal cord. It sends out nerve impulses and receives sensory information, which tells your brain about things you see, hear, smell, taste and feel.**
- **The peripheral nervous system includes the nerves that branch off from the brain and the spinal cord. It carries the nerve impulses from the central nervous system to the muscles and glands.**
- **The autonomic nervous system regulates involuntary action, such as heartbeat and digestion.**

Respiratory System

The respiratory system brings air into the body and removes carbon dioxide. It includes the nose, trachea (windpipe) and lungs. When you inhale, air enters your **nose** and goes down the **trachea**. The trachea branches into two bronchial tubes, which go to the **lungs**. These tubes branch off into even smaller bronchial tubes, which end in air sacs. Oxygen follows this path and passes through the air sacs and blood vessels and enters the blood stream. At the same time, carbon dioxide passes into the lungs and is exhaled.

Skeletal System

The skeletal system is made up of **bones**, **ligaments** and **tendons**. It shapes the body and protects organs. The skeletal system works with the muscular system to help the body move.

 For more about the body and its systems, go to www.FACT MONSTER.com

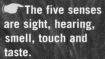

Body Count

☞ The five senses are sight, hearing, smell, touch and taste.

☞ Your body contains eight pints of blood.

☞ You use 14 muscles to smile and 43 to frown.

☞ Kids have 20 first teeth. Adults have 32 teeth.

☞ Most people shed 40 pounds of skin in a lifetime.

☞ Your body is 70% water.

☞ An **eyelash** lives about 150 days before it falls out.

☞ You blink your eyes about 20,000 times a day.

☞ Your heart beats about 100,000 times a day.

☞ When you sneeze, air rushes through your **nose** at a rate of 100 miles per hour.

☞ Humans breathe 20 times per minute, more than 10 million times per year and about 700 million times in a lifetime.

☞ You have about **100,000 hairs** on your head.

☞ Your **tongue** has four taste zones: bitter (back), sour (back sides), salty (front sides) and sweet (front).

The Dirty Truth
About Smoking

There are many reasons not to smoke. Smoking stinks—literally! It makes breath, hair and clothes smell like smoke. It's expensive. It dulls your sense of taste and smell. It raises blood pressure and causes shortness of breath. Some smokers can't stop coughing.

And it kills. Each year, about half a million Americans die from smoking-related illnesses. Cigarettes contain nicotine, a highly addictive drug. Nicotine is also a poison! Arsenic, formaldehyde, hydrogen cyanide, tar and carbon monoxide are some of the other poisons found in cigarettes. No wonder smoking is linked to heart disease and cancer.

Did You Know?

What did antismoking activists **Wayne McLaren** and **David McLean** have in common? They were former "Marlboro Men," the rugged cowboys in ads that helped make Marlboro the world's best-selling cigarette. Both died of lung cancer in the 1990s.

Exercise—It's GOOD for You

Exercise is not only fun, it's also good for your body, mind and overall well-being. Kids who exercise on a regular basis often do better in school, sleep better, don't feel as tired, are less likely to get hurt while exercising and are stronger than less active kids. Exercise can also relieve stress and improve your mood.

There are two types of exercise, **aerobic** and **anaerobic**. When you do aerobic exercise, you increase your heart rate and the flow of oxygen-rich blood to your muscles.

Aerobic exercise builds endurance and burns fat and calories. Doctors recommend that people do 30 minutes of aerobic exercise every day.

When you do anaerobic exercise, such as weight-lifting or push-ups, which involve short bursts of effort, you build strength and muscle mass.

Indoor Exercise

Stuck inside with energy to burn?
Here are some ways you might exercise.

* **dance to your favorite music**
* **see how long you can hula hoop**
* **practice jump-rope tricks**
* **run up and down stairs**

Here are some of kids' favorite kinds of aerobic exercise:

* running
* swimming
* inline skating
* ice skating
* jumping rope
* soccer
* bicycling
* dancing
* playing hockey
* skiing
* skateboarding
* snowboarding

You Are What You Eat

Eat a Variety of Foods

Foods contain nutrients and other healthful substances. No single food can supply all nutrients in the amounts you need. For example, oranges provide vitamin C but no vitamin B_{12}; cheese provides vitamin B_{12} but no vitamin C. To make sure you get all of the nutrients you need, choose the recommended number of daily servings from each of the major food groups.

Build Good Eating Habits

Nutrition experts recommend daily servings from the six food groups in this pyramid. Draw lines to show where each food belongs on the pyramid. **Hint:** Some foods belong to more than one group.

FATS, OILS AND SWEETS
Eat small amounts of fat and sugar. Most Americans eat way too much of these.

MEAT, FISH AND OTHER PROTEIN
Eat three servings a day, including eggs and beans.

MILK, YOGURT AND CHEESE
For bone-building calcium, eat at least three servings a day.

FRUIT
Eat at least three vitamin-packed servings a day.

VEGETABLES
Eat four servings a day.

GRAINS
Try for nine servings throughout the day.

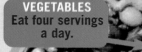
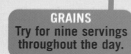

Smart Food, Junk Food

Eating the right foods for health and well-being is not a new idea. According to folklore, the following foods are good for you. Now scientists agree.

❖ **Carrots** are good for your eyes. They contain beta-carotene, which can reduce the chance of eye disease.

❖ **Chicken soup** fights congestion that comes with a cold. It has a protein that thins the lining of the sinuses, thus relieving stuffiness.

❖ **Garlic and onions** kill flu and cold viruses.

❖ **Fish** is good for your brain. The mineral zinc is found in fish and shellfish. Studies show that even a small deficiency of zinc impairs thinking and memory.

❖ **Ginger** fights nausea and helps relieve headaches.

❖ **Yogurt** fights bacteria that can cause infections.

You may love these junk foods, but don't eat too much of them!

❖ **Cakes and cookies** contain lots of sugar and not very many vitamins and minerals.

❖ **Colas** have lots of sugar and few nutrients. Also, they often contain caffeine, which is an addictive drug.

❖ **Ice cream** does have a lot of nutrients, but it is also full of sugar and fat.

❖ **Imitation fruit drinks** are mostly sugar and water, with artificial colors and flavors.

❖ **Potato chips** are deep-fried and contain a lot of fat and salt.

Did You Know?

Grains are part of a healthy diet. But processed grains, such as white flour, aren't so healthy. Whole grains, such as whole wheat, contain more natural nutrients and are higher in fiber. Fiber helps lower cholesterol and may protect against some cancers.

TFK Mystery Person

This Greek physician is often regarded as the "father of medicine." He studied disease and the functions of the body almost 2,500 years ago. The Hippocratic Oath, which is named after him, is often used at the graduation ceremonies of medical schools.

Who is he?

A FAMILY THAT DIGS TOGETHER...

THE CHASES HAVE MADE EXCITING DISCOVERIES IN THE ANCIENT MAYAN CITY OF CARACOL

Adrian, Elyse and Aubrey sift through soil taken from a tomb.

Crawling around creepy tombs is not a typical pastime for a 9-year-old boy, but it's routine for Aubrey Chase, his brother Adrian, 11, and their sister Elyse, 6. Their parents, Arlen and Diane, are archaeologists—scientists who study the remains of old civilizations. Both teach at the University of Central Florida and spend two months a year exploring the ruins of an ancient city called Caracol (car-ah-coal) in Belize, Central America.

Caracol was built more than 2,000 years ago by the Maya, a native people of Central America and Mexico. It is one of the largest Mayan cities ever found. Arlen and Diane Chase have been studying Caracol's ancient temples and tombs for 17 years, searching for clues about the Maya and how they lived.

The kids work with their parents at the dig site every day after morning lessons. The three have found pieces of stone tools and clay pots. "They're really good at fitting the pieces together," says their mom. "It's like a jigsaw puzzle." The kids participate in almost all the excavation activities, including sifting dirt through screens and washing the pieces they find. Soon, Adrian will begin to make detailed technical drawings of the excavation.

The Chases have made many fascinating discoveries at Caracol. Just

BY KATHRYN HOFFMAN

MEXICO

BELIZE

CARIBBEAN SEA

☉ Belize City
Caracol

GUATEMALA

HONDURAS

EL SALVADOR

NICARAGUA

More About the Maya

The Maya built mighty cities and were successful farmers. They had one of the most advanced civilizations of the ancient world. Archaeologists have unearthed many interesting Mayan facts. Here's the dirt:

● **The Maya were very good at math. Their use of the zero allowed them to calculate very large numbers. Scientists say the Maya were the first in the Americas to use the zero.**

● **The Maya created three basic calendars. One was similar to what we have today—it was made up of 365 days. They used it to record daily events, as well as planting and harvesting dates.**

● **Scientists say the Maya had the most advanced writing system of all Native American groups. They used hieroglyphs—pictures or symbols that represent sounds—to record information.**

recently, they found two new tombs as well as a very worn-down monument. They realized that they had walked by the monument many times before—it looked like a large stone.

After examining it more closely, Arlen and Diane noticed an image of a person inside a moon sign. They think the symbol may tell a Mayan myth.

The Chases also found an exciting clue that may help them learn what caused the collapse of Mayan civilization: a huge stash of well-preserved pottery that dates back to A.D. 895. It was found in the last part of Caracol to remain occupied—"literally right before they left," Arlen says. Usually, Mayan artifacts are found in tombs. But these were left in their ordinary environment, which will help the Chases understand what was going on right before the collapse.

The Chase family returns to Florida every spring. The stars and the Mayan secrets are always waiting quietly when the Chases return the next year.

TFK Mystery Person

This famous Roman dictator is one of the most important historical figures of all time. More than 2000 years ago, his social and political beliefs changed the course of history. Fellow politicians who didn't agree with the changes he was proposing eventually killed him. Much later, Shakespeare wrote a play based on his life.

Who is he?

History

Ancient History

10,000–4000 B.C.	In Mesopotamia, settlements develop into cities and people learn to use the wheel.
4500–4000 B.C.	Earliest-known civilization arises in Sumer.
3000–2000 B.C.	The rule of the pharaohs begins in Egypt. King Khufu completes construction of the Great Pyramid at Giza (ca.* 2680 B.C.), and King Khafre builds the Great Sphinx of Giza (ca. 2540 B.C.).
3000–1500 B.C.	The Indus Valley civilization flourishes in what is today Pakistan. In Britain, Stonehenge is erected.
1500–1000 B.C.	Moses leads the Israelites out of Egypt and delivers the Ten Commandments. Chinese civilization develops under the Shang Dynasty.
1000–900 B.C.	Hebrew elders begin to write the books of the Hebrew Bible.
900–800 B.C.	Phoenicians establish Carthage (ca. 810 B.C.). The *Iliad* and the *Odyssey* are composed, probably by the Greek poet Homer.
800–700 B.C.	The first-recorded Olympic games (776 B.C.) take place.
700–600 B.C.	Lao-tse, Chinese philosopher and founder of Taoism, is born around 604 B.C.
600–500 B.C.	Confucius (551–479 B.C.) develops his philosophy in China. Buddha (ca. 563–ca. 483 B.C.) founds Buddhism in India.
500–400 B.C.	Greek culture flourishes during the Age of Pericles (450–400 B.C.); the Parthenon is built in Athens as a temple of the goddess Athena (447–432 B.C.).
400–300 B.C.	Alexander the Great (356–323 B.C.) destroys Thebes (335 B.C.), conquers Tyre and Jerusalem (332 B.C.), occupies Babylon (330 B.C.) and invades India.
300–250 B.C.	The Temple of the Sun is built at Teotihuacán, Mexico (ca. 300 B.C.).
250–200 B.C.	The Great Wall of China is built (ca. 215 B.C.).
100–31 B.C.	Julius Caesar (100–44 B.C.) invades Britain (55 B.C.) and conquers Gaul (France) (ca. 50 B.C.). Cleopatra rules Egypt (51–31 B.C.).
44 B.C.	Julius Caesar is murdered.

*"ca." is an abbreviation for "circa," which means "around."

World History A.D. 1–999

1-49 — Life of Jesus Christ (ca. 1-30). Emperor Kuang Wu Ti founds Han dynasty in China. Buddhism introduced to China.

50-99 — Jews revolt against the Romans; Jerusalem destroyed (A.D. 70).

100-149 — The great emperor Hadrian rules Rome (A.D. 117-138).

150-199 — The earliest Mayan temples are built in Central America.

200-249 — Goths invade Asia Minor (ca. A.D. 220).

250-299 — Mayan civilization (A.D. 250-900) has advances in art, architecture and science.

300-349 — Constantine the Great (rules A.D. 312-337) unites eastern and western Roman empires, with new capital at Constantinople (A.D. 330).

350-399 — Huns (Mongols) invade Europe (ca. A.D. 360).

400-449 — St. Patrick returns to Ireland (A.D. 432) and brings Christianity to the island.

450-499 — Vandals destroy Rome (A.D. 455).

500-549 — Arthur, semi-legendary king of the Britons, is killed around 537.

550-599 — After killing about half the European population, plague in Europe subsides (594).

600-649 — Muhammad, founder of Islam, flees from Mecca to Medina (the *Hegira*, 622). Arabs conquer Jerusalem (637) and destroy the Alexandrian library (641).

650-699 — Arabs attack North Africa (670) and destroy Carthage (697).

700-749 — Arab empire extends from Lisbon to China (by 716).

750-799 — City of Machu Picchu flourishes in Peru.

800-849 — Charlemagne is crowned first Holy Roman Emperor in Rome (800).

850-899 — Russian nation is founded by Vikings under Prince Rurik (855-879).

900-949 — Vikings discover Greenland (ca. 900). Arab Spain under Abd al-Rahman III becomes center of learning (912-961).

950-999 — Eric the Red establishes first Viking colony in Greenland (982).

History

119

World History 1000–1499

ca. 1000–1300 — The Pueblo period of Anasazi culture flourishes; cliff dwellings are built.

ca. 1000 — Viking raider Leif Ericsson reaches North America.

ca. 1008 — Murasaki Shikibu finishes *The Tale of Genji*, the world's first novel.

1066 — William of Normandy invades England, crowned William I (the Conqueror).

1096 — Pope Urban II launches the First Crusade, one of at least 8 European military campaigns between 1095 and 1291 to take the Holy Land from the Muslims.

ca. 1150 — The temple complex of Angkor Wat is completed in Cambodia.

1211 — Genghis Khan invades China, captures Peking (1214), conquers Persia (1218) and invades Russia (1223).

1215 — King John is forced by barons to sign the Magna Carta, limiting royal power.

1231 — The Inquisition begins as the Catholic Church fights heresy; torture is used.

1251 — Kublai Khan governs China.

1271 — Marco Polo of Venice travels to China; visits court of Kublai Khan (1275-1292).

1312–1337 — The Mali Empire reaches its height in Africa under King Mansa Musa.

ca. 1325 — Aztecs establish Tenochtitlán on the site of modern Mexico City.

1337–1453 — In the Hundred Years' War, English and French kings fight for control of France.

1347–1351 — At least 25 million people die in Europe's Black Death (bubonic plague).

1368 — The Ming Dynasty begins in China.

ca. 1387 — Geoffrey Chaucer writes *The Canterbury Tales*.

1428 — Joan of Arc leads the French against the English.

1438 — The Incas rule in Peru.

1450 — Florence, Italy, becomes the center of Renaissance art and learning.

1453 — The Turks conquer Constantinople, thus beginning the Ottoman Empire.

1455 — Johannes Gutenberg invents the printing press.

1462 — Ivan the Great rules Russia until 1505 as first czar.

1492 — Christopher Columbus reaches the New World.

World History 1500–1899

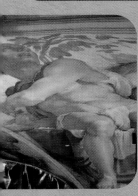

1501 The first African slaves in America are brought to the Spanish colony of Santo Domingo.

ca. 1503 Leonardo da Vinci paints the Mona Lisa.

1509 Henry VIII takes the English throne.
Michelangelo begins painting the ceiling of the Sistine Chapel.

1517 Martin Luther protests wrongdoing in the Catholic Church; start of Protestantism.

1519 Hernando Cortés conquers Mexico for Spain.

1520 Suleiman I ("the Magnificent") becomes Sultan of Turkey.

1522 Portuguese explorer Ferdinand Magellan's expedition circumnavigates the globe.

1543 Copernicus publishes his theory that Earth revolves around the sun.

1547 Ivan IV ("the Terrible") is crowned czar of Russia.

1588 The Spanish Armada is defeated by the English.

1609 Galileo makes the first astronomical observations using a telescope.

1620 Pilgrims, after a three-month voyage in the *Mayflower*, land at Plymouth Rock.

1775 The American Revolution begins with the battle of Lexington and Concord.

1776 The Declaration of Independence is signed.

1787 The American Revolution ends with the Treaty of Paris.

1789 The French Revolution begins with the storming of the Bastille.

1819 Simón Bolívar leads wars for independence throughout South America.

1824 Mexico becomes a republic, three years after declaring independence from Spain.

1846 Failure of potato crop causes famine in Ireland.

1849 The California gold rush begins.

1861 The U.S. Civil War begins as attempts to compromise about slavery fail.

1865 The U.S. Civil War ends.

1884 The Berlin West Africa Conference is held; Europe colonizes the African continent.

1890 U.S. troops kill over 200 Sioux at the Massacre of Wounded Knee.

1898 The Spanish-American War begins.

History

World History 1900–

1903 The Wright brothers fly the first powered airplane at Kitty Hawk, North Carolina.

1904 The Russo-Japanese War begins as competition for Korea and Manchuria heats up.

1909 U.S. explorers Robert E. Peary and Matthew Henson reach the North Pole. The National Association for the Advancement of Colored People (NAACP) is founded in New York City.

1912 The *Titanic* sinks on its maiden voyage; over 1,500 drown.

1914 World War I begins.

1917 U.S. enters World War I. Russian Revolution begins.

1918 World War I fighting ends. A worldwide flu epidemic strikes; by 1920, nearly 20 million are dead.

1919 Mahatma Gandhi begins his nonviolent resistance against British rule in India.

1924 Joseph Stalin begins his rule as Soviet dictator, which lasts until his death in 1953.

1929 In the U.S., stock market prices collapse and the Depression begins.

1933 Adolf Hitler is appointed German chancellor; Nazi oppression begins. Franklin Delano Roosevelt is inaugurated U.S. President; he launches New Deal.

1937 The Nazis open their first concentration camp (Buchenwald); by 1945, the Nazis had murdered some 6 million Jews in what is now called the Holocaust.

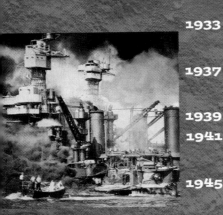

1939 World War II begins.

1941 A Japanese attack on the U.S. fleet at Pearl Harbor in Hawaii (December 7) brings U.S. into World War II. Manhattan Project (atomic bomb research) begins.

1945 War ends in Europe on V-E Day (May 8). The U.S. drops the atomic bomb on Hiroshima, Japan (August 6), and Nagasaki, Japan (August 9). The war ends in the Pacific on V-J day (September 2).

1947 The U.S. Marshall Plan is proposed to help Europe recover from the war. India and Pakistan gain independence from Britain.

1948 The nation of Israel is proclaimed.

1949 The North Atlantic Treaty Organization (NATO) is founded. Communist People's Republic of China is proclaimed by Chairman Mao Zedong. South Africa sets up apartheid (a policy of discrimination against nonwhites).

1950 Korean War begins when North Korean Communist forces invade South Korea. It lasts for three years.

For a year-by-year guide from 1900 onward, go **www.FACT MONSTER.com**

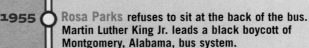

1955 Rosa Parks refuses to sit at the back of the bus. Martin Luther King Jr. leads a black boycott of Montgomery, Alabama, bus system.

1957 Russians launch *Sputnik I*, the first Earth-orbiting satellite; the Space Age begins.

1963 Martin Luther King Jr. delivers his "I have a dream" speech in Washington, D.C. President Kennedy is shot and killed by a sniper in Dallas, Texas.

1965 U.S. planes begin combat missions in Vietnam War.

1967 Israeli and Arab forces battle; Six-Day War ends with Israel occupying Sinai Peninsula, Golan Heights, Gaza Strip and the east bank of the Suez Canal.

1969 Apollo 11 astronauts take man's first walk on the moon.

1973 Vietnam War ends with signing of peace pacts. The Yom Kippur War begins as Egyptian and Syrian forces attack Israel.

1979 Muslim leader Ayatollah Khomeini takes over Iran; U.S. citizens seized and held hostage.

1981 Scientists identify the AIDS virus.

1989 Thousands rallying for democracy are killed in Tiananmen Square, China. After 28 years, the Berlin Wall that divided Germany is torn down.

1990 South Africa frees Nelson Mandela, who was imprisoned 27 years. Iraqi troops invade Kuwait, setting off nine-month Persian Gulf War.

1991 The Soviet Union breaks up after President Mikhail Gorbachev resigns. In Yugoslavia, Slovenia and Croatia secede; a four-year war with Serbia begins.

1994 In Rwanda, murders of Tutsis by Hutus begin; 800,000 killed in about 100 days. South Africa holds first interracial national election; Nelson Mandela elected President.

2000 Elections in Yugoslavia formally end the war-torn rule of Slobodan Milosevic.

2001 Hijackers crash two jetliners into the Twin Towers of New York City's World Trade Center and another into the Pentagon. A fourth hijacked plane crashes 80 miles outside Pittsburgh, Pennsylvania.

go

For more time lines, go to
www.timeforkids.com/timelines

History

Holidays

Federal Holidays

In the U.S., there are **10** federal holidays set by law. Four of these holidays are set by date. The other six are set by a day of the week and month. Most of these are celebrated on Mondays to create three-day weekends.

New Year's Day
January 1
New Year's Day has its origin in ancient Roman times, when sacrifices were offered to Janus, the two-faced Roman god who looked back on the past and forward to the future.

Martin Luther King Jr. Day
Third Monday in January
This holiday honors the civil rights leader. It has been a federal holiday since 1986.

Washington's Birthday
Third Monday in February
Although this holiday is sometimes called Presidents' Day to honor both George Washington and Abraham Lincoln, the federal holiday is officially Washington's Birthday.

Memorial Day
Last Monday in May
Memorial Day originated in 1868 as a day when the graves of Civil War soldiers would be decorated. Later, it became a holiday dedicated to the memory of all war dead.

Independence Day
July 4
The Declaration of Independence was adopted on July 4, 1776. It declared that the 13 colonies were independent of Britain.

TFK TOP 5
MostPopularHoliday Pies in the U.S.

Each Thanksgiving, Americans gobble up more pumpkin pie than their usual favorite—apple! Here are the pies Americans feast on most during the holiday season. Which is your favorite?

1 Pumpkin
2 Apple
3 Cherry
4 Lemon Meringue
5 Pecan, Chocolate Cream, Mincemeat (Three-way tie)

Source: American Pie Council

A Fourth of July celebration

Labor Day
First Monday in September
Labor Day, a day set aside in honor of workers, was first celebrated in New York in 1882 under the sponsorship of the Central Labor Union.

Columbus Day
Second Monday in October
Columbus Day honors Christopher Columbus's landing in the New World in 1492.

Veterans' Day
November 11
Veterans' Day honors all men and women who have served America in its armed forces.

Thanksgiving
Fourth Thursday in November
The first American Thanksgiving took place in 1621, to celebrate the harvest reaped by the Plymouth Colony after a harsh winter.

Christmas Day
December 25
The most popular holiday of the Christian year, Christmas is celebrated as the anniversary of the birth of Jesus.

go For more on these holidays and others www.FACT MONSTER.COM

TFK Puzzles & Games — Turkey Time

Go from the door to the table. You must use the path that has the letters that spell THANKSGIVING. Good luck and good eating!

Other **FUN** Holidays

Groundhog Day
February 2
Legend has it that on this morning, if a groundhog can see its shadow, there will be six more weeks of winter.

Mardi Gras
Last day before Lent
"Mardi Gras," or "Fat Tuesday," is a time of carnivals and parades before Ash Wednesday starts the Christian season of Lent.

Valentine's Day
February 14
Named for the third-century martyr St. Valentine, this day is celebrated with candy, cards and other tokens of love.

Mother's Day
Second Sunday in May
Having a day to honor mothers goes back at least as far as 17th-century England, when Mothering Sunday began.

Father's Day
Third Sunday in June
This U.S. holiday honoring fathers began in 1910 in Spokane, Washington.

Halloween
October 31
Halloween is celebrated with jack-o-lanterns, costumes and the telling of ghost stories.

Kwanzaa
December 26 through January 1
Kwanzaa, an African-American holiday, honors the values of ancient African cultures.

Groundhog Glory

The most famous American groundhog, Punxsutawney Phil, lives in a climate-controlled habitat next to Pennsylvania's Punxsutawney Library. A local celebrity, Phil gained national fame in the 1993 movie *Groundhog Day*. Phil's weather predictions are recorded in the National Archive. So far, he has seen his shadow—and forecast a long winter—about 85% of the time.

Christian Holidays 2003

Ash Wednesday
March 5
The first day of Lent

Easter
April 20
The resurrection of Jesus

Pentecost
June 8
The feast of the Holy Spirit

First Sunday in Advent
November 30
The start of the Christmas season

Christmas Day
December 25
The birth of Jesus

Visit the TFK spooky schoolhouse if you dare!
www.timeforkids.com/halloween

All Jewish and Muslim holidays begin at sundown the day before they are listed here.

Jewish Holidays 2003

Purim
March 18
The feast of lots

Passover
April 17
The feast of unleavened bread

Shavuot
June 6
The feast of first fruits

Sukkot
October 11
The feast of the tabernacles

Rosh Hashanah
September 27
The Jewish New Year

Simchat Torah
October 19
The rejoicing of the law

Yom Kippur
October 6
The day of atonement

Hanukkah
December 20
The festival of lights

Muslim Holidays 2003

Eid al-Adha
February 12
The festival of sacrifice

Muharram
March 5
The Muslim New Year

Mawlid al-Nabi
May 14
The prophet Muhammad's birthday

Ramadan
begins October 27
The month of fasting

Eid al-Fitr
November 26
Ramadan ends

A Chinese Celebration

Legend has it that in ancient times, Buddha asked all the animals to meet him on Chinese New Year. Twelve came, and Buddha named a year after each one. He announced that the people born in each animal's year would have some of that animal's personality. People born in the Year of the Goat (which begins February 1, 2003) are said to be wise and gentle. See page 57 for all the Chinese years.

TFK Mystery Person

This activist was married to one of the most important civil rights leaders in U.S. history. After he was assassinated in 1968, she carried on his message of equality and nonviolence. In 1983, she led a campaign to make his birthday a legal holiday. It's now celebrated by Americans in January.
Who is she?

127

Homework Helper

TIPS
for Being a Good Listener

1. Give your full attention to the teacher. Don't look out the window or at what else is going on in the room.

2. Make sure your mind is focused, too. If you feel your mind wandering, change the position of your body and try to concentrate on the teacher's words.

3. Let the teacher finish before you begin to talk. When you interrupt, it looks like you aren't listening, even if you really are.

4. Listen for main ideas. The main ideas are the most important points someone wants to get across. Pay special attention to statements that begin with phrases such as "The thing to remember is..."

5. Ask questions. If you are not sure you understand what the teacher has said, just ask!

Please Take Notes!

Hearing something once is not enough to really learn it, and that is why it is so important to take notes. Taking notes helps you to focus and learn during class time. Clearly written, accurate notes also help you to study later. Here are some tips.

1. Keep your notes organized. Use a separate notebook for each subject, or use dividers in your loose-leaf notebook to make sections for each subject.

2. Begin each note-taking session at the top of a fresh page. Start by writing the date.

3. Do not try to write down everything the teacher says. Try to record as many facts and ideas as you can. Underline important facts or main ideas.

4. Use short sentences and easy-to-remember abbreviations and symbols.

5. Read over your notes after class. If there is anything you don't understand, ask the teacher at the next class.

I left it in my mom's car.

Don't know something? Look it up at the TFK Information Station: *www.timeforkids.com/info*

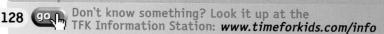

Ten Tips for Taking Tests

1. Read the instructions carefully. Never assume you will know what they will say! Ask the teacher if you are unsure about anything.

2. Read the entire test through before starting. Notice the point value of each section. This will help you to pace yourself.

3. Answer the easiest questions first, then the ones with the highest point value. You don't want to spend 20 minutes trying to figure out a two-point problem!

4. Keep busy! If you get stuck on a question, come back to it later. The answer might come to you while you are working on another part of the test.

5. If you aren't sure how to answer a question fully, try to answer at least part of it. You might get partial credit.

6. Need to guess on a multiple-choice test? First, eliminate the answers that you know are wrong. Then take a guess. Because your first guess is most likely to be correct, you shouldn't go back and change an answer later unless you are certain you were wrong.

7. On an essay test, take a moment to plan your writing. First, jot down the important points you want to make. Then number these points in the order you will cover them.

8. Keep it neat! If your teacher can't read your writing, you might lose points.

9. Don't waste time doing things for which you will not receive credit, such as rewriting test questions.

10. Leave time at the end to look over your work. Did you answer every question? Did you proofread for errors? It is easy to make careless mistakes while taking a test.

AFTER THE TEST

☞ Read the teacher's comments carefully and try to learn from your mistakes.

☞ Save tests to review for end-of-term tests.

I was trying to save the rain forest by saving paper.

How to Write a

Book reports are a way to show how well you understood a book and to tell what you think about it. Many teachers have their own rules about what should be in a book report, so be sure to check with your teacher. Here are some general guidelines.

INTRODUCTION

The introduction starts your report and captures the reader's attention. It should include:

☛ **The title and author of the book**

☛ **Some information about the book (but don't give away the ending)**

☛ **What kind of story it is—adventure, fantasy, animal, nonfiction, biography?**

BODY

This is where you describe the main parts of the story: theme, plot, setting and characters. Then you can give your opinions about the book.

☛ The **theme** is the most important message in the story. An example might be the importance of friendship. Tell what you think the theme is and why you do. Lessons learned by the main character are often important clues to the theme.

☛ The **plot** is the series of events in the book. In your book report, you should explain the main event or conflict in the plot. What events lead up to it? What happens as a result?

Be careful not to re-tell the whole plot in detail—you will need room in your report to write about other things. Just say enough about the plot so that the rest of your report will make sense. If the plot has a big mystery or a surprise, be careful not to give away the ending.

☛ The **setting** is the time and place of the story. Is it set a long time ago, now or in the future? Does it take place in another country or in an imaginary place?

☛ The **characters** are people, animals and creatures in the book. The main character is called the protagonist. Who are the other characters? Do they help or hinder the protagonist?

I left it in my pocket and my mom put it through the wash.

Book Report

An important part of a book report is giving your opinion or telling what you thought about the book. Some questions you might want to answer are:

- ☞ **Did you like the story? Why or why not?**

- ☞ **What was the best part of the book? Why?**

- ☞ **How did the story make you feel? Did you feel different emotions at different points?**

- ☞ **Would you recommend the book to friends?**

- ☞ **Would you read other books by the author?**

- ☞ **What new things did you learn from the book?**

CONCLUSION

The conclusion sums up your report. It tells your overall opinion of the book and the most important thing you want readers to know about it.

Mrs. Coverlet's Magicians:
A Spellbinding Story

The babysitter has been in bed for weeks, and Toad says it's because he put a spell on her. Could it be true? That's the question that runs through *Mrs. Coverlet's Magicians* by Mary Nash. This hilarious novel tells about the troubles that Toad, his sister Mary and his brother Malcolm get into while the one adult in the house lies asleep.

I loved this book because whenever people said Toad's ideas were silly, he found a surprising way to prove them wrong. For example, when Toad announced that he could find a Christmas tree to chop down, Malcolm and Molly laughed, because there are no woods near their town. But soon afterward, Toad led them into the old marsh and began to make a very strange-looking wand.

Tips for Writing Essays

Come up with a Good Topic

1. First, choose a subject that interests you. Let's say you like dogs. That's a good place to start.

2. Then try to narrow the subject down to something you can write about knowledgeably. Let's say you have a beagle and you know a lot about beagles based on your experience as a dog owner.

3. Now come up with a statement about your topic. "Beagles are the best breed of dog." This will be your main idea, or thesis statement.

4. Answer the question "why" at least three times. Why are beagles the best? Some answers might be, "beagles are smart" or "beagles are neither too small nor too big—they're just right."

5. Wrap it up. Write a brief conclusion that sums up the points you have made. "Clearly, beagles are best because they're smart and they're just the right size."

Brainstorm

1. Brainstorming is one way to develop your topic. It is a good way to let ideas you didn't know you had come to the surface.

2. Write down whatever comes into your head about your topic. Don't worry about organizing your thoughts just yet.

3. Keep writing for a short but specific amount of time—maybe five minutes. Don't stop to correct spelling or grammar errors.

4. After a few minutes, read through what you have written. Chances are you came up with some new ideas.

I thought it was due next week!

Organize Your Ideas

Develop an outline to organize your ideas. An outline shows your main ideas and the order in which you are going to write about them. Here is a sample outline.

Worm Composting: A Great Indoor Activity

1. Introduction

2. Worm composting is good for the earth
   a. Worms can turn food waste into rich compost
   b. Worms help you recycle fruit and vegetable scraps
   c. Worm compost makes plants healthy and strong

3. Worm composting is a fun way to learn about worms
   a. Worms make tunnels in soil
   b. Worms seem to have favorite kinds of garbage

4. My personal experience with worm composting
   a. I liked helping my sister to set up the worm bin
   b. It was fun to feed the worms things like potato peels
   c. We put the worm compost on our houseplants

5. Conclusion

Revise the First Draft

Try to set aside your draft for a day or two before revising. This way you can see it with fresh eyes and notice any problems. You may decide you need to develop your ideas in more detail, give more evidence to support your claims or delete material that is unnecessary. You may also reword sentences.

Read your paper out loud. This sometimes makes it easier to identify writing that is awkward or unclear. Have somebody else read the paper and tell you if there's anything that's unclear or confusing.

Proofread the Final Draft

Look for careless errors such as misspelled words and incorrect punctuation and capitalization. If you type your paper on a computer, print out a copy to proofread. Don't rely on spell checkers and grammar checkers—they don't always catch errors!

HOW TO WRITE
A NARRATIVE ESSAY

The first important thing to remember about a narrative essay is that it tells a story. You may write about

❉ an experience or event from your past

❉ a recent or an ongoing experience or event

❉ something that happened to somebody else, such as a parent or a grandparent

Learning something new can be a scary experience. One of the hardest things I've ever had to do was learn how to swim. I was always afraid of the water, but I decided that swimming was an important skill that I should learn.

The second important thing is that in a narrative essay the story should have a point. In the final paragraph, you should come to a conclusion about the story you told.

Learning to swim was not easy for me, but in the end my efforts paid off. Now when I am faced with a new situation I am not so nervous. I may feel uncomfortable at first, but I know that as my skills get better, I will feel more and more comfortable.

The conclusion is where the author reflects on the larger meaning of the experience described. In this case, the author concludes that learning to swim has helped her to feel more confident about herself in new situations. The idea that self-confidence comes from conquering your fears is something that anyone can relate to. It is the point of this essay.

GET PERSONAL!

The writing in an essay should be lively and engaging. Try to keep the reader's interest by adding details or observations. Sharing your thoughts invites the reader into your world and makes the story more personal and more interesting.

I dropped it in the sink while I was doing dishes.

136

TACKLE A DESCRIPTIVE ESSAY

The purpose of a descriptive essay is to describe a person, place or thing in such vivid detail that the reader can easily form a mental picture. You may accomplish this by using words that create a mood, making interesting comparisons and describing images that appeal to the senses.

> **I have always been fascinated by carnival rides. My first experience with a carnival ride was a Ferris wheel at a local fair. It was huge, smoky and noisy. Ever since that first impression years ago, these rides have reminded me of mythical beasts carrying off their screaming passengers. Even the droning sound of their engines brings to mind the great roar of a fire-breathing dragon.**

Mood Words The author uses words that create excitement, like "fascinated," "great roar" and "fire-breathing dragon."

Interesting Comparisons One way the author makes his subject interesting is by comparing the Ferris wheel to a mythical beast.

Sensory Details The author uses his senses for details about how the Ferris wheel looks, sounds and feels. The ride is "huge, smoky and noisy" and its engines "drone."

Like other essays, a descriptive essay should be well organized. This essay began with a general statement—that the author has always been fascinated by carnival rides. The body is made of paragraphs that describe the subject. The conclusion restates the main idea—in this case, that the author continues to find carnival rides fascinating.

> **A trip on the Ferris wheel never fails to thrill me. The fascination I have for Ferris wheels comes back with each and every ride.**

Teenagers stole it.

How to Write a Research Paper

Writing a research paper involves all of the steps for writing an essay plus some additional ones. To write a research paper you must first do some research, that is, investigate your topic by reading about it in different sources, including books, magazines, newspapers and the Internet. The information you gather is used to support the points you make in your paper.

Writing a research paper also involves documenting your sources of information in footnotes or endnotes. This way, the reader knows where you got your information and can judge whether it is reliable.

Eight Steps to a Great Research Paper

1. Find your topic. Try to pick a topic that's fun and interesting. If your topic genuinely interests you, chances are you'll enjoy working on it.

2. Look for sources. Take a trip to the library. Use the electronic catalog or browse the shelves to look for books on your topic. If you find a book that is useful, check the bibliography (list of sources) in the back of that book for other books or articles on that topic. Ask a librarian if you need help finding sources.

Keep a list of all the sources that you use. Include the title of the source, the author, publisher, and place and date of publication.

3. Read your sources and take notes. After you've gathered your sources, begin reading and taking notes.

Use 3 x 5 index cards, writing one fact or idea per card. This way related ideas from different sources can be easily grouped together. Be sure to note the source and the page number on each card.

4. Make an outline. Organize your index cards by topic, then develop an outline to organize your ideas. An outline shows your main ideas and the order in which you are going to write about them. (See page 135 for a sample outline.)

> **My computer crashed.**

5. Write a first draft. Every essay or paper is made up of three parts: the introduction, the body and the conclusion.

☞ The introduction is the first paragraph. It often begins with a general statement about the topic and ends with a more specific statement of your main idea.

☞ The body of the paper follows the introduction. It has a number of paragraphs in which you develop your ideas in detail. Limit yourself to one main idea per paragraph, and use examples and quotations to support your ideas.

☞ The conclusion is the last paragraph of the paper. Its purpose is to sum up your points—leaving out specific examples—and to restate your main idea.

6. Use footnotes or endnotes. These identify the sources of your information. If you are using footnotes, the note will appear on the same page as the information you are documenting, at the bottom (or foot) of the page. If you are using endnotes, the note will appear together with all other notes on a separate page at the end of your report, just before the bibliography.

There are different formats, so be sure to use the one your teacher prefers.

The National Beagle Club held its first show in 1891.[1]

[1] Samantha Lopez, *For the Love of Beagles* (New York: Ribbon Books, 1993), p. 24.

7. Revise your draft. After you've completed your first draft, you'll want to make some changes. (See page 135 for general tips.) Also remember that in a research paper, it's important to check that you have put footnotes or endnotes wherever they are needed.

8. Proofread your final draft. When you are happy with your revision, print it and check spelling, punctuation and grammar. It is good to do this more than once, checking for different kinds of mistakes each time.

Don't Copy This!

Plagiarism means using someone else's work as your own. If you take words or ideas from a source without giving credit, you are plagiarizing. When you copy something directly from a book without putting it in your own words, put quotation marks around it so that you know it is an exact quotation. This will help you avoid plagiarism.

The cat shredded it.

How to Write a Biography

A biography is the story of a life. Biographies can be just a few sentences long, or they can fill an entire book. Biographers (people who write biographies) use primary and secondary sources.

❊ Primary sources convey first-hand experience. They include letters, diaries, interview tapes and other accounts of personal experience.

❊ Secondary sources convey second-hand experience. They include articles, textbooks, reference books and other information sources.

To write a biography, you should

1. Select a person you find interesting.

2. Find out the basic facts of the person's life. You might want to start by looking in an encyclopedia.

3. Think about what else you would like to know about the person.

❊ What makes this person special or interesting?

❊ What kind of effect did he or she have on the world?

❊ What are the adjectives you would use to describe the person?

❊ What examples from the person's life show those qualities?

❊ What events shaped or changed this person's life?

And Furthermore: Transition Words and Phrases

Transition words and phrases help establish clear connections between ideas and ensure that sentences and paragraphs flow together smoothly, making them easier to read. Use the following words and phrases in the following circumstances.

To indicate more information:	To indicate an example:	To indicate a cause or reason:	To indicate a result or an effect:
Besides	For example	As	Accordingly
Furthermore	For instance	Because	Consequently
In addition	In particular	Because of	Finally
In fact	Particularly	Due to	Therefore
Moreover	Specifically	Since	Thus

There was a blackout so I couldn't see to do my homework.

Giving Credit Where It Is Due:
Putting Together a
Bibliography

A bibliography is a list of the sources you used to get information for your report. It is included at the end of your report. You will find it easy to prepare your bibliography if you keep track of each source you use as you are reading and taking notes.

When putting together a final bibliography, list your sources (texts, articles, interviews and so on) in alphabetical order by authors' last names. Sources that don't have authors should be alphabetized by title. There are different formats for bibliographies, so be sure to use the one your teacher prefers.

General Guide for Bibliographies

Book
Author (last name first). *Title of the book*. City: Publisher, Date of publication.
Dahl, Roald. *The BFG*. New York: Farrar, Straus and Giroux, 1982.

Encyclopedia
Encyclopedia title, edition, date. Volume number, "Article title," page numbers.
The Encyclopaedia Britannica, 1997. Volume 7, "Gorillas," pp. 50-51.

Magazine
Author (last name first), "Article Title." *Name of magazine*. Volume number (Date): page numbers.
Jordan, Jennifer, "Filming at the Top of the World." *Museum of Science Magazine*. Volume 47, No. 1 (Winter 1998): p. 11.

Newspaper
Author (last name first), "Article title." *Name of newspaper*, city, state of publication. (Date): edition if available, section, page number(s).
Powers, Ann, "New Tune for the Material Girl." *The New York Times*, New York, N.Y. (3/1/98): Atlantic Region, Section 2, p. 34.

Person
Full name (last name first). Occupation. Date of interview.
Smeckleburg, Sweets. Bus driver. April 1, 2002.

CD-ROM
Disc title: version, date. "Article title," pages if given. Publisher.
Compton's Multimedia Encyclopedia: Macintosh version, 1995. "Civil rights movement," p. 3. Compton's Newsmedia.

Internet
Author of message (Date). Subject of message. Electronic conference or bulletin board (Online). Available e-mail: LISTSERV@ e-mail address
Ellen Block (September 15, 1995). New Winners. Teen Booklist (Online). Helen Smith@wellington.com

Doing Research on the **Internet**

The Internet has become a convenient tool for finding information on just about anything. Here are some things to keep in mind when you're doing research on the Internet.

> **Choose your key words carefully.** The more words you use, the more specific your search will be. For example, if you use the key word "animals," you will find sites with all kinds of information about animals. If you use the key words "endangered animals," you will find sites with information on that particular topic. If you don't find what you want, try using different key words.

> **Know your source!** Anybody can put up information on the Internet and call himself an expert. The information you read on someone's home page may be incorrect. The web sites of government sources, schools, and magazine and newspaper publishers are more accurate.

> **Search in different ways.** Just as one encyclopedia at the library may not have all the information you want, one search engine may not have just what you are looking for. If you don't find what you want through one search, try another.

Here is a list of web sites that you might find useful.

Search Engines
Ask Jeeves Kids: *www.ajkids.com*
Google: *www.google.com*
Yahooligans!: *www.yahooligans.com*

Kids
Fact Monster: *www.factmonster.com*
Sports Illustrated For Kids: *www.sikids.com*
TIME For Kids: *www.timeforkids.com*

News
BBC TV & Radio: *www.bbc.co.uk*
CNN Interactive: *www.cnn.com*
The New York Times: *www.nytimes.com*
The Washington Post: *www.washingtonpost.com*

Government Sites
Census Bureau: *www.census.gov*
Department of the Treasury: *www.ustreas.gov*
Environmental Protection Agency (EPA): *www.epa.gov*
Federal Bureau of Investigation: *www.fbi.gov*
FedStats (statistics) for Kids: *www.fedstats.gov/kids.html*
House of Representatives: *www.house.gov*
National Weather Service: *www.nws.noaa.gov*
Senate: *www.senate.gov*
U.S. Postal Service: *www.usps.gov*
White House: *www.whitehouse.gov*

I swear I gave it to you yesterday.

Conducting an Interview

Books, magazines and the Internet aren't the only sources for research. Conducting an interview can be a great way to learn about a subject, too! You may learn unexpected things, and you'll feel like a reporter.

BEFORE THE INTERVIEW

Make a list of questions you plan to ask. What would you like to learn about? Let's say your subject is the assassination of President Kennedy. You could ask the person you are interviewing where they were when they heard the news. Who were they with? How did they feel? What concerns did they have for the country?

DURING THE INTERVIEW

1. If the person gives you permission, tape-record the interview. Even if you tape the interview, you should take notes so that you'll remember important points.

2. At the beginning of the interview, ask when and where the person was born. This will save you from having to backtrack and figure out dates later.

3. Don't interrupt or correct the person you are talking to. People sometimes remember things wrong. That's okay—you can check dates and facts later. The important thing is to hear about the person's impressions and feelings.

4. Listen carefully. Something the person says may inspire you to ask a question you hadn't planned. For example, let's say the person mentions that she will never forget seeing television footage of the Kennedy children at the President's funeral. You might ask why it was so unforgettable. What did the children do? How old were they?

AFTER THE INTERVIEW

Look back over the questions you prepared before the interview. Did the interview help to answer them? If you are going to do an oral report, think about how you will present your information. You might talk about what you had hoped to get out of the interview, and what you learned from it that was unexpected. You could also talk about the difference between reading a book and getting a personal view.

How to Give an Oral Report

In many ways, planning an oral report is similar to planning a written report.

☛ **Choose a subject that is interesting to you.** What do you care about? What would you like to learn more about? Follow your interests, and you'll find your topic.

☛ **Be clear about your purpose.** Do you want to persuade your audience? Inform them about a topic? Or just tell an entertaining story?

An oral report also has the same three basic parts as a written report.

☛ The **introduction** should "hook" your audience. Catch their interest with a question, a dramatic tale or a personal experience that relates to your topic.

☛ The **body** is the main part of your report, and will use most of your time. Make an outline of the body so that you can share information in an organized way.

☛ The **conclusion** is the time to summarize and get across your most important point. What do you want the audience to remember?

1. Research!

It's important to really know your subject and be well organized. If you know your material well, you will be confident and able to answer questions. If your report is well organized, the audience will find it informative and easy to follow.

Think about your audience. If you were listening to a report on your subject, what would you want to know? Too much information can seem overwhelming, and too little can be confusing. Organize your outline around your key points, and focus on getting them across.

Remember—enthusiasm is contagious! If you're interested in your subject, the audience will be interested, too.

2. Rehearse!

Practicing your report is a key to success. At first, some people find it helpful to go through the report alone. You might practice in front of a mirror or in front of your stuffed animals. Then, try out your report in front of a practice audience—friends or family. Ask your practice audience:

☛ **Could you follow my presentation?**

☛ **Did I seem knowledgeable about my subject?**

☛ **Was I speaking clearly? Could you hear me? Did I speak too fast or too slow?**

If you are using visual aids, such as posters or overhead transparencies, practice using them while you rehearse. Also, you might want to time yourself to see how long your report actually takes. The time will probably go by faster than you expect.

3. Report!

Stand up straight. Hold your upper body straight, but not stiff, and keep your chin up. Try not to distract your audience by shifting around or fidgeting.

Make eye contact. You will seem more sure of yourself, and the audience will listen better, if you make eye contact during your report.

Use gestures. Your body language can help you make your points and keep the audience interested. Lean forward at key moments, and use your hands and arms for emphasis.

Use your voice effectively. Vary your tone and speak clearly. If you're nervous, you might speak too fast. If you find yourself hurrying, take a breath and try to slow it down.

It fell in the mud.

Nerves!

Almost everyone is nervous when speaking before a group. Many people say public speaking is their Number 1 fear. Being well prepared is the best way to prevent nerves from getting the better of you. Also, try breathing deeply before you begin your report, and remember to breathe during the report. Being nervous isn't all bad—it can help to keep you on your toes!

One last thing!

Have you prepared and practiced your report? Then go get 'em! Remember: you know your stuff, and your report is interesting and important.

Puzzles & Games

Order in the Classroom!

Going to school is nothing to lose your head over. Tell that to this teacher! Help his students stay on the right track. Circle 13 things that are wrong in this crazy, mixed-up classroom.

BONUS: One math problem is wrong. What's the right answer?

145

Did You Ever Wonder?

Here are some questions that kids have sent to www.factmonster.com. You can find all the answers in this book!

What do the colors in the Olympic rings mean? **Page 286**

What are the two kinds of mammals that lay eggs? What do you call them? **Page 30**

Where can I find a times table to memorize? **Page 163**

What is the world's tallest building? **Page 49**

I need to find a list of birthstones. **Page 57**

What's the smallest bone in the body? The largest? **Page 108**

How were chocolate chip cookies invented? **Page 152**

I was born in 1989. What is my Chinese animal year? **Page 57**

What language is spoken by the most people? **Page 155**

How do I convert pounds to kilograms? **Page 171**

Does it hurt a woodpecker to hammer like that? **Page 32**

When did Joan of Arc live? **Page 120**

What was the smartest dinosaur? **Page 68**

How do I write my age in Roman numerals? **Page 160**

If the stars on the flag stand for the 50 states, what do the stripes stand for? **Page 295**

What did people wear in the 1920s? **Page 86**

When you mix a color with white to make it lighter, what do you call that? What do you call it when you mix it with black? **Page 38**

How many people died when the *Titanic* sank? **Page 73**

What is the planet Jupiter's big red spot made of? **Page 271**

I need to know which three Presidents died on the Fourth of July. **Page 238**

What is the highest mountain in the world? **Page 88**

When was the telephone invented? **Page 151**

Which is the biggest movie hit of all time, *Star Wars* or *Titanic?* **Page 179**

What's Idaho's state bird? **Page 311**

Who can run for President? Do you have to have been in the military? **Page 106**

What is J. K. Rowling's middle name? **Page 47**

I need to research biomes. What are the main types? **Pages 80 to 81**

What's the name of that groundhog in Pennsylvania that forecasts the weather? **Page 126**

Which state gets the most tornadoes? **Page 338**

What does Italy's flag look like? **Page 203**

Why did people think the cancan dance was so shocking? **Page 65**

What country has the most people? **Page 188**

I know dinosaurs lived in the Jurassic period. What period do we live in now? **Page 262**

What do you call a mother pig? A baby pig? **Page 31**

What are the different kinds of musical instruments? **Page 186**

I need to learn how to spell my name using American Sign Language. **Page 156**

When was Donkey Kong invented? **Page 60**

What is the oldest religion in the world? **Page 253**

TFK Mystery Person

George W. Bush narrowly defeated this person in his run for President in 2000. After getting over his close loss, this former Vice President (under Bill Clinton) decided to go into another career in which he could make a difference: teaching! So he worked as a visiting professor at Columbia University's Graduate School of Journalism in New York.

Who is he?

Inventions

Just a few highlights

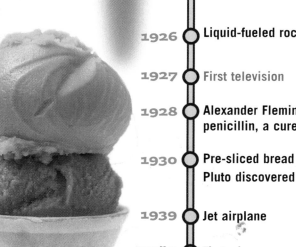

Model T car

1901	First transatlantic radio signals
1903	**Wright brothers fly first motorized plane**
1904	Ice-cream cone
1907	**Plastic**
1908	Model T car
1911	**Oreo cookies**
1913	**First moving assembly line**
1916	Einstein's theory of relativity published
1926	**Liquid-fueled rocket**
1927	First television
1928	**Alexander Fleming discovers penicillin, a cure for infections**
1930	**Pre-sliced bread Pluto discovered**
1939	**Jet airplane**
1945	**First microwave oven ENIAC, the first electronic computer**
1949	**Silly Putty**

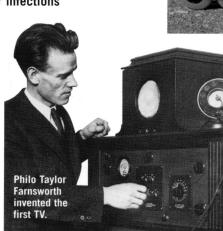

Philo Taylor Farnsworth invented the first TV.

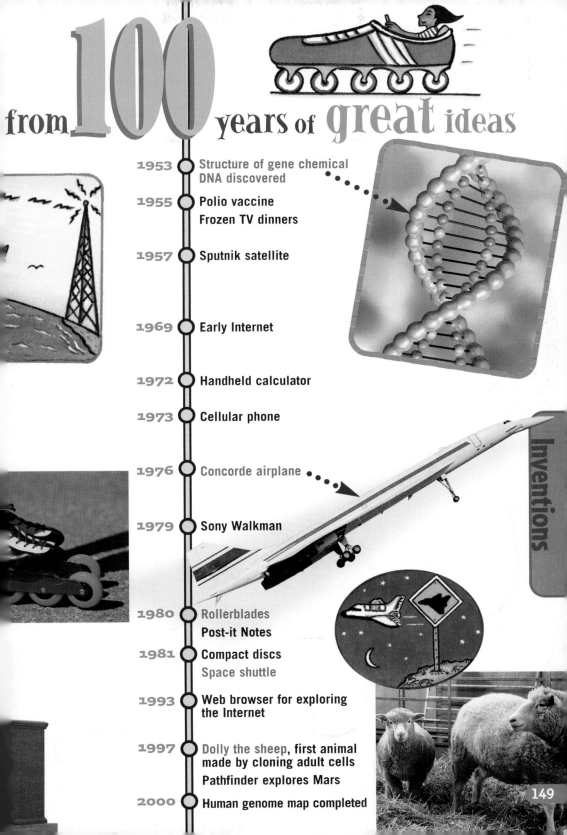

from 100 years of great ideas

1953	**Structure of gene chemical DNA discovered**
1955	**Polio vaccine** **Frozen TV dinners**
1957	**Sputnik satellite**
1969	**Early Internet**
1972	**Handheld calculator**
1973	**Cellular phone**
1976	**Concorde airplane**
1979	**Sony Walkman**
1980	**Rollerblades** **Post-it Notes**
1981	**Compact discs** **Space shuttle**
1993	**Web browser for exploring the Internet**
1997	**Dolly the sheep, first animal made by cloning adult cells** **Pathfinder explores Mars**
2000	**Human genome map completed**

Inventions

149

TFK Puzzles & Games

Great Ideas

African-American inventors may not be household names, but we use their inventions every day! Read the clues, then match these inventors to the invention.

Granville T. Woods, called the black Edison, invented more than 50 items. This 1901 invention was right on track.

Peanut butter

There's a beautiful secret behind the success of **Madame C. J. Walker,** the first U.S. businesswoman to earn millions.

Automatic traffic signal

George Washington Carver was nuts about an ordinary seed. He came up with more than 300 uses for it.

Improved light bulb

In 1881 Lewis Latimer improved on Thomas Edison's electric lamp with this bright idea! Do you see his invention?

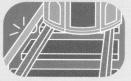

Hair and beauty products

In 1923 Garrett A. Morgan's invention stopped traffic!

Third rail

Did You Know?

A tailor in New York City, **Thomas L. Jennings (1791-1857),** is believed to be the first African American to hold a U.S. patent. The patent, which was issued in 1821, was for a dry-cleaning process. Jennings used the money he earned from his invention to help abolitionist (anti-slavery) causes.

STARS

from the
National Inventors Hall of Fame

These inventors changed our lives. They are all honored in the National Inventors Hall of Fame, which is located in Akron, Ohio.

Luther Burbank
More than 800 plant varieties
(1870s-1920s)

Alexander Graham Bell
Telephone
(1876)

Henry Ford
Automobile
(1896)

Orville and Wilbur Wright
Airplane
(1903)

Thomas Alva Edison
Electric lamp
(1879)

Ernst F. W. Alexanderson
Radio that transmits speech and music (1906)

Philo Taylor Farnsworth
Television
(1927)

Eli Whitney
Cotton gin
(1794)

John Deere
Steel plow
(1838)

Charles Goodyear
Vulcanized rubber
(1844)

Elisha Graves Otis
Elevator brake
(1854)

Louis Pasteur
Pasteurization of food products
(1860s)

Emile Berliner
Record player
(1887)

Nikola Tesla
Induction motor
(1888)

George Washington Carver
Peanut butter
(1890s)

George Eastman
Handheld camera
(1888)

Guglielmo Marconi
Wireless telegraph
(1895)

Rudolf Diesel
Internal-combustion engine
(1896)

Walt Disney
Animated cartoons
(1928)

Roy J. Plunkett
Teflon
(1938)

Igor Sikorsky
Helicopter
(1938)

Percy L. Spencer
Microwave oven
(1945)

George D. Mestral
Velcro
(1955)

Alfred Nobel
Dynamite
(1863)

Inventions

For more about inventors
go www.FACT MONSTER.com

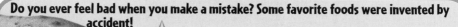

ACCIDENTAL
Food Inventions

Do you ever feel bad when you make a mistake? Some favorite foods were invented by accident!

★ In 1905, an 11-year-old Frank Epperson was mixing powdered soda and water to make soda pop. He accidentally left the mixing bucket outside, and overnight the mixture froze solid, with the wooden stirrer standing up. But the frozen pop tasted great! Frank started selling "Epperson icicles," later known as **Popsicles**.

★ One day in the 1700s, the Earl of Sandwich was so busy gambling that he did not want to go to eat. So he ordered some food to be piled between two slices of bread, which he ate while gambling. The **sandwich** has been popular ever since.

★ In 1930, Ruth Wakefield was making chocolate cookies at the Toll House Inn in Whitman, Massachusetts. When she ran out of baking chocolate, Wakefield broke a bar of semi-sweet chocolate into pieces and added them to the dough. When the cookies were baked, the chocolate hadn't melted. Instead there were little chips of chocolate throughout the cookies. Wakefield was soon selling **chocolate chip cookies**.

★ One day in 1853, a diner at Moon Lake Lodge in Saratoga Springs, New York, refused to eat an order of French fries because they were too thick. The chef, George Crum, fried a thinner batch, but the customer also rejected these. Crum decided to teach the diner a lesson. He sliced a potato paper-thin and fried it so heavily it could not be cut with a fork. But the customer loved them. Soon other customers were asking for **potato chips**.

★ Ernest Hamwi was selling Syrian pastry at the St. Louis World's Fair in 1904. When a nearby ice-cream vendor ran out of dishes, Hamwi rolled some pastry into a cone so that ice cream could be put inside. It was a hit. However, earlier that same year a man named Italo Marchiony received a patent to manufacture **ice cream cones**, suggesting that more than one person invented them.

INVENTIONS that Became Big Fads

Silly Putty (1944)

Chemists at General Electric first stumbled across this stretchy material. In 1949, ad man Peter Hodgson began selling little bags of the putty in plastic eggs. It was an instant success. Millions of eggs of Silly Putty have been sold and continue to sell to this day.

Slinky (1945)

Richard James of Philadelphia invented the Slinky. The Slinky's ability to "walk" down stairs and open and close like an accordion made it a favorite toy during the 1950s, and it is still popular today.

Hula Hoop (1958)

The founders of the Wham-O Toy Company took an idea from Australia, where gym students exercised using bamboo hoops, and turned it into the biggest fad of all time. More than 25 million had been sold only four months after it was introduced.

Pet Rocks (1975)

More than a million people bought Pet Rocks in 1975. Salesman Gary Dahl had the idea while joking with friends about his easy-to-care-for pet, a rock. Pet Rocks were sold with a funny manual that included tips on how to teach a rock tricks.

Rubik's Cube (1977)

Hungarian architect Erno Rubik designed a colorful cube with each face consisting of nine smaller cubes. A Hungarian company saw its potential as a puzzle and began marketing it. By 1980, more than 100 million Rubik's Cubes had been sold.

TFK Mystery Person

This 19th-century inventor, researcher and poet died on December 10, 1896. Before he died, he requested that his fortune be used to honor great work in chemistry, physics, medicine, literature and peace. For more than 100 years since, a committee in Stockholm, Sweden, has awarded the ultimate prize for scientists and scholars in his name. An economics prize was added in 1968.

Who is he?

MESSAGE ON A MUMMY

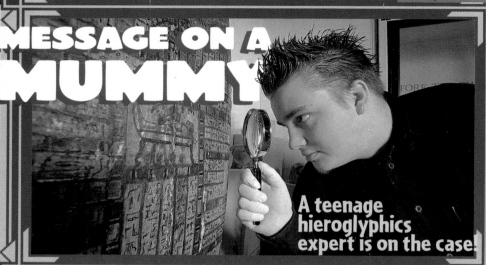

A teenage hieroglyphics expert is on the case!

BY GAIL HENNESSEY

Adam Caldwell, 17, of South Yorkshire, England, spends much of his spare time with a 2,600-year-old mummy. His dog, Pepi, is named after an Egyptian pharaoh. These may seem like unusual pals for a teenager, but Adam is no ordinary teen!

Over the last year, Adam has been working to translate hundreds of hieroglyphics—pictures of symbols that represent sounds—on the case of an unknown mummy. "The most exciting discovery was when I learned her name," says Adam. "That was my aim when I began the project." Adam also learned that the mummy, Djedma'atiuesankh (pronounced jed-mar-art-ee-you-ess-ank), came from a wealthy Egyptian family.

The mummy first caught Adam's eye last year on a visit to the Sheffield City Museum, in Sheffield, England. The mummy had been in the museum since 1893, but the head-to-toe hieroglyphics had never been translated.

Adam had taught himself to read hieroglyphics several years earlier, after a family trip to Egypt sparked his interest in the country's ancient culture. Now, he has translated nearly all of the writings on the mummy and found that they offer prayers to the Egyptian god of the dead, Osiris (oh-SIGH-ris).

ABOVE: **Adam decodes the ancient text.** BELOW: **The top of the case shows a young girl.**

SPEAKING of Home

About **14%** of Americans speak a non-English language at home. It's estimated that besides English, more than 300 languages are spoken in the U.S. today! Here's a look at the **20** most common.

1. Spanish
2. French
3. German
4. Italian
5. Chinese
6. Tagalog (spoken in the Philippines)
7. Polish
8. Korean
9. Vietnamese
10. Portuguese
11. Japanese
12. Greek
13. Arabic
14. Hindi (Urdu)
15. Russian
16. Yiddish
17. Thai (Laotian)
18. Persian
19. French Creole
20. Armenian

A mural in Los Angeles, California, celebrates the city's diversity.

TFK TOP 5
Languages Spoken Around the World

language	number of people
1. Mandarin Chinese	885 million
2. Spanish	332 million
3. English	322 million
4. Bengali	189 million
5. Hindi	182 million

Source: Ethnologue, 13th edition

Language

155

American **Sign Language** (ASL)

American Sign Language (ASL) was developed at the American School for the Deaf in Hartford, Connecticut, which was founded in 1817. Teachers at the school created ASL by combining French Sign Language with several American visual languages. It includes signs, gestures, facial expressions and the hand alphabet shown below. Today, ASL is the fourth most used language in the U.S.

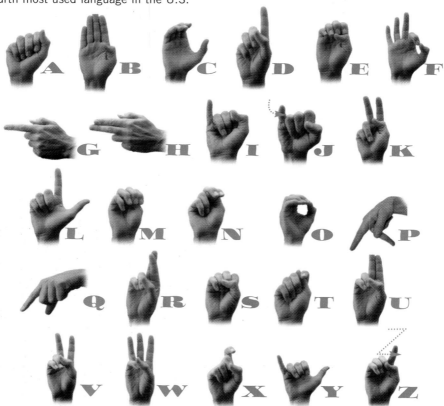

Braille System

In the 1800s **Louis Braille** developed the Braille System to help teach blind children to read and write. Braille, a Frenchman, had himself been blind since an accident at the age of three. His system of letters, numbers and punctuation marks is made up of raised points or dots.

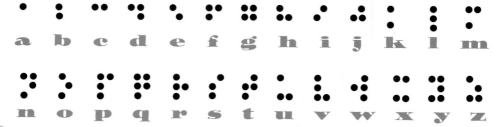

Hello World!

In any language, "hello" may be the most important thing you can say.
Now you can dazzle your friends and family by greeting them in different languages.

Language	HELLO	Pronunciation
Arabic	Ahalan	AH-hah-lan
Afrikaans	Hallo	hah-LOH
French	Bonjour	bohn-ZHOOR
German	Guten Tag	GOO-ten tahk
Greek	Geia sou	YAH-sooh
Hawaiian	Aloha	ah-LOH-hah
Hebrew	Shalom	SHAH-lohm
Hindustani	Namaste	nah-MAH-stay
Italian	Buon giorno	bwohn JOR-noh
Japanese	Konnichi-wa	koh-nee-chee-wah
Russian	Zdravstvuite	z-DRAST-vet-yah
Spanish	Hola	OH-lah
Swahili	Jambo	JAHM-boh
Zulu	Sawubona	sow-BOH-nah

Guten Tag

Did You Know?

There are more than 2,700 languages in the world. In addition, there are more than 7,000 dialects. A dialect is a variety of a language that is spoken in a certain area or by a certain group of people.

A NOT-SO-SECRET LANGUAGE

Pig Latin is the most popular and well-known secret language. Move the first letter to the end of the word and add "ay" to it.

"Mary had a little lamb" in Pig Latin is "Arymay adhay aay ittlelay amblay."

Idioms

If you say, "The cat's out of the bag" instead of "The secret is given away," you're using an idiom. The meaning of an idiom is different from the actual meaning of the words used.

"A chip on your shoulder."

In 19th-century America, a boy who thought he was pretty tough would put a wood chip on his shoulder and dare anyone to knock it off. Today the idiom refers to anyone who takes offense easily.

"Raining cats and dogs."

In Norse mythology, the dog is associated with wind and the cat with storms. This expression means that it's raining very heavily.

"Dot the i's and cross the t's."

When only handwritten documents were used, it was very important for the clerk to write everything properly, especially letters like *i* and *t*, which could easily be confused. The idiom has since come to mean paying attention to every little detail.

"Crocodile tears."

Crocodiles have a reflex that causes their eyes to tear when they open their mouths. This makes it look as though they are crying while devouring their prey. In fact, neither crocodiles nor people who shed "crocodile" tears feel sorry for their actions.

"ONYMS"

ACRONYM

An acronym is a word or name formed by combining the first letters of words in a phrase. For example, SCUBA comes from self-contained underwater breathing apparatus.

ANTONYM

Antonyms are words with opposite meanings. *Sweet* and *bitter* are antonyms.

HETERONYM

Heteronyms are words with identical spellings but different meanings and pronunciations. For example, *bow* and arrow, and to *bow* on stage.

HOMONYM

Homonyms are words that sound alike (and are sometimes spelled alike) but name different things. *Die* (to stop living) and *dye* (color) are homonyms.

PSEUDONYM

From the Greek *pseud* (false) and *onym* (name), a pseudonym is a false name or pen name used by an author. Mark Twain is a pseudonym for Samuel Langhorne Clemens.

SYNONYMS

Synonyms are words with the same or similar meanings. *Cranky* and *grumpy* are synonyms.

Word Relationships: Analogies

An analogy is a type of word problem. It is made up of two word pairs, like this:

GRACEFUL : CLUMSY :: late : _____

Your goal in solving an analogy is to find a word that correctly completes the second pair. Both pairs of words have the same kind of relationship. To solve the analogy you need to find that relationship. Read the analogy like this:

"Graceful is to clumsy as late is to 'blank.'"
Ask yourself: What is the relationship between graceful and clumsy? They are antonyms—words that have opposite meanings. The second pair of words must also be antonyms. Early is the best answer—it means the opposite of late.

Here are some other types of relationships the word pairs might have:

Synonyms	or words that have similar meanings, as in WORK : LABOR
Descriptives	in which one word describes the other word, as in BLUE : SKY
Part to Whole	in which one word is a part of the other, as in ARM : BODY
Item to Category	in which one word names something that falls into the group named by the other word, as in MILK : BEVERAGE

TFK Mystery Person

Many people are familiar with this person because of his fairy tales. He and his brother were the original publishers of such famous stories as "Hansel and Gretel" and "Snow White and the Seven Dwarfs." They traveled around Germany in the 19th century and collected their tales. But you might not know that this brother (on the left) was an expert in linguistics—the study of languages.

Who is he?

TFK Puzzles & Games — Try It! The Analogy Game
Circle the word that best completes the analogy.

1) HOPSCOTCH : GAME :: apple : _____ (banana, fruit, cider)

2) NEW : ANTIQUE :: sorrow : _____ (joy, tears, sadness)

3) SLEEVE : COAT :: page : _____ (writing, book, turn)

4) RUBY : RED :: skunk : _____ (burrow, claws, furry)

5) DESTROY : DEMOLISH :: repair : _____ (fix, break, make)

Language

To practice online, try the Analogy of the Day at
 www.FACT MONSTER.COM

159

Math

Numerical Prefixes

A prefix is an element at the beginning of a word. A numerical prefix lets you know how many there are of a particular thing.

PREFIX	MEANING	EXAMPLE
uni-	1	unicorn: mythical creature with one horn
mono-	1	monorail: train that runs on one track
bi-	2	bicycle: two-wheeled vehicle
tri-	3	triceratops: three-horned dinosaur
quadr-	4	quadruped: four-footed animal
quint-	5	quintuplets: five babies born at a single birth
penta-	5	pentagon: figure with five sides
hex-	6	hexapod: having six legs—an insect, for example
sex-	6	sextet: group of six musicians
hept-	7	heptathlon: athletic contest with seven events
sept-	7	septuplets: seven babies at a single birth
octo-	8	octopus: sea creature with eight arms
nove-	9	novena: prayers said over nine days
deka- or deca-	10	decade: a period of 10 years
cent-	100	century: a period of 100 years
hecto-	100	hectogram: 100 grams
milli-	1,000	millennium: a period of 1,000 years
kilo-	1,000	kilogram: 1,000 grams
mega-	1,000,000	megaton: one million tons
giga-	1,000,000,000	gigabyte: one billion bytes

 How much do you weigh in basketballs? Crunch this and more conversions at *www.timeforkids.com/numbers*

Roman Numerals

The ancient Romans gave us this numbering system. The year 2003 in Roman numerals is **MMIII**.

One	I
Two	II
Three	III
Four	IV
Five	V
Six	VI
Seven	VII
Eight	VIII
Nine	IX
Ten	X
Eleven	XI
Twelve	XII
Thirteen	XIII
Fourteen	XIV
Fifteen	XV
Sixteen	XVI
Seventeen	XVII
Eighteen	XVIII
Nineteen	XIX
Twenty	XX
Thirty	XXX
Forty	XL
Fifty	L
Sixty	LX
Seventy	LXX
Eighty	LXXX
Ninety	XC
One hundred	C
Five hundred	D
One thousand	M

I am **VIII** years old!

Integers

Integers are **whole numbers. They include positive numbers, negative numbers and zero.** Integers can be shown as a **number line:**

$$\longleftarrow \quad -4 \quad -3 \quad -2 \quad -1 \quad 0 \quad 1 \quad 2 \quad 3 \quad 4 \quad \longrightarrow$$

The arrows on each end of the number line mean that you can keep counting in either direction.

Adding and Subtracting Integers

Whether you are adding or subtracting two integers, **start by using the number line to find the first number.** Put your finger on it. Let's say the first number is 3:

● **If you are adding a positive number, move your finger to the right as many places as the value of that number. For example, if you are adding 4, move your finger 4 places to the right.**

$3 + 4 = 7$

● **If you are adding a negative number, move your finger to the left as many places as the value of that number. For example, if you are adding -4, move your finger 4 places to the left.**

$3 + -4 = -1$

● **If you are subtracting a positive number, move your finger to the left as many places as the value of that number. For example, if you are subtracting 4, move your finger 4 places to the left.**

$3 - 4 = -1$

● **If you are subtracting a negative number, move your finger to the right as many places as the value of that number. For example, if you are subtracting -4, move your finger 4 places to the right.**

$3 - -4 = 7$

Here are two rules to remember:

● **Adding a negative number is the same as subtracting a positive number.**

$3 + -4 = 3 - 4$

● **Subtracting a negative number is the same as adding a positive number. The two negatives cancel out each other.**

$3 - -4 = 3 + 4$

Multiplying and Dividing Integers

● **If you multiply or divide two positive numbers, the result will be positive.**

$6 \times 2 = 12$

● **If you multiply or divide a positive number with a negative number, the result will be negative.**

$6 \times -2 = -12$

● **If you multiply or divide two negative numbers, the result will be positive—the two negatives will cancel out each other.**

$-6 \times -2 = 12$

Is It an Integer?

Only whole numbers are integers. Therefore, these numbers can never be integers:

● **fractions**

● **decimals**

● **percents**

● **exponents**

EVEN and ODD Numbers

Even numbers are numbers that can be divided evenly by 2. Odd numbers are numbers that cannot be divided evenly by 2. Zero is considered an even number.

Is It Even or Odd?

To tell whether a number is even or odd, look at the number in the ones place. That single number will tell you whether the entire number is odd or even.

An even number ends in 0, 2, 4, 6 or 8.

An odd number ends in 1, 3, 5, 7 or 9.

Consider the number 3,842,917. It is an odd number because it ends in 7, an odd number. Likewise, 8,322 is an even number because it ends in 2.

Adding Even and Odd Numbers

even + even = even
$$4 + 2 = 6$$

even + odd = odd
$$4 + 3 = 7$$

odd + odd = even
$$5 + 3 = 8$$

Subtracting Even and Odd Numbers

even - even = even
$$4 - 2 = 2$$

even - odd = odd
$$4 - 3 = 1$$

odd - odd = even
$$5 - 3 = 2$$

Multiplying Even and Odd Numbers

even x even = even
$$4 \times 2 = 8$$

even x odd = even
$$4 \times 3 = 12$$

odd x odd = odd
$$5 \times 3 = 15$$

Division, or The Fraction Problem

As you can see, there are rules that determine what happens when you add, subtract or multiply even and odd numbers. In all of these operations, you will always get a particular kind of whole number.

But when you divide numbers, something tricky can happen—you might be left with a fraction. Fractions are not even numbers or odd numbers, because they are not whole numbers. They are only parts of numbers, and can be written in different ways.

For example, you can't say that the fraction $1/3$ is odd because the denominator is an odd number. You could just as well write that same fraction as $2/6$, in which the denominator is an even number.

The terms even number and odd number are only used for whole numbers.

To find the answer to an addition or a multiplication problem, pick one number from the top of the box and one number from the side. Follow each row into the center. The place where they meet is the answer.

Addition Table

+	0	1	2	3	4	5	6	7	8	9	10
0	0	1	2	3	4	5	6	7	8	9	10
1	1	2	3	4	5	6	7	8	9	10	11
2	2	3	4	5	6	7	8	9	10	11	12
3	3	4	5	6	7	8	9	10	11	12	13
4	4	5	6	7	8	9	10	11	12	13	14
5	5	6	7	8	9	10	11	12	13	14	15
6	6	7	8	9	10	11	12	13	14	15	16
7	7	8	9	10	11	12	13	14	15	16	17
8	8	9	10	11	12	13	14	15	16	17	18
9	9	10	11	12	13	14	15	16	17	18	19
10	10	11	12	13	14	15	16	17	18	19	20

Multiplication Table

X	0	1	2	3	4	5	6	7	8	9	10	11	12
0	0	0	0	0	0	0	0	0	0	0	0	0	0
1	0	1	2	3	4	5	6	7	8	9	10	11	12
2	0	2	4	6	8	10	12	14	16	18	20	22	24
3	0	3	6	9	12	15	18	21	24	27	30	33	36
4	0	4	8	12	16	20	24	28	32	36	40	44	48
5	0	5	10	15	20	25	30	35	40	45	50	55	60
6	0	6	12	18	24	30	36	42	48	54	60	66	72
7	0	7	14	21	28	35	42	49	56	63	70	77	84
8	0	8	16	24	32	40	48	56	64	72	80	88	96
9	0	9	18	27	36	45	54	63	72	81	90	99	108
10	0	10	20	30	40	50	60	70	80	90	100	110	120
11	0	11	22	33	44	55	66	77	88	99	110	121	132
12	0	12	24	36	48	60	72	84	96	108	120	132	144

Prime Numbers

A prime number is a number that can be divided, without a remainder, only by itself and by 1. For example, 17 is a prime number. It can be divided only by 17 and by 1.

Some facts:

● The only even prime number is 2. All other even numbers can be divided by 2.

● No prime number greater than 5 ends in a 5. Any number greater than 5 that ends in a 5 can be divided by 5.

● Zero and 1 are not considered prime numbers.

● Except for 0 and 1, a number is either a prime number or a composite number. A composite number is defined as any number greater than 1 that is not prime.

To prove whether a number is a prime number, first try dividing it by 2, and see if you get a whole number. If you do, it can't be a prime number. If you don't get a whole number, next try dividing it by 3, then by 5, then by 7 and so on, always dividing by an odd number.

Cardinal, Ordinal and Nominal Numbers

A cardinal number tells **how many.** Cardinal numbers are also known as "counting numbers," because they show quantity.

● 8 puppies

● 14 friends

Ordinal numbers tell the **order of things in a set**—first, second, third, etc. Ordinal numbers do not show quantity. They only **show rank or position**.

● 3rd fastest

● 6th in line

A **nominal number names something**, such as a telephone number or a player on a team. Nominal numbers do not show quantity or rank. They are used only **to identify something**.

● jersey number 2

● ZIP code 02116

Decimal Places

One decimal place to the left of the decimal point is the **ones** place. One decimal place to the right of the decimal place is the **tenths** place.

Keep your eye on the **9** *to see where the decimal places fall.*

millions	9,000,000.0
hundred thousands	900,000.0
ten thousands	90,000.0
thousands	9,000.0
hundreds	900.0
tens	90.0
ones	9.0
tenths	0.9
hundredths	0.09
thousandths	0.009
ten thousandths	0.0009
hundred thousandths	0.00009
millionths	0.000009

To add or subtract decimals, line up the decimal points and use zeros to fill in the blanks:

$$9 - 2.67 =$$

$$
\begin{array}{r}
9.00 \\
-2.67 \\
\hline
6.33
\end{array}
$$

Math

Fractions, Decimals & Percents

To change
A fraction to a decimal:
  Divide the denominator (the bottom part) into the numerator (the top part):

  $1/4 = 1.00 \div 4 = 0.25$

A fraction to a percent:
  Multiply the fraction by 100 and reduce it. Then, attach a percent sign.

  $1/4 \times 100/1 = 100/4 = 25/1 = 25\%$

A decimal to a fraction:
  Starting from the decimal point, count the decimal places. If there is one decimal place, put the number over 10 and reduce. If there are two places, put the number over 100 and reduce. If there are three places, put it over 1,000 and reduce, and so on.

  $0.25 = 25/100 = 1/4$

A decimal to a percent:
  Move the decimal point two places to the right. Then, attach a percent sign.

  $0.25 = 25\%$

A percent to a decimal:
  Move the decimal point two places to the left. Then, drop the percent sign.

  $25\% = 0.25$

A percent to a fraction:
  Put the number over 100 and reduce. Then drop the percent sign.

  $25\% = 25/100 = 1/4$

Rounding Numbers

A rounded number has about the same value as the number you start with, but it is less exact. For example, 341 rounded to the nearest hundred is 300. That is because 341 is closer in value to 300 than to 400.

Rules for Rounding

Here's the general rule for rounding:

- **If the number you are rounding ends with 5, 6, 7, 8 or 9, round the number up.**

    Example: **38 rounded to the nearest ten is 40**

- **If the number you are rounding ends with 0, 1, 2, 3 or 4, round the number down.**

    Example: **33 rounded to the nearest ten is 30**

What Are You Rounding To?

When rounding a number, ask: What are you rounding it to? Numbers can be rounded to the nearest ten, the nearest hundred, the nearest thousand and so on.

Consider the number 4,827.

- **4,827 rounded to the nearest ten is 4,830**

- **4,827 rounded to the nearest hundred is 4,800**

- **4,827 rounded to the nearest thousand is 5,000**

Rounding and Decimals

Rounding decimals works exactly the same way as rounding whole numbers. The only difference is that you round to tenths, hundredths, thousandths and so on.

- **7.8199 rounded to the nearest tenth is 7.8**

- **1.0621 rounded to the nearest hundredth is 1.06**

- **3.8792 rounded to the nearest thousandth is 3.879**

Rounding Tip

When rounding long decimals, look only at the number in the place you are rounding to and the number that follows it. For example, to round 5.3824791 to the nearest hundredth, just look at the number in the hundredths place—8—and the number that follows it—2. Then you can easily round it to 5.38.

Powers & Exponents

A power is the product of multiplying a number by itself.

Usually, a power is represented with **a base number** and an **exponent**. The **base number** tells **what number is being multiplied.** The exponent, a small number written above and to the right of the base number, tells how many times the base number is being multiplied.

For example, "6 to the 5th power" may be written as 6^5. Here, the base number is 6 and the exponent is 5. This means that 6 is being multiplied by itself 5 times: 6 x 6 x 6 x 6 x 6

6 x 6 x 6 x 6 x 6 = 7,776

or $6^5 = 7,776$

BASE NUMBER	2ND POWER	3RD POWER	4TH POWER	5TH POWER
1	1	1	1	1
2	4	8	16	32
3	9	27	81	243
4	16	64	256	1,024
5	25	125	625	3,125
6	36	216	1,296	7,776
7	49	343	2,401	16,807
8	64	512	4,096	32,768
9	81	729	6,561	59,049
10	100	1,000	10,000	100,000
11	121	1,331	14,641	161,051
12	144	1,728	20,736	248,832

More than a MILLION

**Googol is a number followed by 100 zeros.
The googolplex is the number followed by a googol of zeros.**

Million: **1,000,000**

Billion: **1,000,000,000**

Trillion: **1,000,000,000,000**

Quintillion: **1,000,000,000,000,000,000**

Centillion: **1 followed by 303 zeros**

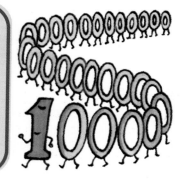

TFK Puzzles & Games Number Stumper

Multiply the number of feet in a yard by the number of teaspoons in a tablespoon. Add the number of days in the month of October. Divide the total by the number of fingers on a gorilla's hand. Now, subtract the number of days in a week. What is the answer?

Common Formulas

Finding Area

SQUARE
Multiply the length of the side by itself. (For example, if the side is 6 inches long, multiply 6 x 6.)

RECTANGLE
Multiply the base by the height.

CIRCLE
Multiply the radius by itself, then multiply the result by 3.1416.

TRAPEZOID
Add the two parallel sides, multiply by the height and divide by 2.

TRIANGLE
If you know the base and the height, multiply them and then divide by 2.

Finding Circumference and Perimeter

The CIRCUMFERENCE of a circle is the complete distance around it. To find the circumference of a circle, multiply its diameter by 3.1416.

The PERIMETER of a geometrical figure is the complete distance around that figure. To find the perimeter, simply add up the lengths of the figure's sides.

Types of Triangles

A **triangle** has three sides and is made of straight lines. A triangle may be classified by how many of its sides are of equal length.

In an **equilateral** triangle, all three sides are the same length.

In an **isosceles** triangle, two sides are the same length.

In a **scalene** triangle, none of the sides are the same length.

A triangle may also be classified by what kind of angles it has.

In an **equiangular** triangle, all the angles are equal—each one measures 60 degrees. An equiangular triangle is always equilateral.

In a **right** triangle, one of the angles is a right angle—an angle of 90 degrees. A right triangle may be isosceles or scalene.

In an **obtuse** triangle, one angle is greater than a right angle—it is more than 90 degrees. An obtuse triangle may be isosceles or scalene.

In an **acute** triangle, all angles are less than right angles—each one is less than 90 degrees. An acute triangle may be equilateral, isosceles or scalene.

Origins of Measurements

In ancient times, the body ruled when it came to measuring. The length of a foot, the width of a finger and the distance of a step were all accepted measurements.

Inch: At first an inch was the width of a man's thumb. In the 14th century, King Edward II of England ruled that 1 inch equals 3 grains of barley placed end to end lengthwise.

Hand: A hand was approximately 5 inches across. Today, a hand is 4 inches and is used to measure horses (from the ground to the horse's withers, or shoulder).

Span: A span was the length of the hand stretched out, about 9 inches.

Foot: In ancient times, the foot was 11¼ inches. Today it is 12 inches.

Yard: A yard was originally the length of a man's belt. Today it is 36 inches, about the distance from the nose to the tip of the outstretched arm of a man.

U.S. Weights and Measures

MEASURING LENGTH

12 inches = 1 foot
3 feet = 1 yard
5½ yards = 1 rod
40 rods = 1 furlong
8 furlongs = 1 mile

MEASURING AREA

144 square inches = 1 square foot
9 square feet = 1 square yard
30¼ square yards = 1 square rod
160 square rods = 1 acre
640 acres = 1 square mile

MEASURING WEIGHT

16 ounces = 1 pound
2,000 pounds = 1 ton

MEASURING LIQUID

2 cups = 1 pint
2 pints = 1 quart
4 quarts = 1 gallon

COOKING MEASURES

3 teaspoons = 1 tablespoon
4 tablespoons = ¼ cup
5 tablespoons + 1 teaspoon = ⅓ cup
16 tablespoons = 1 cup

Metric Weights

Most of the world uses the metric system. The only countries not on this system are the U.S., Burma and Liberia.

The metric system is based on **10s**. For example, 10 decimeters make a meter.

Units smaller than a meter have Latin prefixes:

Deci- means 10; 10 decimeters make a meter.
Centi- means 100; 100 centimeters make a meter.
Milli- means 1,000; 1,000 millimeters make a meter.

Units larger than a meter have Greek prefixes:

Deka- means 10; a dekameter is 10 meters.
Hecto- means 100; a hectometer is 100 meters.
Kilo- means 1,000; a kilometer is 1,000 meters.

Helpful Hints

Remember:
A meter is a little more than a yard. A kilometer is less than a mile. A liter is a little more than a quart.

Length

UNIT	VALUE
Millimeter (mm)	0.001 meters
Centimeter (cm)	0.01 meters
Decimeter (dm)	0.1 meter
Meter (m)	1 meter
Dekameter (dam)	10 meters
Hectometer (hm)	100 meters
Kilometer (km)	1,000 meters

Mass and Weight

UNIT	VALUE
Milligram (mg)	0.001 grams
Centigram (cg)	0.01 grams
Decigram (dg)	0.10 grams
Gram (g)	1 gram
Dekagram (dag)	10 grams
Hectogram (hg)	100 grams
Kilogram (kg)	1,000 grams
Metric ton (t)	1,000,000 grams

Capacity

UNIT	VALUE
Milliliter (ml)	0.001 liters
Centiliter (cl)	0.01 liters
Deciliter (dl)	0.10 liters
Liter (l)	1 liter
Dekaliter (dal)	10 liters
Hectoliter (hl)	100 liters
Kiloliter (kl)	1,000 liters

Did You Know?

The average door is about a meter wide.

and Measures

Metric Conversions

MULTIPLY	BY	TO FIND
centimeters	.3937	inches
feet	.3048	meters
gallons	3.7853	liters
grams	.0353	ounces
inches	2.54	centimeters
kilograms	2.2046	pounds
kilometers	.6214	miles
liters	1.0567	quarts
liters	.2642	gallons
meters	3.2808	feet
meters	1.0936	yards
miles	1.6093	kilometers
ounces	28.3495	grams
pounds	.4536	kilograms
quarts	.946	liters
square kilometers	.3861	square miles
square meters	1.196	square yards
square miles	2.59	square kilometers
square yards	.8361	square meters
yards	.9144	meters

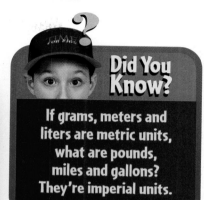

Did You Know?

If grams, meters and liters are metric units, what are pounds, miles and gallons? They're imperial units.

TFK Mystery Person

None of his writings have survived, but the work of this influential thinker still affects mathematicians today. Working mostly in Italy, he changed how we view music and many other fields. He was also one of the first vegetarians!

Who is he?

A paper clip weighs about one gram.

171

Money

From TFK magazine

Europe's New Money

By Ritu Upadhyay

Twelve countries make a historic switch in currency

As spectacular New Year's Eve fireworks lit up the skies, thousands of people across Europe lined up at cash machines to get crisp new bills.

When the clock struck midnight in Europe the night of December 31, 2001, it didn't just usher in a new year, it marked the beginning of a new era. The 304 million residents of 12 European countries switched from their local coins and bills to a single currency: the euro.

Preparations for the largest monetary changeover ever have been going on for a long time. Banks worldwide started using euros three years ago. At stores, prices were given in local currency and euros. In July 1999, mints began printing 15 billion bills and 56 billion coins. But it wasn't until January 1, 2002, that the euro became part of everyday life.

The euros are very different from the old currencies that included France's franc, Italy's lira and Germany's mark.

The colorful, old bills honored each country's unique history. The euro notes show general styles of architecture from different periods in European history. Since euros will be used in many countries, none of the images on the bills or coins could be associated with a specific place or historical figure.

The changeover caused a bit of confusion as people adjusted to counting euros. But despite the small glitches, European leaders believe the euro will build a bond among Europe's citizens and improve trade. Most people are buying into that idea. "It makes me feel like I am part of something bigger," said Alice Magnoni in Italy.

(For a list of the countries that switched to the euro, see "The Switch Is On" on page 177.)

Front: A silvery foil hologram prevents counterfeiting. When the bill is tilted, the euro symbol and the value of the bill appear. **Back:** A map of Europe (above) appears on each bill.

go See what dollars are worth in euros at www.timeforkids.com/currency

Did You Know?

On Yap Island in the Pacific Ocean, money is a stone with a hole in the middle. The hole is there so the stone can be rolled from place to place with a long pole. Yap money stones can weigh more than 500 pounds and be as large as 12 feet across.

Money in History

Before they made coins, the ancient Greeks used iron nails as money, the ancient Britons used sword blades and the ancient Chinese used swords and knives. The Hercules coin was introduced by Alexander the Great in 325 B.C.

Cowrie shells have been used as money in many cultures.

Native Americans used wampum, woven material, as money.

A Hebrew coin called a shekel dates from around A.D. 80.

Arsinoë, an Egyptian ruler's wife, is on a gold coin from 170-117 B.C.

A Roman coin shows the double-faced god Janus. It dates from 240-220 B.C.

In ancient times the Lydians in Asia Minor stamped their coins with pictures as a guarantee that they were made of pure precious metals. This custom soon spread to Greece and Persia, and eventually throughout the world.

People used banks even before they used paper money or coins! In ancient Mesopotamia, grains and other valuable trade goods were stored in palaces and temples for safe-keeping.

173

U.S. PAPER MONEY

BILL	PORTRAIT	DESIGN ON BACK
$1	Washington	ONE between the front and back of the Great Seal of the U.S.
$2 (1976)	Jefferson	Monticello
$2 (1998)	Jefferson	The signing of the Declaration of Independence
$5	Lincoln	Lincoln Memorial
$10	Hamilton	U.S. Treasury Building
$20 (1998)	Jackson	White House
$50 (1997)	Grant	U.S. Capitol
$100 (1996)	Franklin	Independence Hall in Philadelphia, Pennsylvania
$500	McKinley	Ornate FIVE HUNDRED
$1,000	Cleveland	Ornate ONE THOUSAND
$5,000	Madison	Ornate FIVE THOUSAND
$10,000	Chase	Ornate TEN THOUSAND
$100,000	Wilson	Ornate ONE HUNDRED THOUSAND

- The Treasury first printed paper money in 1862, during a coin shortage. The bills were issued in denominations of 1, 5, 25 and 50 cents.

- U.S. paper money is made of 75% cotton and 25% linen, with some colored synthetic fibers woven throughout.

- In 1929, the size of paper money was reduced by about one-third, to its current size. The old bills measured about 3.1 by 7.4 inches; the new ones measure about 2.6 by 6.1 inches.

- About half the bills printed every year are one-dollar bills, mostly because these much-used bills wear out in an average of 18 months.

- About 95% of the money printed in the U.S. is made to replace worn-out currency.

- The thousands of tiny lines and dots that make up pictures on U.S. currency are still engraved by hand on steel plates. Computers cannot create images that are as detailed or as difficult to counterfeit.

- The $100 bill is the largest that is now in circulation.

- The $100,000 note was printed only from December 18, 1934, to January 9, 1935. The largest bill ever printed, it was used for transactions between Federal Reserve banks.

U.S. Coins

COIN	PORTRAIT	DESIGN ON BACK
Cent	Lincoln	Lincoln Memorial
Nickel	Jefferson	Monticello
Dime	F. D. Roosevelt	Torch, olive branch, oak branch
Quarter	Washington	Eagle*
Half-dollar	Kennedy	Presidential coat of arms
Dollar	Sacagawea and her infant son	Eagle in flight

*The 50 State Quarters Program Act features quarters with unique state designs on the back. The program began in 1999 and is expected to run until 2008, with five new quarters released every year over ten years.

- Lincoln is the only President on a coin who faces right. However, on the new dollar coin Sacagawea faces right, as did Susan B. Anthony on the old dollar coin.

- The dime is the only coin that does not say how many cents it is worth. Words printed on the dime simply say that it is worth "one dime."

- A half-cent coin was issued from 1793 to 1857, and a 20-cent piece was issued from 1875 to 1878. A two-cent piece (1864-1873) and a three-cent piece (1851-1873, 1865-1889) are also among discontinued U.S. coins.

- The first U.S. pennies were large coins made of pure copper. Today's pennies are mostly zinc, though they are plated with copper.

- Circulating coins last about 25 years.

- In the early days of U.S. money, the main coin was the Spanish dollar, which was sometimes cut (like a pie) into eight "bits." Each bit was worth $12\frac{1}{2}$ cents. In slang, the American quarter dollar is said to be worth "two bits."

- The image on the reverse (tails side) of a U.S. coin always appears upside down. No one is sure how or why this practice began, but it has been continued by tradition for more than two centuries.

Did You Know?

A person who collects coins is called a numismatist.

Money Man Match-up

Below are some Presidents who appear on money. Match the name with the face!

THOMAS JEFFERSON $2

He was the third President of the United States.

ANDREW JACKSON $20

He was a hero in the War of 1812 before becoming President.

WILLIAM MCKINLEY $500

He guided America through the Spanish-American War in 1898.

GROVER CLEVELAND $1,000

He was the only President to get married while in the White House.

WOODROW WILSON $100,000

He was known for his New Freedom plan, which stressed the rights of individuals.

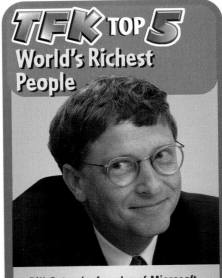

1. **Bill Gates** (cofounder of Microsoft software company)
2. **Warren Buffett** (chairman of Berkshire Hathaway, which owns Dairy Queen and others)
3. **Paul Allen** (cofounder of Microsoft)
4. **Lawrence Ellison** (founder of Oracle software company)
5. **Theo and Karl Albrecht** (brothers who own Aldi discount stores)

Source: Forbes

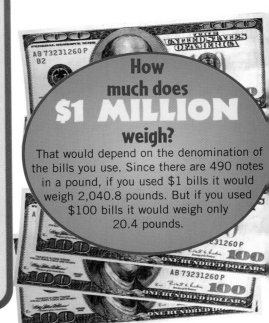

How much does $1 MILLION weigh?

That would depend on the denomination of the bills you use. Since there are 490 notes in a pound, if you used $1 bills it would weigh 2,040.8 pounds. But if you used $100 bills it would weigh only 20.4 pounds.

Money Around the World

Would you like to pay for your purchase in camels or cocoa beans? Throughout history, all kinds of things have been used as money. Here are some ways that cold cash is measured around the world today.

Country	Currency
AUSTRALIA	DOLLAR
BRAZIL	REAL
CHINA	YUAN
ETHIOPIA	BIRR
GHANA	CEDI
HAITI	GOURDE
INDIA	RUPEE
ISRAEL	SHEKEL
JAPAN	YEN
MEXICO	PESO
MOROCCO	DIRHAM
RUSSIA	RUBLE
SAUDI ARABIA	RIYAL
SOUTH AFRICA	RAND
THAILAND	BAHT
UNITED KINGDOM	POUND STERLING
VENEZUELA	BOLIVAR
ZAMBIA	KWACHA

The Switch Is On

On January 1, 2002, these 12 countries made the switch from their own currencies to the euro:

Austria	Ireland
Belgium	Italy
Finland	Luxembourg
France	The Netherlands
Germany	Portugal
Greece	Spain

Money

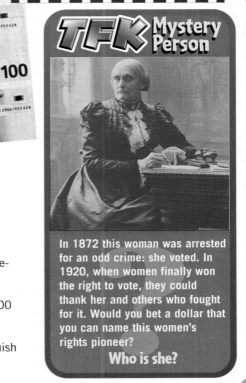

TFK Mystery Person

In 1872 this woman was arrested for an odd crime: she voted. In 1920, when women finally won the right to vote, they could thank her and others who fought for it. Would you bet a dollar that you can name this women's rights pioneer?

Who is she?

Counterfeit Money

Counterfeiting of money is one of the oldest crimes in history. It was an especially serious problem in the U.S. during the 19th century, when banks issued their own currency. At the time of the Civil War, it was estimated that one-third of all currency in circulation was counterfeit.

At that time, there were approximately 1,600 state banks designing and printing their own notes (paper money). Each note carried a different design, making it difficult to distinguish the 4,000 varieties of counterfeits from the 7,000 varieties of genuine notes.

Source: The U.S. Secret Service

Behind the Magic

A look at the making of the first Harry Potter movie

In 2001, the world got the chance to see Daniel Radcliffe as Harry Potter for the first time. That's when the movie *Harry Potter and the Sorcerer's Stone*, based on J. K. Rowling's best-selling book, hit theaters. What was it like to make the film? How did it feel to fly on a broomstick and have an owl for a pal?

Making the movie took about six months. Most of it was shot in London's Leavesden Studios. That's where the team of director Chris Columbus created such Harry hotspots as Diagon Alley, the wizard's shopping district, and the vast Great Hall at Hogwarts School of Witchcraft and Wizardry.

For Daniel, there was nothing better than being a wizard, with magical powers provided by special effects. "You'd flick your wand," he says, "and there'd be this huge flash of light and then something really cool would happen."

Harry's "invisibility cloak" was Daniel's favorite magical effect. But flying was also a high point. "It's a weird sensation when you're up there 22 feet in the air," says Daniel. He did most of his own stunts, even in scenes where the actor's playing the high-flying game of quidditch. "The broomsticks are really fast!" he says.

For Rupert Grint, who plays Harry's buddy Ron Weasley, the best part of being a wizard was the candy, especially Bertie Bott's Every Flavor Beans. "It was wicked," he gushes. "They were every flavor: grass, vomit, everything!"

BY CLAUDIA WALLIS

Columbus was amazed by the chemistry between Daniel, Rupert and Emma Watson, who played Hermione Granger. Many children tested for the roles but "those three just clicked," recalls the director.

The kids personally feel that they are each like their characters. "I've never been at the top of my class," says Emma, "but I am very bossy." Rupert, like Ron, "has an amazingly good sense of humor," says Columbus. Dan, like Harry, says he's "loyal to my friends."

In a spooky scene, the young wizards must play their way across a giant chessboard. "It was intense," says Rupert Grint, who plays Ron.

Try our Hogwarts challenge at

All-Time Box-Office Hits*

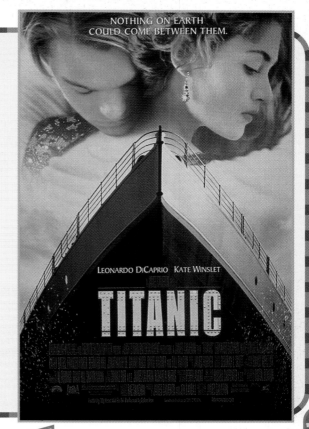

NOTHING ON EARTH COULD COME BETWEEN THEM.

LEONARDO DiCAPRIO KATE WINSLET

TITANIC

1. Titanic   1997
2. Star Wars   1977
3. E.T. the Extra-Terrestrial   1982
4. Star Wars: Episode One—   1999
   The Phantom Menace
5. Jurassic Park   1993
6. Forrest Gump   1994
7. Harry Potter and the
   Sorcerer's Stone   2001
8. The Lion King   1994
9. Return of the Jedi   1983
10. Independence Day   1996
11. The Lord of the Rings:
    The Fellowship of the Ring   2001
12. The Sixth Sense   1999
13. The Empire Strikes Back   1980
14. Home Alone   1990
15. Shrek   2001

*Films that have made the most money

American Film Institute's Greatest Screen Legends

The American Film Institute defines an American screen legend as "an actor or a team of actors with a significant screen presence in American feature-length films whose screen debut occurred in or before 1950, or whose screen debut occurred after 1950 but whose death has marked a completed body of work."

Men

★ 1. Humphrey Bogart
★ 2. Cary Grant
★ 3. James Stewart
★ 4. Marlon Brando
★ 5. Fred Astaire
★ 6. Henry Fonda
★ 7. Clark Gable
★ 8. James Cagney
★ 9. Spencer Tracy
★ 10. Charlie Chaplin

Women

★ 1. Katharine Hepburn
★ 2. Bette Davis
★ 3. Audrey Hepburn
★ 4. Ingrid Bergman
★ 5. Greta Garbo
★ 6. Marilyn Monroe
★ 7. Elizabeth Taylor
★ 8. Judy Garland
★ 9. Marlene Dietrich
★ 10. Joan Crawford

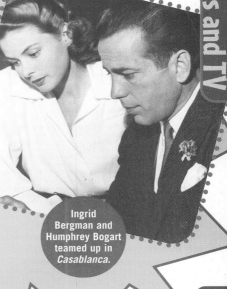

Ingrid Bergman and Humphrey Bogart teamed up in *Casablanca*.

Movies and TV

179

Movie

1889 — William Dickson, commissioned by Thomas Edison, builds the first movie camera and names it the Kinetograph.

1894 — The Edison Corporation opens the first motion-picture studio. The first Kinetoscope parlor opens in New York City, where people can see films for 25¢.

1903 — *The Great Train Robbery* is the first film with a plot. It is also the first western.

1905 — The first movie theater opens in Pittsburgh, Pennsylvania.

1910 — Thomas Edison introduces his Kinetophone, which makes talkies a reality.

1912 — Photoplay debuts as the first magazine for movie fans.

1914 — Winsor McCay unleashes *Gertie the Dinosaur*, the first animated cartoon.

1923 — German Shepherd Rin Tin Tin becomes film's first dog star.

1924 — Walt Disney creates his first cartoon, *Alice's Wonderland*.

1927 — Al Jolson performs his nightclub act in *The Jazz Singer*, the first feature-length talkie.

1928 — Walt Disney introduces the first cartoons with sound. The Academy Awards are handed out for the first time. *Wings* wins best picture.

Milestones

1935 Although a two-color process had been first used in 1922, audiences didn't love Technicolor until a three-color system appears in *Becky Sharp*.

1937 Walt Disney's first full-length animated feature, *Snow White and the Seven Dwarfs*, hits theaters.

1946 The Cannes Film Festival debuts in France.

1953 Hollywood develops wide-screen processes such as CinemaScope, first seen in *The Robe*.

1955 70mm film is introduced with *Oklahoma!*

1968 The motion-picture rating system debuts with G, PG, R and X.

1977 *Star Wars* hits theaters for the first time.

1998 *Titanic* becomes the highest-grossing film of all time.

1999 *Star Wars: Episode I—The Phantom Menace* opens and breaks a string of box-office records.

2001 The first Harry Potter movie premieres.

Movies and TV

181

Television Time Line

1928	John Baird beams a television image from England to the U.S. GE introduces a television set with a 3-inch to 4-inch screen.
1931	There are nearly 40,000 television sets in the U.S.; 9,000 of them are in New York City alone.
1947	The Yankees beat the Dodgers in the first televised World Series. *Meet the Press* debuts on NBC. The first news show will become television's longest-running program.
1949	The first Emmy Awards are handed out on January 25. *These Are My Children*, a live, 15-minute show, premieres on NBC. It is the first continuing daytime drama, or soap opera.
1950	Saturday-morning children's programming begins.
1951	Color television is introduced in the U.S. For the first time, a nationwide program airs: Edward R. Murrow's *See It Now* series.
1952	Television's first magazine-style program, the *Today* show, debuts on NBC.
1954	NBC broadcasts the World Series in color for the first time.
1956	*Gone With the Wind* and *The Wizard of Oz* are shown on television for the first time.
1960	Seventy million people watch the presidential debate between Senator John F. Kennedy and Vice President Richard Nixon. Ninety percent of U.S. homes have a television set.
1966	The first *Star Trek* episode is broadcast.
1967	Congress creates the Public Broadcasting System (PBS).
1968	*60 Minutes* airs on CBS, beginning its reign as the longest-running prime-time newsmagazine.
1969	Children's Television Workshop introduces *Sesame Street* and *Big Bird*.
1980	Ted Turner launches CNN, the first all-news network.
1988	Ninety-eight percent of U.S. homes have at least one television set.
1990	*The Simpsons* debuts on Fox and becomes an instant hit.
2002	The average cost of a 30-second ad during the Super Bowl is $1.9 million.

182

The Museum of Television and Radio

More than 70 years of broadcasting history are celebrated at the Museum of Television and Radio. Founded in 1975, the museum has one branch in New York City and one in Beverly Hills, California. It features a variety of exhibitions and special screenings. Most days the museum hosts discussions with actors, directors and other broadcasting stars.

But what really brings television history to life is the museum's collection of more than 100,000 programs on tape. Visitors can sit at private consoles to watch their favorite shows or search for news, cartoons, commercials and more.

TFK Mystery Person

This hard-working actress left her mark on television when her show *I Love Lucy* hit the airwaves in 1951. She and her husband Desi Arnaz, who also played her husband on television, helped the show become one of TV's greatest hits.
Who is she?

Did You Know?

The first television commercial aired in 1941 on NBC. It ran 60 seconds and featured a Bulova clock ticking. The Bulova Watch Company paid $9.00 for the minute-long spot.

Music♭♮

High Notes in American

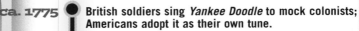

ca. 1775	British soldiers sing *Yankee Doodle* to mock colonists; Americans adopt it as their own tune.
1815	Francis Scott Key publishes *The Star-Spangled Banner*.
1861	Julia Ward Howe writes the poem *Battle Hymn of the Republic;* set to music, it becomes a popular Civil War song.
1891	Carnegie Hall opens in New York.
1893	The *Happy Birthday* tune is written by two teachers in Louisville, Kentucky.
1900s	Jazz develops in New Orleans. It is based on Mississippi River boat music, as well as African-American, French and Spanish piano music.
1907	Florenz Ziegfeld launches the elaborate musical stage shows known as the *Ziegfeld Follies*.
1911	Popular songwriter Irving Berlin writes *Alexander's Ragtime Band*.
1922	Jazz musician Duke Ellington moves to New York and forms the band that becomes the legendary Duke Ellington Orchestra.
1927	*Show Boat,* with music by Jerome Kern and lyrics by Oscar Hammerstein, is the first hugely popular musical comedy.
1932	Radio City Music Hall opens with a musical show featuring the Rockettes.
1935	George Gershwin's folk opera *Porgy and Bess* premieres.
1936	Electric guitar debuts.
1948	Columbia Records introduces the "long playing" vinyl record.
1951	Cleveland disc jockey Alan Freed coins the term "rock and roll."
1955	*Rock Around the Clock* by Bill Haley and the Comets is the first rock hit.
ca. 1955	Elvis Presley becomes the first rock star.
1957	Leonard Bernstein's musical *West Side Story* debuts.
1958	*Billboard* magazine begins their Hot 100 chart listing popular songs. The National Academy of Recording Arts and Sciences presents the first Grammy Award.
1959	Berry Gordy Jr. founds Motown record company; in the 1960s Motown stars include the Supremes, Stevie Wonder and Marvin Gaye.
1961	Country singer Patsy Cline becomes a mainstream popular (pop) music star.

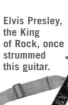

Elvis Presley, the King of Rock, once strummed this guitar.

Alicia Keys won five Grammys in 2002.

Ricky Martin in his Menudo days

Popular Music

1964 The Beatles' *I Want to Hold Your Hand* is a sensation, igniting the "British invasion."

1969 The Woodstock Music and Art Fair, featuring such artists as Janis Joplin, Jimi Hendrix, The Who and Joan Baez, is attended by hundreds of thousands of fans.

1971 The *Sonny and Cher Comedy Hour* popularizes such hits as *I Got You Babe*.

ca. 1975 CBGB (Country Bluegrass & Blues) club in New York showcases "punk rock."

1977 The movie *Saturday Night Fever* brings the Bee Gees' disco music to the silver screen.

1978 Hip hop, a blend of rock, jazz and soul with African drumming, is born in New York City's South Bronx.

1981 MTV music television debuts with nonstop music videos.

1982 *Cats* begins its 18-year run on Broadway in New York City.

1983 Compact discs begin to replace vinyl records. Madonna releases her debut album; the single *Holiday* becomes a hit.

The Backstreet Boys wanted their outfits *that way*.

1984 Cyndi Lauper's *Girls Just Wanna Have Fun* moves up the charts. Twelve-year-old Ricky Martin begins his five-year stint with Menudo.

1985 Michael Jackson releases *Thriller*; the video becomes a classic.

1989 Eight-year-old Britney Spears makes her musical television debut on *Star Search*.

early 1990s Grunge rock rises in Seattle, featuring such bands as Nirvana and Pearl Jam.

1992 Backstreet Boys and Blackstreet, two of the top male groups of the 1990s, form.

1995 The Rock and Roll Hall of Fame and Museum opens in Cleveland, Ohio.

1998 Celine Dion's *My Heart Will Go On*, from the movie *Titanic*, is the top song of the year.

2001 More than 30 years after breaking up, the Beatles top the chart with the greatest-hits album *1*.

2002 Satellite radio companies hope their high-quality sound will create "car potatoes."

Music

Good Vibrations:
Families of Instruments

Musical instruments are grouped into families based on how they make sounds. In an orchestra, musicians sit together in these family groupings. But not every instrument fits neatly into a group. For example, the piano has strings that vibrate and hammers that strike. Is it a string instrument or a percussion instrument? Some say it is both!

Brass

Brass instruments are made of brass or some other metal and make sounds when air is blown inside. The musician's lips must buzz, as though making a "raspberry" noise against the mouthpiece. Air then vibrates inside the instrument, which produces a sound.

Brass instruments include the trumpet, trombone, tuba, French horn, cornet and bugle.

Percussion

Most percussion instruments, such as drums and tambourines, make sounds when they are hit. Others are shaken, like maracas, and still others may be rubbed, scratched or whatever else will make the instrument vibrate and thus produce a sound.

Percussion instruments include drums, cymbals, triangles, chimes, bells and xylophones.

Strings

Yes, the sounds of string instruments come from their strings. The strings may be plucked, as with a guitar or harp; bowed, as with a cello or a violin; or struck, as with a dulcimer. This creates a vibration that causes a unique sound. **Stringed instruments include the violin, viola, cello, bass, harp and dulcimer.**

Woodwinds

Woodwind instruments produce sound when air (wind) is blown inside. Air might be blown across an edge, as with a flute; between a reed and a surface, as with a clarinet; or between two reeds, as with a bassoon. The sound happens when the air vibrates inside.

Woodwind instruments include the flute, piccolo, clarinet, recorder, bassoon and oboe.

THE ROCK AND ROLL
HALL OF FAME

The **Rock and Roll Hall of Fame and Museum** is located in Cleveland, Ohio. It showcases musical instruments, recordings and everything you can think of that relates to rock and roll and the artists that helped create it. Collections of personal items include David Bowie's red leather platform boots and John Lennon's report card!

Since 1986, the Rock and Roll Hall of Fame has honored musicians and music-industry figures who have contributed to rock music. To be eligible for inclusion, musicians and bands must have released a record at least 25 years prior to the year of induction. Inductees in 2002 included Brenda Lee, the Talking Heads and the Ramones.

Elton John and Ginger, one of the Spice Girls, wore these boots made for walking—and performing!

TOP-SELLING
Albums of All Time

- ★ Their Greatest Hits 1971-1975 **Eagles (Elektra)**
- ★ Thriller **Michael Jackson (Epic)**
- ★ The Wall **Pink Floyd (Columbia)**
- ★ Led Zeppelin IV **Led Zeppelin (Swan Song)**
- ★ Greatest Hits Volumes I & II **Billy Joel (Columbia)**
- ★ Back in Black **AC/DC (ATCO)**
- ★ The Beatles **The Beatles (Capitol)**
- ★ Come On Over **Shania Twain (Mercury Nashville)**
- ★ Rumours **Fleetwood Mac (Warner Bros.)**
- ★ The Bodyguard (Soundtrack) **Whitney Houston (Arista)**
- ★ Boston **Boston (Epic)**
- ★ Cracked Rear View **Hootie & the Blowfish (Atlantic)**
- ★ Hotel California **Eagles (Elektra)**
- ★ Jagged Little Pill **Alanis Morissette (Maverick)**
- ★ No Fences **Garth Brooks (Capitol Nashville)**
- ★ The Beatles 1967-1970 **The Beatles (Capitol)**
- ★ Appetite for Destruction **Guns N' Roses (Geffen)**
- ★ Born in the U.S.A. **Bruce Springsteen (Columbia)**
- ★ Dark Side of the Moon **Pink Floyd (Capitol)**
- ★ Greatest Hits **Elton John (Rocket)**

TFK Mystery Person

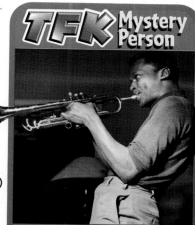

This legendary giant of jazz from Illinois began playing trumpet at age 10. He later moved to New York and helped create a new form of jazz called "cool jazz" in the 1940s and 1950s. He continued making influential music until his death in 1991.

Who is he?

Music

Source: The Recording Industry Association of America

Nations

A New Nation!

The newest country in the world is East Timor, which became independent in May 2002. It is located in Southeast Asia, just north of Australia. East Timor occupies half of the island of Timor. The rest of the island is part of Indonesia.

For 400 years, East Timor was a colony of Portugal. In 1975 Indonesia invaded East Timor. Indonesia took over East Timor the following year.

However, many of the East Timorese people wanted to be independent and began fighting against the Indonesians. In 1999, the Indonesian government allowed the East Timorese to vote on whether they wanted to remain part of Indonesia or become an independent nation. A large majority, 79%, of East Timorese voted for independence.

After the vote, the United Nations ran the country while an East Timorese government was created. In 2001, the East Timorese elected members to sit in an assembly and write a constitution for the country. A new President was elected in 2002.

East Timor has a population of about 800,000. Between 100,000 and 200,000 died during the Indonesian occupation. Most East Timor residents are Roman Catholic. Coffee and marble are major exports. The official languages of East Timor are Tetun, a local language, and Portuguese. English and Indonesian are also spoken.

More than 6 billion of us

The world population reached 6 billion in 1999—just 12 years after it hit the 5 billion mark! Experts predict that the world population will level off around the year 2220, after reaching almost 10 billion.

Most populous nation: China, 1.3 billion people

Least populous nation: Vatican City, 890 people

TFK TOP 5
World's Largest Nations

You think it's a long way from New York to Los Angeles? You should try going from Magnitogorsk to Cherskiy in Russia! Yes, the United States is a very big country, but Russia is even bigger. The United States isn't even the biggest country in North America! Here are the biggest countries in the world:

1. Russia ----> 6.59 million sq mi
2. Canada ----> 3.85 million sq mi
3. U.S. ------> 3.72 million sq mi
4. China ----> 3.71 million sq mi
5. Brazil ----> 3.29 million sq mi

The United Nations

The **United Nations (U.N.)** was created after World War II to provide an international meeting place to help develop good relationships between countries, promote peace and security around the world and encourage international cooperation in solving international problems.

The major organizations of the U.N. are the Secretariat, the Security Council and the General Assembly.

The Secretariat is the management center of U.N. operations and is headed by the Secretary-General, who is the director of the U.N.

The Security Council is responsible for making and keeping international peace. Its main purpose is to prevent war by settling disputes between nations. The Security Council has 15 members. There are five permanent members: the U.S., the Russian Federation, Britain, France and China. There are also 10 temporary members that serve two-year terms.

The General Assembly is the world's forum for discussing matters affecting world peace and security, and for making recommendations concerning them. It has no power of its own to enforce decisions. It is made up of the 51 original member nations and those admitted since, for a total of 185.

Nations

Did You Know?

Including East Timor, there are 193 nations in the world. There are also six disputed territories and more than 60 dependent areas.

193 nations!!!!

The World's Nations from A to Z

On the following pages you will find information about the world's nations. Here's an example.

If you divide the population by the area, you can find out the population density—how many people there are per square mile.

These are the main languages and the official languages (if any) in a nation. In this case, most people in the nation speak Spanish, and a smaller number speak native Indian languages.

This is the type of money used in the nation.

Mexico

Where? North America
Capital: Mexico City
Area: 761,600 sq mi (1,972,550 sq km)
Population estimate (2002): 103,400,165
Government: Federal republic
Languages: Spanish, Indian languages
Monetary unit: Peso
Per capita GDP: $9,100
Literacy rate: 87%

The per capita GDP is a way to estimate the wealth of a nation. It represents the value of all goods and services produced by a nation in one year, divided by that nation's population.

This is the percentage of people who can read and write.

Afghanistan

Where? Asia

Capital: Kabul

Area: 251,737 sq mi (652,000 sq km)

Population estimate (2002):
27,755,775

Government: Transitional

Languages: Pushtu, Dari Persian, other Turkic and minor languages

Monetary unit: Afghani

Per capita GDP: $800

Literacy rate: 29%

At press time, the new Afghan flag had not been finalized.

Albania

Where? Europe

Capital: Tiranë

Area: 11,100 sq mi (28,750 sq km)

Population estimate (2002): 3,544,841

Government: Emerging democracy

Languages: Albanian (Tosk is the official dialect), Greek

Monetary unit: Lek

Per capita GDP: $3,000

Literacy rate: 72%

Algeria

Where? Africa

Capital: Algiers

Area: 919,590 sq mi (2,381,740 sq km)

Population estimate (2002): 32,277,942

Government: Republic

Languages: Arabic (official), French, Berber dialects

Monetary unit: Dinar

Per capita GDP: $5,500

Literacy rate: 57%

Andorra

Where? Europe

Capital:
Andorra la Vella

Area: 181 sq mi (468 sq km)

Population estimate (2002): 68,403

Government: Parliamentary democracy

Languages: Catalán (official), French, Spanish

Monetary units: French franc and Spanish peseta

Per capita GDP: $18,000

Literacy rate: 100%

Angola

Where? Africa

Capital: Luanda

Area: 481,350 sq mi (1,246,700 sq km)

Population estimate (2002): 10,593,171

Government: Transitional, nominally a multiparty democracy

Languages: Bantu, Portuguese (official)

Monetary unit: Kwanza

Per capita GDP: $1,000

Literacy rate: 42%

Antigua and Barbuda

Where? North America

Capital: St. John's

Area: 171 sq mi (442 sq km)

Population estimate (2002): 67,448

Government: Constitutional monarchy

Language: English

Monetary unit: East Caribbean dollar

Per capita GDP: $8,200

Literacy rate: 89%

Argentina

Where? South America
Capital: Buenos Aires
Area: 1,068,296 sq mi (2,766,890 sq km)
Population estimate (2002): 37,812,817
Government: Republic
Languages: Spanish (official), English, Italian, German, French
Monetary unit: Peso
Per capita GDP: $12,900
Literacy rate: 96%

Armenia

Where? Asia
Capital: Yerevan
Area: 11,500 sq mi (29,800 sq km)
Population estimate (2002): 3,330,099
Government: Republic
Language: Armenian
Monetary unit: Dram
Per capita GDP: $2,900
Literacy rate: 99%

Australia

Where? Pacific Islands
Capital: Canberra
Area: 2,967,893 sq mi (7,686,850 sq km)
Population estimate (2002): 19,546,792
Government: Democratic
Language: English
Monetary unit: Australian dollar
Per capita GDP: $22,200
Literacy rate: 100%

Austria

Where? Europe
Capital: Vienna
Area: 32,375 sq mi (83,850 sq km)
Population estimate (2002): 8,169,929
Government: Federal republic
Language: German
Monetary unit: Euro (formerly schilling)
Per capita GDP: $25,000
Literacy rate: 99%

Azerbaijan

Where? Asia
Capital: Baku
Area: 33,400 sq mi (86,600 sq km)
Population estimate (2002): 7,798,497
Government: Republic
Languages: Azerbaijani Turkic, Russian, Armenian
Monetary unit: Manat
Per capita GDP: $3,000
Literacy rate: 97%

Bahamas

Where? North America
Capital: Nassau
Area: 5,380 sq mi (13,940 sq km)
Population estimate (2002): 300,529
Government: Constitutional parliamentary democracy
Language: English
Monetary unit: Bahamian dollar
Per capita GDP: $15,000
Literacy rate: 90%

Bahrain

Where? Asia
Capital: Manamah
Area: 240 sq mi (620 sq km)
Population estimate (2002): 656,397
Government: Constitutional monarchy
Languages: Arabic (official), English, Farsi, Urdu
Monetary unit: Bahrain dinar
Per capita GDP: $15,900
Literacy rate: 77%

Bangladesh

Where? Asia
Capital: Dhaka
Area: 55,598 sq mi (144,000 sq km)
Population estimate (2002): 133,376,684
Government: Parliamentary democracy
Languages: Bangla (official), English
Monetary unit: Taka
Per capita GDP: $1,570
Literacy rate: 36%

Barbados

Where? North America
Capital: Bridgetown
Area: 166 sq mi (430 sq km)
Population estimate (2002): 276,607
Government: Parliamentary democracy
Language: English
Monetary unit: Barbados dollar
Per capita GDP: $14,500
Literacy rate: 99%

Belarus

Where? Europe
Capital: Minsk
Area: 80,154 sq mi (207,600 sq km)
Population estimate (2002): 10,335,382
Government: Republic
Language: Belarussian
Monetary unit: Belarussian ruble
Per capita GDP: $7,500
Literacy rate: 100%

Belgium

Where? Europe
Capital: Brussels
Area: 11,781 sq mi (30,510 sq km)
Population estimate (2002): 10,274,595
Government: Federal parliamentary democracy under a constitutional monarch
Languages: Dutch (Flemish), French, German (all official)
Monetary unit: Euro (formerly Belgian franc)
Per capita GDP: $25,300
Literacy rate: 99%

Belize

Where? Central America
Capital: Belmopan
Area: 8,865 sq mi (22,960 sq km)
Population estimate (2002): 262,999
Government: Parliamentary democracy
Languages: English (official), Creole, Spanish, Garifuna, Mayan
Monetary unit: Belize dollar
Per capita GDP: $3,200
Literacy rate: 91%

Benin

Where? Africa

Capital: Porto-Novo (official)

Area: 43,483 sq mi (112,620 sq km)

Population estimate (2002): 6,787,625

Government: Republic under multiparty democratic rule

Languages: French (official), African languages

Monetary unit: CFA franc

Per capita GDP: $1,030

Literacy rate: 23%

Bhutan

Where? Asia

Capital: Thimphu

Area: 18,147 sq mi (47,000 sq km)

Population estimate (2002): 2,094,176

Government: Monarchy

Language: Dzongkha

Monetary unit: Ngultrum

Per capita GDP: $1,100

Literacy rate: 42%

Bolivia

Where? South America

Capital: Sucre

Area: 424,162 sq mi (1,098,580 sq km)

Population estimate (2002): 8,445,134

Government: Republic

Languages: Spanish (official), Quechua, Aymara, Guarani

Monetary unit: Boliviano

Per capita GDP: $2,600

Literacy rate: 82%

Bosnia and Herzegovina

Where? Europe

Capital: Sarajevo

Area: 19,741 sq mi (51,129 sq km)

Population estimate (2002): 3,964,388

Government: Emerging democracy

Languages: The language is called Serbian, Croatian or Bosnian depending on the speaker

Monetary unit: Dinar

Per capita GDP: $1,700

Literacy rate: NA

Botswana

Where? Africa

Capital: Gaborone

Area: 231,800 sq mi (600,370 sq km)

Population estimate (2002): 1,591,232

Government: Parliamentary republic

Languages: English (official), Setswana

Monetary unit: Pula

Per capita GDP: $6,600

Literacy rate: 69%

Brazil

Where? South America

Capital: Brasília

Area: 3,286,470 sq mi (8,511,965 sq km)

Population estimate (2002): 176,029,560

Government: Federative republic

Language: Portuguese

Monetary unit: Real

Per capita GDP: $6,500

Literacy rate: 81%

Brunei

Where? Asia

Capital: Bandar Seri Begawan

Area: 2,228 sq mi (5,770 sq km)

Population estimate (2002): 350,898

Government: Constitutional sultanate

Languages: Malay (official), Chinese, English

Monetary unit: Brunei dollar

Per capita GDP: $17,600

Literacy rate: 80%

Bulgaria

Where? Europe

Capital: Sofia

Area: 48,822 sq mi (110,910 sq km)

Population estimate (2002): 7,621,337

Government: Parliamentary democracy

Language: Bulgarian

Monetary unit: Lev

Per capita GDP: $6,200

Literacy rate: 93%

Burkina Faso

Where? Africa

Capital: Ouagadougou

Area: 105,870 sq mi (274,200 sq km)

Population estimate (2002): 12,603,185

Government: Parliamentary

Languages: French (official), tribal languages

Monetary unit: CFA franc

Per capita GDP: $1,000

Literacy rate: 18%

Burundi

Where? Africa

Capital: Bujumbura

Area: 10,745 sq mi (27,830 sq km)

Population estimate (2002): 6,373,002

Government: Republic

Languages: Kirundi and French (both official), Swahili

Monetary unit: Burundi franc

Per capita GDP: $720

Literacy rate: 41%

Cambodia

Where? Asia

Capital: Phnom Penh

Area: 69,900 sq mi (181,040 sq km)

Population estimate (2002): 12,775,324

Government: Multiparty liberal democracy under a constitutional monarchy

Languages: Khmer (official), French, English

Monetary unit: Riel

Per capita GDP: $1,300

Literacy rate: 69%

Cameroon

Where? Africa

Capital: Yaoundé

Area: 183,567 sq mi (475,440 sq km)

Population estimate (2002): 16,184,748

Government: Unitary republic

Languages: French and English (both official), African languages

Monetary unit: CFA franc

Per capita GDP: $1,700

Literacy rate: 54%

Canada

Where? North America
Capital: Ottawa, Ontario
Area: 3,851,788 sq mi (9,976,140 sq km)
Population estimate (2002): 31,902,268
Government: Confederation with parliamentary democracy
Languages: English and French (both official)
Monetary unit: Canadian dollar
Per capita GDP: $24,800
Literacy rate: 96%

Cape Verde

Where? Africa
Capital: Praia
Area: 1,557 sq mi (4,033 sq km)
Population estimate (2002): 408,760
Government: Republic
Languages: Portuguese, Crioulo
Monetary unit: Cape Verdean escudo
Per capita GDP: $1,700
Literacy rate: 67%

Central African Republic

Where? Africa
Capital: Bangui
Area: 240,534 sq mi (622,984 sq km)
Population estimate (2002): 3,642,739
Government: Republic
Languages: French (official), Sangho, Arabic, Hansa, Swahili
Monetary unit: CFA franc
Per capita GDP: $1,700
Literacy rate: 38%

Chad

Where? Africa
Capital: N'Djamena
Area: 495,752 sq mi (1,284,000 sq km)
Population estimate (2002): 8,997,237
Government: Republic
Languages: French (official), Sangho, Arabic, Hansa, Swahili
Monetary unit: CFA franc
Per capita GDP: $1,000
Literacy rate: 30%

Chile

Where? South America
Capital: Santiago
Area: 292,258 sq mi (756,950 sq km)
Population estimate (2002): 15,498,930
Government: Republic
Language: Spanish
Monetary unit: Peso
Per capita GDP: $10,100
Literacy rate: 95%

China

Where? Asia
Capital: Beijing
Area: 3,705,386 sq mi (9,596,960 sq km)
Population estimate (2002): 1,284,303,705
Government: Communist state
Languages: Chinese (Mandarin), local dialects
Monetary unit: Yuan
Per capita GDP: $3,600
Literacy rate: 84%

Colombia

Where? South America
Capital: Bogotá
Area: 439,733 sq mi (1,138,910 sq km)
Population estimate (2002): 41,008,227
Government: Republic
Language: Spanish
Monetary unit: Peso
Per capita GDP: $6,200
Literacy rate: 87%

Comoros

Where? Africa
Capital: Moroni
Area: 838 sq mi (2,170 sq km)
Population estimate (2002): 614,382
Government: Independent republic
Languages: French and Arabic (both official), Shaafi Islam (Swahili dialect), Malagasu
Monetary unit: CFA franc
Per capita GDP: $720
Literacy rate: 48%

Congo, Democratic Republic of the

Where? Africa
Capital: Kinshasa
Area: 905,562 sq mi (2,345,410 sq km)
Population estimate (2002): 55,225,478
Government: Dictatorship
Languages: French (official), Swahili, Lingala, Ishiluba, Kikongo, others
Monetary unit: Congolese franc
Per capita GDP: $600
Literacy rate: 72%

Congo, Republic of the

Where? Africa
Capital: Brazzaville
Area: 132,046 sq mi (342,000 sq km)
Population estimate (2002): 2,958,448
Government: Republic
Languages: French (official), Lingala, Kikongo, others
Monetary unit: CFA franc
Per capita GDP: $1,100
Literacy rate: 57%

Costa Rica

Where? Central America
Capital: San José
Area: 19,730 sq mi (51,100 sq km)
Population estimate (2002): 3,834,934
Government: Democratic republic
Language: Spanish
Monetary unit: Colón
Per capita GDP: $6,700
Literacy rate: 93%

Côte d'Ivoire

Where? Africa
Capital: Yamoussoukro
Area: 124,502 sq mi (322,460 sq km)
Population estimate (2002): 16,804,784
Government: Republic
Languages: French (official), African languages
Monetary unit: CFA franc
Per capita GDP: $1,600
Literacy rate: 54%

Croatia

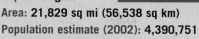

Where? Europe
Capital: Zagreb
Area: 21,829 sq mi (56,538 sq km)
Population estimate (2002): 4,390,751
Government: Presidential/parliamentary democracy
Language: Croatian
Monetary unit: Kuna
Per capita GDP: $5,800
Literacy rate: 97%

Cuba

Where? North America
Capital: Havana
Area: 42,803 sq mi (110,860 sq km)
Population estimate (2002): 11,224,321
Government: Communist state
Language: Spanish
Monetary unit: Peso
Per capita GDP: $1,700
Literacy rate: 94%

Cyprus

Where? Middle East
Capital: Lefkosia (Nicosia)
Area: 3,572 sq mi (9,250 sq km)
Population estimate (2002): 767,314
Government: Republic
Languages: Greek, Turkish
Monetary unit: Cyprus pound
Per capita GDP: $16,000
Literacy rate: 94%

Czech Republic

Where? Europe
Capital: Prague
Area: 30,450 sq mi (78,866 sq km)
Population estimate (2002): 10,256,760
Government: Parliamentary democracy
Language: Czech
Monetary unit: Koruna
Per capita GDP: $12,900
Literacy rate: 99%

Denmark

Where? Europe
Capital: Copenhagen
Area: 16,639 sq mi (43,094 sq km)
Population estimate (2002): 5,368,854
Government: Constitutional monarchy
Languages: Danish, Faeroese, Greenlandic, German
Monetary unit: Krone
Per capita GDP: $25,500
Literacy rate: 99%

Djibouti

Where? Africa
Capital: Djibouti
Area: 8,494 sq mi (22,000 sq km)
Population estimate (2002): 472,810
Government: Republic
Languages: Arabic and French (both official), Afar, Somali
Monetary unit: Djibouti franc
Per capita GDP: $1,300
Literacy rate: 46%

Dominica

Where? North America
Capital: Roseau
Area: 290 sq mi
(750 sq km)
Population estimate (2002): 70,158
Government: Parliamentary democracy
Languages: English (official), French patois
Monetary unit: East Caribbean dollar
Per capita GDP: $4,000
Literacy rate: 94%

Dominican Republic

Where? North America
Capital: Santo Domingo
Area: 18,815 sq mi
(48,730 sq km)
Population estimate (2002): 8,721,594
Government: Representative democracy
Languages: Spanish, English
Monetary unit: Peso
Per capita GDP: $5,700
Literacy rate: 84%

Ecuador

Where? South America
Capital: Quito
Area: 109,483 sq mi
(283,560 sq km)
Population estimate (2002): 13,447,494
Government: Republic
Languages: Spanish (official), Quechua
Monetary unit: U.S. dollar
Per capita GDP: $2,900
Literacy rate: 90%

Egypt

Where? Africa
Capital: Cairo
Area: 386,660 sq mi
(1,001,450 sq km)
Population estimate (2002): 70,712,345
Government: Republic
Language: Arabic
Monetary unit: Egyptian pound
Per capita GDP: $3,600
Literacy rate: 48%

El Salvador

Where?
Central America
Capital: San Salvador
Area: 8,124 sq mi (21,040 sq km)
Population estimate (2002): 6,353,681
Government: Republic
Language: Spanish
Monetary unit: Colón
Per capita GDP: $4,000
Literacy rate: 73%

Equatorial Guinea

Where? Africa
Capital: Malabo
Area: 10,830 sq mi
(28,050 sq km)
Population estimate (2002): 498,144
Government: Republic
Languages: Spanish (official), French (second official), pidgin English, Fang, Bubi, Creole
Monetary unit: CFA franc
Per capita GDP: $2,000
Literacy rate: 50%

Eritrea

Where? Africa
Capital: Asmara
Area: 46,842 sq mi (121,320 sq km)
Population estimate (2002): 4,465,651
Government: Transitional
Languages: Afar, Bilen, Kunama, Nara, Arabic, Tobedawi, Saho, Tigre, Tigrinya
Monetary unit: Birr
Per capita GDP: $710
Literacy rate: 20%

Estonia

Where? Europe
Capital: Tallinn
Area: 17,462 sq mi (45,226 sq km)
Population estimate (2002): 1,415,681
Government: Parliamentary democracy
Languages: Estonian (official), Russian, Finnish, English
Monetary unit: Kroon
Per capita GDP: $10,000
Literacy rate: 100%

Ethiopia

Where? Africa
Capital: Addis Ababa
Area: 485,184 sq mi (1,127,127 sq km)
Population estimate (2002): 67,673,031
Government: Federal republic
Languages: Amharic (official), English, Orominga, Tigrigna, others
Monetary unit: Birr
Per capita GDP: $600
Literacy rate: 28%

Fiji

Where? Oceania
Capital: Suva
Area: 7,054 sq mi (18,270 sq km)
Population estimate (2002): 856,346
Government: Republic
Languages: Fijian, Hindustani, English (official)
Monetary unit: Fiji dollar
Per capita GDP: $7,300
Literacy rate: 79%

Finland

Where? Europe
Capital: Helsinki
Area: 130,127 sq mi (337,030 sq km)
Population estimate (2002): 5,183,545
Government: Republic
Languages: Finnish and Swedish (both official)
Monetary unit: Euro (formerly markka)
Per capita GDP: $22,900
Literacy rate: 100%

France

Where? Europe
Capital: Paris
Area: 211,208 sq mi (547,030 sq km)
Population estimate (2002): 59,765,983
Government: Republic
Language: French
Monetary unit: Euro (formerly French franc)
Per capita GDP: $24,400
Literacy rate: 99%

Gabon

Where? **Africa**
Capital: **Libreville**
Area: **103,347 sq mi (267,670 sq km)**
Population estimate (2002): **1,233,353**
Government: **Republic**
Languages: **French (official), Fang, Myene, Bateke, Bapounou/Eschira, Bandjabi**
Monetary unit: **CFA franc**
Per capita GDP: **$6,500**
Literacy rate: **61%**

The Gambia

Where? **Africa**
Capital: **Banjul**
Area: **4,363 sq mi (11,300 sq km)**
Population estimate (2002): **1,455,842**
Government: **Republic**
Languages: **English (official), native tongues**
Monetary unit: **Dalasi**
Per capita GDP: **$1,030**
Literacy rate: **27%**

Georgia

Where? **Asia**
Capital: **T'bilisi**
Area: **26,911 sq mi (69,700 sq km)**
Population estimate (2002): **4,960,951**
Government: **Republic**
Languages: **Georgian (official), Russian, Armenian, Azerbaijani**
Monetary unit: **Lari**
Per capita GDP: **$2,300**
Literacy rate: **99%**

Germany

Where? **Europe**
Capital: **Berlin**
Area: **137,846 sq mi (357,021 sq km)**
Population estimate (2002): **83,251,851**
Government: **Federal republic**
Language: **German**
Monetary unit: **Euro (formerly Deutsche mark)**
Per capita GDP: **$22,700**
Literacy rate: **99%**

Ghana

Where? **Africa**
Capital: **Accra**
Area: **92,100 sq mi (238,540 sq km)**
Population estimate (2002): **20,244,154**
Government: **Constitutional democracy**
Languages: **English (official), native tongues**
Monetary unit: **Cedi**
Per capita GDP: **$1,900**
Literacy rate: **60%**

Greece

Where? **Europe**
Capital: **Athens**
Area: **50,942 sq mi (131,940 sq km)**
Population estimate (2002): **10,645,343**
Government: **Parliamentary republic**
Language: **Greek**
Monetary unit: **Euro (formerly drachma)**
Per capita GDP: **$13,900**
Literacy rate: **93%**

Grenada

Where? North America
Capital: Saint George's
Area: 131 sq mi (340 sq km)
Population estimate (2002): 89,227
Government: Constitutional monarchy
Language: English
Monetary unit: East Caribbean dollar
Per capita GDP: $3,700
Literacy rate: 98%

Guatemala

Where? Central America
Capital: Guatemala City
Area: 42,042 sq mi (108,890 sq km)
Population estimate (2002): 13,314,079
Government: Constitutional democratic republic
Languages: Spanish (official), Indian languages
Monetary unit: Quetzal
Per capita GDP: $3,900
Literacy rate: 55%

Guinea

Where? Africa
Capital: Conakry
Area: 94,925 sq mi (245,860 sq km)
Population estimate (2002): 7,775,065
Government: Republic
Languages: French (official), native tongues
Monetary unit: Guinean franc
Per capita GDP: $1,200
Literacy rate: 24% in French; 48% in local languages

Guinea-Bissau

Where? Africa
Capital: Bissau
Area: 13,946 sq mi (36,120 sq km)
Population estimate (2002): 1,345,479
Government: Republic
Languages: Portuguese (official), African languages
Monetary unit: Guinea-Bissau peso
Per capita GDP: $900
Literacy rate: 37%

Guyana

Where? South America
Capital: Georgetown
Area: 83,000 sq mi (214,970 sq km)
Population estimate (2002): 698,209
Government: Republic
Languages: English (official), Amerindian dialects
Monetary unit: Guyana dollar
Per capita GDP: $2,500
Literacy rate: 96%

Haiti

Where? North America
Capital: Port-au-Prince
Area: 10,714 sq mi (27,750 sq km)
Population estimate (2002): 7,063,722
Government: Elected government
Languages: Creole and French (both official)
Monetary unit: Gourde
Per capita GDP: $1,340
Literacy rate: 53%

Honduras

Where?
Central America

Capital: Tegucigalpa

Area: 43,278 sq mi (112,090 sq km)

Population estimate (2002): 6,560,608

Government: Democratic constitutional republic

Languages: Spanish, Amerindian dialects

Monetary unit: Lempira

Per capita GDP: $2,050

Literacy rate: 73%

Hungary

Where? Europe

Capital: Budapest

Area: 35,919 sq mi (93,030 sq km)

Population estimate (2002): 10,075,034

Government: Parliamentary democracy

Language: Magyar (Hungarian)

Monetary unit: Forint

Per capita GDP: $7,800

Literacy rate: 98%

Iceland

Where? Europe

Capital: Reykjavik

Area: 39,768 sq mi (103,000 sq km)

Population estimate (2002): 279,384

Government: Constitutional republic

Language: Icelandic

Monetary unit: Icelandic króna

Per capita GDP: $23,500

Literacy rate: 100%

India

Where? Asia

Capital: Delhi

Area: 1,269,338 sq mi (3,287,590 sq km)

Population estimate (2002): 1,045,845,226

Government: Federal republic

Languages: Hindi (national), English; 24 major languages plus more than 1600 dialects

Monetary unit: Rupee

Per capita GDP: $1,800

Literacy rate: 52%

Indonesia

Where? Asia

Capital: Jakarta

Area: 741,096 sq mi (1,919,440 sq km)

Population estimate (2002): 232,073,071

Government: Republic

Languages: Bahasa Indonesia (official), Dutch, English; more than 500 languages and dialects

Monetary unit: Rupiah

Per capita GDP: $2,800

Literacy rate: 84%

Iran

Where? Middle East

Capital: Tehran

Area: 636,293 sq mi (1,648,000 sq km)

Population estimate (2002): 66,622,704

Government: Theocratic republic

Languages: Farsi (Persian), Azari, Kurdish, Arabic

Monetary unit: Rial

Per capita GDP: $5,300

Literacy rate: 54%

Iraq

Where? Middle East
Capital: Baghdad
Area: 168,753 sq mi (437,072 sq km)
Population estimate (2002): 24,001,816
Government: Republic
Languages: Arabic, Kurdish
Monetary unit: Iraqi dinar
Per capita GDP: $2,700
Literacy rate: 60%

Ireland

Where? Europe
Capital: Dublin
Area: 27,136 sq mi (70,280 sq km)
Population estimate (2002): 3,883,159
Government: Republic
Languages: English, Irish Gaelic
Monetary units: Euro (formerly Irish pound [punt])
Per capita GDP: $20,300
Literacy rate: 98%

Israel

Where? Middle East
Capital: Jerusalem
Area: 8,020 sq mi (20,770 sq km)
Population estimate (2002): 6,029,529
Government: Parliamentary democracy
Languages: Hebrew (official), Arabic, English
Monetary unit: Shekel
Per capita GDP: $18,300
Literacy rate: 92%

Italy

Where? Europe
Capital: Rome
Area: 116,305 sq mi (301,230 sq km)
Population estimate (2002): 57,715,625
Government: Republic
Language: Italian
Monetary unit: Euro (formerly lira)
Per capita GDP: $21,400
Literacy rate: 97%

Jamaica

Where? North America
Capital: Kingston
Area: 4,243 sq mi (10,990 sq km)
Population estimate (2002): 2,680,029
Government: Constitutional parliamentary democracy
Languages: English, Jamaican Creole
Monetary unit: Jamaican dollar
Per capita GDP: $3,350
Literacy rate: 98%

Japan

Where? Asia
Capital: Tokyo
Area: 145,882 sq mi (377,835 sq km)
Population estimate (2002): 126,974,628
Government: Constitutional monarchy with a parliamentary government
Language: Japanese
Monetary unit: Yen
Per capita GDP: $23,400
Literacy rate: 99%

Jordan

Where? Middle East
Capital: Amman
Area: 34,445 sq mi (89,213 sq km)
Population estimate (2002): 5,307,470
Government: Constitutional monarchy
Languages: Arabic (official), English
Monetary unit: Jordanian dinar
Per capita GDP: $3,500
Literacy rate: 86%

Kazakhstan

Where? Asia
Capital: Astana
Area: 1,049,150 sq mi (2,717,300 sq km)
Population estimate (2002): 16,741,519
Government: Republic
Languages: Kazak (Qazaq) and Russian (both official)
Monetary unit: Tenge
Per capita GDP: $3,200
Literacy rate: 98%

Kenya

Where? Africa
Capital: Nairobi
Area: 224,960 sq mi (582,650 sq km)
Population estimate (2002): 31,138,735
Government: Republic
Languages: English (official), Swahili, several others
Monetary unit: Kenyan shilling
Per capita GDP: $1,600
Literacy rate: 69%

Kiribati

Where? Pacific Islands
Capital: Tarawa
Area: 280 sq mi (717 sq km)
Population estimate (2002): 96,335
Government: Republic
Languages: English (official), I-Kiribati (Gilbertese)
Monetary unit: Australian dollar
Per capita GDP: $860
Literacy rate: 90%

Korea, North

Where? Asia
Capital: Pyongyang
Area: 46,540 sq mi (120,540 sq km)
Population estimate (2002): 22,224,195
Government: Authoritarian socialist; one-man dictatorship
Language: Korean
Monetary unit: Won
Per capita GDP: $1,000
Literacy rate: 100%

Korea, South

Where? Asia
Capital: Seoul
Area: 38,023 sq mi (98,480 sq km)
Population estimate (2002): 48,324,000
Government: Republic
Language: Korean
Monetary unit: Won
Per capita GDP: $13,300
Literacy rate: 98%

Kuwait

Where? Middle East
Capital: Kuwait
Area: 6,880 sq mi (17,820 sq km)
Population estimate (2002): 2,111,561
Government: Nominal constitutional monarchy
Languages: Arabic (official), English
Monetary unit: Kuwaiti dinar
Per capita GDP: $15,000
Literacy rate: 73%

Kyrgyzstan

Where? Asia
Capital: Bishkek
Area: 76,641 sq mi (198,500 sq km)
Population estimate (2002): 4,822,166
Government: Republic
Languages: Kyrgyz (official), Russian
Monetary unit: Som
Per capita GDP: $2,700
Literacy rate: 97%

Laos

Where? Asia
Capital: Vientiane
Area: 91,429 sq mi (236,800 sq km)
Population estimate (2002): 5,777,180
Government: Communist state
Languages: Lao (official), French, English
Monetary unit: Kip
Per capita GDP: $1,700
Literacy rate: 45%

Latvia

Where? Europe
Capital: Riga
Area: 24,938 sq mi (64,589 sq km)
Population estimate (2002): 2,366,515
Government: Parliamentary democracy
Language: Latvian
Monetary unit: Lats
Per capita GDP: $7,200
Literacy rate: 99%

Lebanon

Where? Middle East
Capital: Beirut
Area: 4,015 sq mi (10,400 sq km)
Population estimate (2002): 3,677,780
Government: Republic
Languages: Arabic (official), French, English
Monetary unit: Lebanese pound
Per capita GDP: $5,000
Literacy rate: 80%

Lesotho

Where? Africa
Capital: Maseru
Area: 11,720 sq mi (30,350 sq km)
Population estimate (2002): 2,207,954
Government: Parliamentary constitutional monarchy
Languages: English and Sesotho (both official), Zulu, Xhosa
Monetary unit: Loti
Per capita GDP: $2,400
Literacy rate: 56%

Liberia

Where? Africa
Capital: Monrovia
Area: 43,000 sq mi (111,370 sq km)
Population estimate (2002): 3,288,198
Government: Republic
Languages: English (official), tribal dialects
Monetary unit: Liberian dollar
Per capita GDP: $1,100
Literacy rate: 40%

Libya

Where? Africa
Capital: Tripoli
Area: 679,358 sq mi (1,759,540 sq km)
Population estimate (2002): 5,368,585
Government: Military dictatorship
Languages: Arabic, Italian, English
Monetary unit: Libyan dinar
Per capita GDP: $8,900
Literacy rate: 64%

Liechtenstein

Where? Europe
Capital: Vaduz
Area: 62 sq mi (160 sq km)
Population estimate (2002): 32,842
Government: Hereditary constitutional monarchy
Languages: German (official), Alemmanic dialect
Monetary unit: Swiss franc
Per capita GDP: $23,000
Literacy rate: 100%

Lithuania

Where? Europe
Capital: Vilnius
Area: 25,174 sq mi (65,200 sq km)
Population estimate (2002): 3,601,138
Government: Parliamentary democracy
Languages: Lithuanian (official), Polish, Russian
Monetary unit: Litas
Per capita GDP: $7,300
Literacy rate: 98%

Luxembourg

Where? Europe
Capital: Luxembourg
Area: 999 sq mi (2,586 sq km)
Population estimate (2002): 448,569
Government: Constitutional monarchy
Languages: Luxembourgian, French, German
Monetary unit: Euro (formerly Luxembourg franc)
Per capita GDP: $36,400
Literacy rate: 100%

Macedonia

Where? Europe
Capital: Skopje
Area: 9,781 sq mi (25,333 sq km)
Population estimate (2002): 2,054,800
Government: Emerging democracy
Languages: Macedonian, Albanian
Monetary unit: Denar
Per capita GDP: $4,400
Literacy rate: NA

Madagascar

Where? Africa
Capital: Antananarivo
Area: 226,660 sq mi (587,040 sq km)
Population estimate (2002): 16,473,477
Government: Republic
Languages: Malagasy and French (both official)
Monetary unit: Malagasy franc
Per capita GDP: $800
Literacy rate: 80%

Malawi

Where? Africa
Capital: Lilongwe
Area: 45,745 sq mi (118,480 sq km)
Population estimate (2002): 10,701,824
Government: Multiparty democracy
Languages: English and Chichewa (both official)
Monetary unit: Kwacha
Per capita GDP: $900
Literacy rate: 49%

Malaysia

Where? Asia
Capital: Kuala Lumpur
Area: 127,316 sq mi (329,750 sq km)
Population estimate (2002): 22,662,365
Government: Constitutional monarchy
Languages: Malay (official), Chinese, Tamil, English
Monetary unit: Ringgit
Per capita GDP: $10,300
Literacy rate: 78%

Maldives

Where? Asia
Capital: Malé
Area: 116 sq mi (300 sq km)
Population estimate (2002): 320,165
Government: Republic
Languages: Dhivehi (official), Arabic, Hindi, English
Monetary unit: Maldivian rufiyaa
Per capita GDP: $2,000
Literacy rate: 91%

Mali

Where? Africa
Capital: Bamako
Area: 478,764 sq mi (1,240,000 sq km)
Population estimate (2002): 11,340,480
Government: Republic
Languages: French (official), African languages
Monetary unit: CFA franc
Per capita GDP: $850
Literacy rate: 32%

Malta

Where? Europe
Capital: Valletta
Area: 122 sq mi (316 sq km)
Population estimate (2002): 397,499
Government: Republic
Languages: Maltese and English (both official)
Monetary unit: Maltese lira
Per capita GDP: $14,300
Literacy rate: 88%

Marshall Islands

Where? Pacific Islands
Capital: Majuro
Area: 70 sq mi (181.3 sq km)
Population estimate (2002): 73,630
Government: Constitutional government
Languages: Marshallese and English (both official)
Monetary unit: U.S. dollar
Per capita GDP: $1,670
Literacy rate: 91%

Mauritania

Where? Africa
Capital: Nouakchott
Area: 397,953 sq mi (1,030,700 sq km)
Population estimate (2002): 2,828,858
Government: Republic
Languages: Arabic (official), French
Monetary unit: Ouguiya
Per capita GDP: $2,000
Literacy rate: 34%

Mauritius

Where? Africa
Capital: Port Louis
Area: 718 sq mi (1,860 sq km)
Population estimate (2002): 1,200,206
Government: Parliamentary democracy
Languages: English (official), French, Creole, Hindi, Urdu, Hakka, Bojpoori
Monetary unit: Mauritian rupee
Per capita GDP: $10,400
Literacy rate: 81%

Mexico

Where? North America
Capital: Mexico City
Area: 761,600 sq mi (1,972,550 sq km)
Population estimate (2002): 103,400,165
Government: Federal republic
Languages: Spanish, Indian languages
Monetary unit: Peso
Per capita GDP: $9,100
Literacy rate: 87%

Micronesia

Where? Pacific Islands
Capital: Palikir
Area: 271 sq mi (702 sq km)
Population estimate (2002): 135,869
Government: Constitutional government
Languages: English (official), native languages
Monetary unit: U.S. dollar
Per capita GDP: $2,000
Literacy rate: 85%

Moldova

Where? Europe
Capital: Chisinau
Area: 13,067 sq mi (33,843 sq km)
Population estimate (2002): 4,434,547
Government: Republic
Languages: Moldovan (official), Russian, Gagauz
Monetary unit: Moldovan lem
Per capita GDP: $2,500
Literacy rate: 97%

Monaco

Where? **Europe**
Capital: **Monaco**
Area: **0.75 sq mi (1.95 sq km)**
Population estimate (2002): **31,987**
Government: **Constitutional monarchy**
Languages: **French (official), English, Italian, Monégasque**
Monetary unit: **French franc**
Per capita GDP: **$27,000**
Literacy rate: **99%**

Mongolia

Where? **Asia**
Capital: **Ulaanbaatar**
Area: **604,250 sq mi (1,565,000 sq km)**
Population estimate (2002): **2,694,432**
Government: **Parliamentary**
Languages: **Mongolian (official), Turkic, Russian, Chinese**
Monetary unit: **Tugrik**
Per capita GDP: **$1,780**
Literacy rate: **97%**

Morocco

Where? **Africa**
Capital: **Rabat**
Area: **172,413 sq mi (446,550 sq km)**
Population estimate (2002): **31,167,783**
Government: **Constitutional monarchy**
Languages: **Arabic (official), French, Berber dialects, Spanish**
Monetary unit: **Dirham**
Per capita GDP: **$3,500**
Literacy rate: **50%**

Mozambique

Where? **Africa**
Capital: **Maputo**
Area: **309,494 sq mi (801,590 sq km)**
Population estimate (2002): **19,607,519**
Government: **Republic**
Languages: **Portuguese (official), Bantu languages**
Monetary unit: **Metical**
Per capita GDP: **$1,000**
Literacy rate: **33%**

Myanmar (Burma)

Where? **Asia**
Capital: **Rangoon**
Area: **261,969 sq mi (678,500 sq km)**
Population estimate (2002): **42,238,224**
Government: **Military regime**
Languages: **Burmese, minority languages**
Monetary unit: **Kyat**
Per capita GDP: **$1,500**
Literacy rate: **81%**

Namibia

Where? **Africa**
Capital: **Windhoek**
Area: **318,694 sq mi (825,418 sq km)**
Population estimate (2002): **1,820,916**
Government: **Republic**
Languages: **Afrikaans, German, English (official), native languages**
Monetary unit: **Namibian dollar**
Per capita GDP: **$4,300**
Literacy rate: **38%**

Nauru

Where?
Pacific Islands
Capital: **Yaren District (unofficial)**
Area: **8.2 sq mi (21 sq km)**
Population estimate (2002): **12,329**
Government: **Republic**
Languages: **Nauruan (official), English**
Monetary unit: **Australian dollar**
Per capita GDP: **$5,000**
Literacy rate: **99%**

Nepal

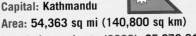

Where? Asia
Capital: **Kathmandu**
Area: **54,363 sq mi (140,800 sq km)**
Population estimate (2002): **25,873,917**
Government: **Parliamentary democracy and constitutional monarchy**
Languages: **Nepali (official), Newari, Bhutia, Maithali**
Monetary unit: **Nepalese rupee**
Per capita GDP: **$1,360**
Literacy rate: **38%**

The Netherlands

Where? Europe
Capital: **Amsterdam**
Area: **16,036 sq mi (41,532 sq km)**
Population estimate (2002): **16,067,754**
Government: **Constitutional monarchy**
Language: **Dutch**
Monetary unit: **Euro (formerly guilder)**
Per capita GDP: **$24,400**
Literacy rate: **99%**

New Zealand

Where?
Pacific Islands
Capital: **Wellington**
Area: **103,737 sq mi (268,680 sq km)**
Population estimate (2002): **3,908,037**
Government: **Parliamentary democracy**
Languages: **English (official), Maori**
Monetary unit: **New Zealand dollar**
Per capita GDP: **$17,700**
Literacy rate: **99%**

Nicaragua

Where?
Central America
Capital: **Managua**
Area: **49,998 sq mi (129,494 sq km)**
Population estimate (2002): **5,023,818**
Government: **Republic**
Language: **Spanish**
Monetary unit: **Cordoba**
Per capita GDP: **$2,700**
Literacy rate: **57%**

Niger

Where? Africa
Capital: **Niamey**
Area: **489,189 sq mi (1,267,000 sq km)**
Population estimate (2002): **10,639,744**
Government: **Republic**
Languages: **French (official), Hausa, Songhai, Arabic**
Monetary unit: **CFA franc**
Per capita GDP: **$1,000**
Literacy rate: **28%**

Nigeria

Where? Africa
Capital: Abuja
Area: 356,700 sq mi (923,770 sq km)
Population estimate (2002): 129,934,911
Government: Republic transitioning from military to civilian rule
Languages: English (official), Hausa, Yoruba, Ibo, more than 200 others
Monetary unit: Naira
Per capita GDP: $950
Literacy rate: 51%

Norway

Where? Europe
Capital: Oslo
Area: 125,181 sq mi (324,220 sq km)
Population estimate (2002): 4,525,116
Government: Constitutional monarchy
Languages: Two official forms of Norwegian, Bokmål and Nynorsk
Monetary unit: Krone
Per capita GDP: $27,700
Literacy rate: 99%

Oman

Where? Middle East
Capital: Muscat
Area: 82,030 sq mi (212,460 sq km)
Population estimate (2002): 2,713,462
Government: Monarchy
Languages: Arabic (official), English, Indian languages
Monetary unit: Omani rial
Per capita GDP: $7,700
Literacy rate: 80%

Pakistan

Where? Asia
Capital: Islamabad
Area: 310,400 sq mi (803,940 sq km)
Population estimate (2002): 147,663,429
Government: Federal republic
Languages: Punjabi, Sindhi, Siraiki, Pashtu, Urdu (official), others
Monetary unit: Pakistan rupee
Per capita GDP: $2,000
Literacy rate: 35%

Palau

Where? Pacific Islands
Capital: Koror
Area: 177 sq mi (458 sq km)
Population estimate (2002): 19,409
Government: Constitutional government
Languages: Palauan, English (official)
Monetary unit: U.S. dollar
Per capita GDP: $7,100
Literacy rate: 86%

Panama

Where: Central America
Capital: Panama City
Area: 30,193 sq mi (78,200 sq km)
Population estimate (2002): 2,882,329
Government: Constitutional democracy
Languages: Spanish (official), English
Monetary unit: Balboa
Per capita GDP: $6,000
Literacy rate: 89%

Papua New Guinea

Where?
Pacific Islands

Capital: Port Moresby

Area: 178,703 sq mi (462,840 sq km)

Population estimate (2002): 5,172,033

Government: Constitutional monarchy with parliamentary democracy

Languages: English, Tok Pisin, Hiri Motu, 717 native languages

Monetary unit: Kina

Per capita GDP: $2,500

Literacy rate: 50%

Paraguay

Where? South America

Capital: Asunción

Area: 157,046 sq mi (406,750 sq km)

Population estimate (2002): 5,884,491

Government: Constitutional republic

Languages: Spanish (official), Guaraní

Monetary unit: Guaraní

Per capita GDP: $4,750

Literacy rate: 90%

Peru

Where? South America

Capital: Lima

Area: 496,223 sq mi (1,285,220 sq km)

Population estimate (2002): 27,949,639

Government: Constitutional republic

Languages: Spanish and Quechua (both official), Aymara, other native languages

Monetary unit: Nuevo sol

Per capita GDP: $4,550

Literacy rate: 85%

The Philippines

Where? Asia

Capital: Manila

Area: 115,830 sq mi (300,000 sq km)

Population estimate (2002): 84,525,639

Government: Republic

Languages: Filipino (based on Tagalog) and English (both official), regional languages

Monetary unit: Peso

Per capita GDP: $3,800

Literacy rate: 94%

Poland

Where? Europe

Capital: Warsaw

Area: 120,727 sq mi (312,683 sq km)

Population estimate (2002): 38,625,478

Government: Republic

Language: Polish

Monetary unit: Zloty

Per capita GDP: $8,500

Literacy rate: 98%

Portugal

Where? Europe

Capital: Lisbon

Area: 35,672 sq mi (92,391 sq km)

Population estimate (2002): 10,084,245

Government: Parliamentary democracy

Language: Portuguese

Monetary unit: Euro (formerly escudo)

Per capita GDP: $15,800

Literacy rate: 85%

Qatar

Where? Middle East
Capital: Doha
Area: 4,416 sq mi (11,439 sq km)
Population estimate (2002): 793,341
Government: Traditional monarchy
Languages: Arabic (official), English
Monetary unit: Qatari riyal
Per capita GDP: $20,300
Literacy rate: 76%

Romania

Where? Europe
Capital: Bucharest
Area: 91,700 sq mi (237,500 sq km)
Population estimate (2002): 22,317,730
Government: Republic
Languages: Romanian (official), Hungarian, German
Monetary unit: Leu
Per capita GDP: $5,900
Literacy rate: 96%

Russia

Where? Europe and Asia
Capital: Moscow
Area: 6,592,735 sq mi (17,075,200 sq km)
Population estimate (2002): 144,978,573
Government: Federation
Languages: Russian, others
Monetary unit: Ruble
Per capita GDP: $7,700
Literacy rate: 98%

Rwanda

Where? Africa
Capital: Kigali
Area: 10,169 sq mi (26,338 sq km)
Population estimate (2002): 7,398,074
Government: Republic
Languages: Kinyarwanda, French, English (all official)
Monetary unit: Rwandan franc
Per capita GDP: $900
Literacy rate: 50%

Saint Kitts and Nevis

Where? North America
Capital: Basseterre
Area: 101 sq mi (261 sq km)
Population estimate (2002): 38,736
Government: Constitutional monarchy
Language: English
Monetary unit: East Caribbean dollar
Per capita GDP: $7,000
Literacy rate: 98%

Saint Lucia

Where? North America
Capital: Castries
Area: 239 sq mi (620 sq km)
Population estimate (2002): 160,145
Government: Parliamentary democracy
Languages: English (official), patois
Monetary unit: East Caribbean dollar
Per capita GDP: $4,500
Literacy rate: 67%

Saint Vincent and the Grenadines

Where? North America
Capital: Kingstown
Area: 150 sq mi (389 sq km)
Population estimate (2002): 116,394
Government: Parliamentary democracy
Languages: English (official), French patois
Monetary unit: East Caribbean dollar
Per capita GDP: $2,800
Literacy rate: 96%

Samoa

Where?
Pacific Islands
Capital: Apia
Area: 1,104 sq mi (2,860 sq km)
Population estimate (2002): 178,631
Government: Constitutional monarchy under native chief
Languages: Samoan, English
Monetary unit: Tala
Per capita GDP: $3,200
Literacy rate: 98%

San Marino

Where? Europe
Capital: San Marino
Area: 24 sq mi (61 sq km)
Population estimate (2002): 27,730
Government: Independent republic
Language: Italian
Monetary unit: Italian lira
Per capita GDP: $32,000
Literacy rate: 96%

São Tomé and Principe

Where? Africa
Capital: São Tomé
Area: 386 sq mi (1,001 sq km)
Population estimate (2002): 170,372
Government: Republic
Language: Portuguese
Monetary unit: Dobra
Per capita GDP: $1,100
Literacy rate: 57%

Saudi Arabia

Where? Middle East
Capital: Riyadh
Area: 756,981 sq mi (1,960,582 sq km)
Population estimate (2002): 23,513,330
Government: Monarchy
Language: Arabic
Monetary unit: Riyal
Per capita GDP: $10,500
Literacy rate: 62%

Senegal

Where? Africa
Capital: Dakar
Area: 75,749 sq mi (196,190 sq km)
Population estimate (2002): 9,979,752
Government: Republic under multiparty democratic rule
Languages: French (official), Wolof, Serer, other dialects
Monetary unit: CFA franc
Per capita GDP: $1,600
Literacy rate: 38%

Seychelles

Where? Africa
Capital: Victoria
Area: 176 sq mi (455 sq km)
Population estimate (2002): 80,098
Government: Republic
Languages: English and French (both official), Seselwa
Monetary unit: Seychelles rupee
Per capita GDP: $7,700
Literacy rate: 58%

Sierra Leone

Where? Africa
Capital: Freetown
Area: 27,699 sq mi (71,740 sq km)
Population estimate (2002): 5,614,743
Government: Constitutional democracy
Languages: English (official), Mende, Temne, Krio
Monetary unit: Leone
Per capita GDP: $510
Literacy rate: 21%

Singapore

Where? Asia
Capital: Singapore
Area: 250 sq mi (648 sq km)
Population estimate (2002): 4,452,732
Government: Parliamentary republic
Languages: Malay, Chinese (Mandarin), Tamil, English (all official)
Monetary unit: Singapore dollar
Per capita GDP: $26,500
Literacy rate: 90%

Slovakia

Where? Europe
Capital: Bratislava
Area: 18,859 sq mi (48,845 sq km)
Population estimate (2002): 5,422,366
Government: Parliamentary democracy
Languages: Slovak (official), Hungarian
Monetary unit: Koruna
Per capita GDP: $10,200
Literacy rate: 99%

Slovenia

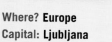

Where? Europe
Capital: Ljubljana
Area: 7,820 sq mi (20,253 sq km)
Population estimate (2002): 1,932,917
Government: Parliamentary democratic republic
Languages: Slovenian, Serbo-Croatian
Monetary unit: Slovenian tolar
Per capita GDP: $12,000
Literacy rate: 99%

Solomon Islands

Where? Pacific Islands
Capital: Honiara
Area: 10,985 sq mi (28,450 sq km)
Population estimate (2002): 494,786
Government: Parliamentary democracy
Languages: English, Solomon Pidgin, more than 60 Melanesian languages
Monetary unit: Solomon Islands dollar
Per capita GDP: $2,000
Literacy rate: 30%

Somalia

Where? **Africa**
Capital: **Mogadishu**
Area: **246,199 sq mi (637,657 sq km)**
Population estimate (2002): **7,753,310**
Government: **Parliamentary**
Languages: **Somali (official), Arabic, English, Italian**
Monetary unit: **Somali shilling**
Per capita GDP: **$600**
Literacy rate: **24%**

South Africa

Where? **Africa**
Capital (administrative): **Pretoria**
Area: **471,008 sq mi (1,219,912 sq km)**
Population estimate (2002): **43,647,658**
Government: **Republic**
Languages: **11 official languages: Afrikaans, English, Ndebele, Pedi, Sotho, Swazi, Tsonga, Tswana, Venda, Xhosa, Zulu**
Monetary unit: **Rand**
Per capita GDP: **$8,500**
Literacy rate: **60%**

Spain

Where? **Europe**
Capital: **Madrid**
Area: **194,896 sq mi (504,782 sq km)**
Population estimate (2002): **40,077,100**
Government: **Parliamentary monarchy**
Languages: **Castilian Spanish (official), Catalan, Galician, Basque**
Monetary unit: **Euro (formerly peseta)**
Per capita GDP: **$18,000**
Literacy rate: **95%**

Sri Lanka

Where? **Asia**
Capital: **Colombo**
Area: **25,332 sq mi (65,610 sq km)**
Population estimate (2002): **19,576,783**
Government: **Republic**
Languages: **Sinhala (official), Tamil, English**
Monetary unit: **Sri Lankan rupee**
Per capita GDP: **$3,250**
Literacy rate: **88%**

Sudan

Where? **Africa**
Capital: **Khartoum**
Area: **967,493 sq mi (2,505,810 sq km)**
Population estimate (2002): **37,090,298**
Government: **Transitional**
Languages: **Arabic (official), English, tribal dialects**
Monetary unit: **Sudanese pound**
Per capita GDP: **$1,000**
Literacy rate: **27%**

Suriname

Where? **South America**
Capital: **Paramaribo**
Area: **63,039 sq mi (163,270 sq km)**
Population estimate (2002): **436,494**
Government: **Constitutional democracy**
Languages: **Dutch (official), Surinamese, English**
Monetary unit: **Suriname guilder**
Per capita GDP: **$3,400**
Literacy rate: **95%**

Swaziland

Where? **Africa**
Capital: **Mbabane**
Area: **6,704 sq mi (17,360 sq km)**
Population estimate (2002): **1,123.605**
Government: **Monarchy**
Languages: **Swazi (official), English**
Monetary unit: **Lilangeni**
Per capita GDP: **$4,000**
Literacy rate: **70%**

Sweden

Where? **Europe**
Capital: **Stockholm**
Area: **173,731 sq mi (449,964 sq km)**
Population estimate (2002): **8,876,744**
Government: **Constitutional monarchy**
Language: **Swedish**
Monetary unit: **Krona**
Per capita GDP: **$22,200**
Literacy rate: **99%**

Switzerland

Where? **Europe**
Capital: **Bern**
Area: **15,942 sq mi (41,290 sq km)**
Population estimate (2002): **7,301,994**
Government: **Federal republic**
Languages: **German, French, Italian (all official), Romansch**
Monetary unit: **Swiss franc**
Per capita GDP: **$28,600**
Literacy rate: **99%**

Syria

Where? **Middle East**
Capital: **Damascus**
Area: **71,498 sq mi (185,180 sq km)**
Population estimate (2002): **17,155,814**
Government: **Republic under military regime**
Languages: **Arabic (official), French, English**
Monetary unit: **Syrian pound**
Per capita GDP: **$3,100**
Literacy rate: **65%**

Taiwan

Where? **Asia**
Capital: **Taipei**
Area: **13,892 sq mi (35,980 sq km)**
Population estimate (2002): **22,548,009**
Government: **Multiparty democratic regime**
Language: **Chinese (Mandarin)**
Monetary unit: **New Taiwan dollar**
Per capita GDP: **$17,400**
Literacy rate: **92%**

Tajikistan

Where? **Asia**
Capital: **Dushanbe**
Area: **55,251 sq mi (143,100 sq km)**
Population estimate (2002): **6,719,567**
Government: **Republic**
Language: **Tajik**
Monetary unit: **Tajik ruble**
Per capita GDP: **$1,140**
Literacy rate: **98%**

Tanzania

Where? Africa
Capital: Dar es Salaam
Area: 364,898 sq mi (945,087 sq km)
Population estimate (2002): 37,187,939
Government: Republic
Languages: Swahili and English (both official), local languages
Monetary unit: Tanzanian shilling
Per capita GDP: $710
Literacy rate: 52%

Thailand

Where? Asia
Capital: Bangkok
Area: 198,455 sq mi (514,000 sq km)
Population estimate (2002): 62,354,402
Government: Constitutional monarchy
Languages: Thai (Siamese), Chinese, English
Monetary unit: Baht
Per capita GDP: $6,700
Literacy rate: 93%

Togo

Where? Africa
Capital: Lomé
Area: 21,925 sq mi (56,790 sq km)
Population estimate (2002): 5,285,501
Government: Republic under transition to multiparty democratic rule
Languages: French (official), Éwé, Mina, Kabyé, Cotocoli
Monetary unit: CFA franc
Per capita GDP: $1,500
Literacy rate: 43%

Tonga

Where? Pacific Islands
Capital: Nuku'alofa
Area: 290 sq mi (748 sq km)
Population estimate (2002): 106,137
Government: Hereditary constitutional monarchy
Languages: Tongan, English
Monetary unit: Pa'anga
Per capita GDP: $2,200
Literacy rate: 47%

Trinidad and Tobago

Where? North America
Capital: Port-of-Spain
Area: 1,980 sq mi (5,130 sq km)
Population estimate (2002): 1,163,724
Government: Parliamentary democracy
Languages: English (official), Hindi, French, Spanish
Monetary unit: Trinidad and Tobago dollar
Per capita GDP: $9,500
Literacy rate: 95%

Tunisia

Where? Africa
Capital: Tunis
Area: 63,170 sq mi (163,610 sq km)
Population estimate (2002): 9,815,644
Government: Republic
Languages: Arabic (official), French
Monetary unit: Tunisian dinar
Per capita GDP: $6,500
Literacy rate: 65%

Turkey

Where? Europe and Asia
Capital: Ankara
Area: 301,388 sq mi (780,580 sq km)
Population estimate (2002): 67,308,928
Government: Republican parliamentary democracy
Language: Turkish
Monetary unit: Turkish lira
Per capita GDP: $6,800
Literacy rate: 81%

Turkmenistan

Where? Asia
Capital: Ashgabat
Area: 188,455 sq mi (488,100 sq km)
Population estimate (2002): 4,688,963
Government: Republic
Languages: Turkmen, Russian, Uzbek
Monetary unit: Manat
Per capita GDP: $4,300
Literacy rate: 98%

Tuvalu

Where? Pacific Islands
Capital: Funafuti
Area: 10 sq mi (26 sq km)
Population estimate (2002): 11,146
Government: Constitutional monarchy with a parliamentary democracy
Languages: Tuvaluan, English
Monetary unit: Tuvaluan dollar
Per capita GDP: $1,100
Literacy rate: Less than 50%

Uganda

Where? Africa
Capital: Kampala
Area: 91,135 sq mi (236,040 sq km)
Population estimate (2002): 24,699,073
Government: Republic
Languages: English (official), Swahili, Luganda, Ateso, Luo
Monetary unit: Ugandan shilling
Per capita GDP: $1,100
Literacy rate: 54%

Ukraine

Where? Europe
Capital: Kyiv (Kiev)
Area: 233,089 sq mi (603,700 sq km)
Population estimate (2002): 48,396,470
Government: Republic
Language: Ukrainian
Monetary unit: Hryvnia
Per capita GDP: $3,850
Literacy rate: 100%

United Arab Emirates

Where? Middle East
Capital: Abu Dhabi
Area: 32,000 sq mi (82,880 sq km)
Population estimate (2002): 2,445,989
Government: Federation
Languages: Arabic (official), English
Monetary unit: U.A.E. dirham
Per capita GDP: $22,800
Literacy rate: 68%

United Kingdom

Where? **Europe**
Capital: **London**
Area: **94,525 sq mi (244,820 sq km)**
Population estimate (2002): **59,778,002**
Government: **Constitutional monarchy**
Languages: **English, Welsh, Scots Gaelic**
Monetary unit: **Pound sterling**
Per capita GDP: **$22,800**
Literacy rate: **99%**

United States

Where? **North America**
Capital: **Washington, D.C.**
Area: **3,717,792 sq mi (9,629,091 sq km)**
Population estimate (2002): **280,562,489**
Government: **Federal republic**
Languages: **English; Spanish spoken by a sizable minority**
Monetary unit: **U.S. dollar**
Per capita GDP: **$36,200**
Literacy rate: **97%**

Uruguay

Where? **South America**
Capital: **Montevideo**
Area: **68,040 sq mi (176,220 sq km)**
Population estimate (2002): **3,386,575**
Government: **Constitutional republic**
Language: **Spanish**
Monetary unit: **Peso**
Per capita GDP: **$9,300**
Literacy rate: **96%**

Uzbekistan

Where? **Asia**
Capital: **Tashkent**
Area: **172,741 sq mi (447,400 sq km)**
Population estimate (2002): **25,563,441**
Government: **Republic**
Languages: **Uzbek, Russian, Tajik**
Monetary unit: **Uzbekistani som**
Per capita GDP: **$2,400**
Literacy rate: **99%**

Vanuatu

Where? **Pacific Islands**
Capital: **Port Vila**
Area: **5,700 sq mi (14,760 sq km)**
Population estimate (2002): **198,176**
Government: **Republic**
Languages: **English and French (both official), Bislama**
Monetary unit: **Vatu**
Per capita GDP: **$1,300**
Literacy rate: **55%**

Vatican City (Holy See)

Where? **Europe**
Capital: **none**
Area: **0.17 sq mi (0.44 sq km)**
Population estimate (2002): **890**
Government: **Ecclesiastical**
Languages: **Latin, Italian, various others**
Monetary unit: **Italian lira**
Per capita GDP: **NA**
Literacy rate: **100%**

Venezuela

Where? South America
Capital: Caracas
Area: 352,143 sq mi (912,050 sq km)
Population estimate (2002): 24,287,670
Government: Federal republic
Languages: Spanish (official), native languages
Monetary unit: Bolivar
Per capita GDP: $6,200
Literacy rate: 91%

Vietnam

Where? Asia
Capital: Hanoi
Area: 127,243 sq mi (329,560 sq km)
Population estimate (2002): 81,098,416
Government: Communist state
Languages: Vietnamese (official), French, English, Khmer, Chinese
Monetary unit: Dong
Per capita GDP: $1,950
Literacy rate: 94%

Yemen

Where? Middle East
Capital: Sanaa
Area: 203,850 sq mi (527,970 sq km)
Population estimate (2002): 18,701,257
Government: Republic
Language: Arabic
Monetary unit: Rial
Per capita GDP: $820
Literacy rate: 39%

Yugoslavia

Where? Europe
Capital: Belgrade
Area: 39,517 sq mi (102,350 sq km)
Population estimate (2002): 10,656,929
Government: Republic
Languages: Serbian, Albanian
Monetary unit: Yugoslav new dinar
Per capita GDP: $2,300
Literacy rate: 91%

Zambia

Where? Africa
Capital: Lusaka
Area: 290,584 sq mi (752,610 sq km)
Population estimate (2002): 9,959,037
Government: Republic
Languages: English (official), local dialects
Monetary unit: Kwacha
Per capita GDP: $880
Literacy rate: 73%

Zimbabwe

Where? Africa
Capital: Harare
Area: 150,803 sq mi (390,580 sq km)
Population estimate (2002): 11,376,676
Government: Parliamentary democracy
Languages: English (official), Ndebele, Shona
Monetary unit: Zimbabwean dollar
Per capita GDP: $2,500
Literacy rate: 80%

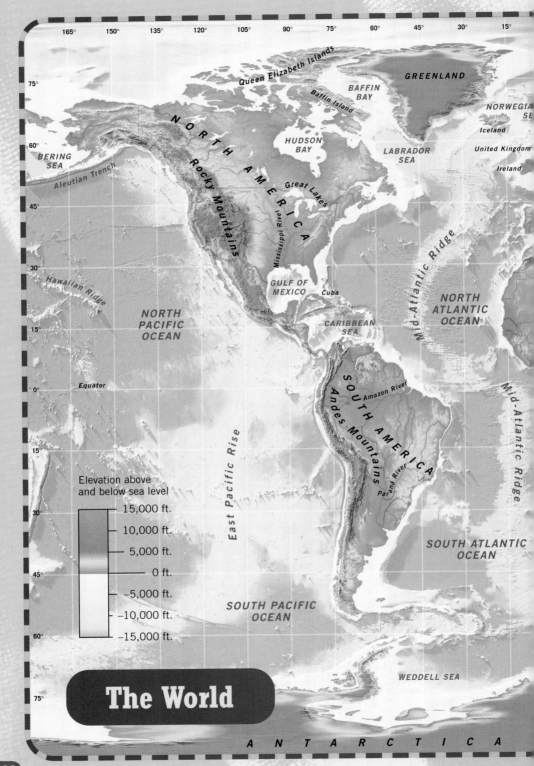

165° 150° 135° 120° 105° 90° 75° 60° 45° 30° 15°

75°

Queen Elizabeth Islands

GREENLAND

Baffin Island

BAFFIN BAY

NORWEGIAN SEA

60°

BERING SEA

NORTH AMERICA

HUDSON BAY

LABRADOR SEA

Iceland

United Kingdom

Ireland

Aleutian Trench

Rocky Mountains

45°

Great Lakes

Mississippi River

30°

Hawaiian Ridge

GULF OF MEXICO

Cuba

Mid-Atlantic Ridge

NORTH ATLANTIC OCEAN

NORTH PACIFIC OCEAN

15°

CARIBBEAN SEA

0° Equator

SOUTH AMERICA

Amazon River

Andes Mountains

Mid-Atlantic Ridge

15°

East Pacific Rise

Paraná River

Elevation above and below sea level

30°

15,000 ft.

10,000 ft.

SOUTH ATLANTIC OCEAN

5,000 ft.

0 ft.

45°

−5,000 ft.

−10,000 ft.

SOUTH PACIFIC OCEAN

60°

−15,000 ft.

WEDDELL SEA

The World

75°

ANTARCTICA

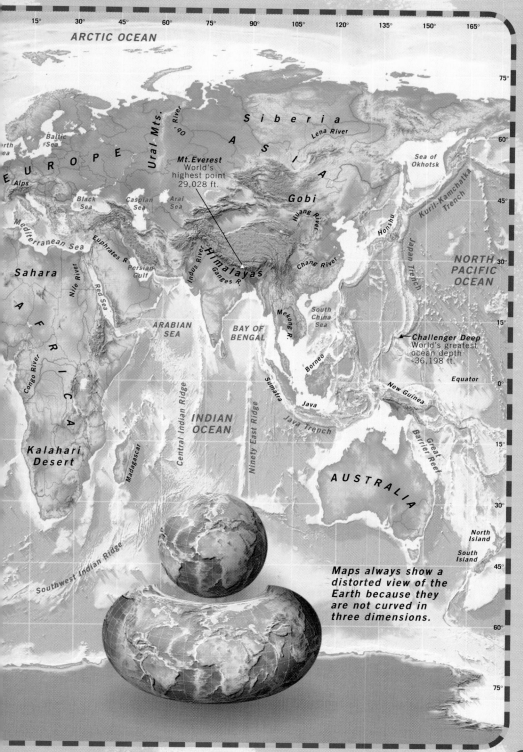

ARCTIC OCEAN

15° 30° 45° 60° 75° 90° 105° 120° 135° 150° 165°

75°

60°

S i b e r i a

Lena River

A

S

I

A

Sea of Okhotsk

45°

Ural Mts.

90 River

EUROPE

North Sea

Baltic Sea

Alps

Black Sea

Caspian Sea

Aral Sea

Mt. Everest
World's highest point
29,028 ft.

Gobi

Huang River

Honshu

Kuril-Kamchatka Trench

Mediterranean Sea

Euphrates R.

Persian Gulf

Indus River

Himalayas

Ganges R.

Chang River

Japan Trench

NORTH PACIFIC OCEAN

30°

Sahara

Nile River

Red Sea

ARABIAN SEA

BAY OF BENGAL

Mekong R.

South China Sea

15°

A
F
R
I
C
A

Congo River

Central Indian Ridge

INDIAN OCEAN

Sumatra

Borneo

Java

Challenger Deep
World's greatest
ocean depth
-36,198 ft.

Equator

0°

New Guinea

Java Trench

Ninety East Ridge

15°

Kalahari Desert

Madagascar

A U S T R A L I A

Great Barrier Reef

30°

Southwest Indian Ridge

Maps always show a
distorted view of the
Earth because they
are not curved in
three dimensions.

North Island

45°

South Island

60°

75°

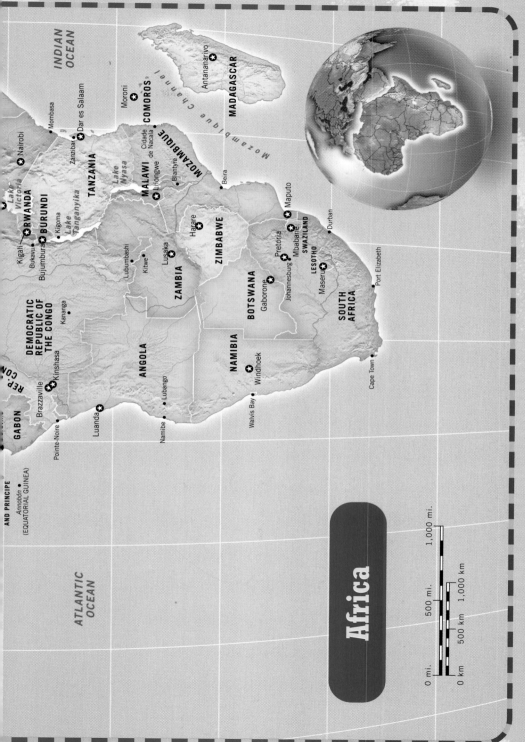

INDIAN
OCEAN

Antananarivo

MADAGASCAR

Mombasa

Moroni

COMOROS

Nairobi

Dar es Salaam

Zanzibar

Mozambique Channel

TANZANIA

Lake
Victoria

Lake
Nyasa

Cidade
de Nacala

MALAWI

RWANDA

Kigali

Lilongwe

Blantyre

MOZAMBIQUE

Beira

Bukavu

BURUNDI

Lake
Tanganyika

Bujumbura

Kigoma

Harare

Maputo

Lubumbashi

ZIMBABWE

Pretoria

Mbabane

Durban

Lusaka

Kitwe

SWAZILAND

Johannesburg

DEMOCRATIC
REPUBLIC OF
THE CONGO

ZAMBIA

BOTSWANA

LESOTHO

Maseru

Port Elizabeth

Kananga

Gaborone

SOUTH
AFRICA

Kinshasa

REP. CONGO

Brazzaville

ANGOLA

NAMIBIA

GABON

Pointe-Noire

Luanda

Lubango

Windhoek

Walvis Bay

Namibe

Cape Town

AND PRINCIPE

Annobón
(EQUATORIAL GUINEA)

ATLANTIC
OCEAN

Africa

0 mi.
500 mi.
1,000 mi.

0 km
500 km
1,000 km

225

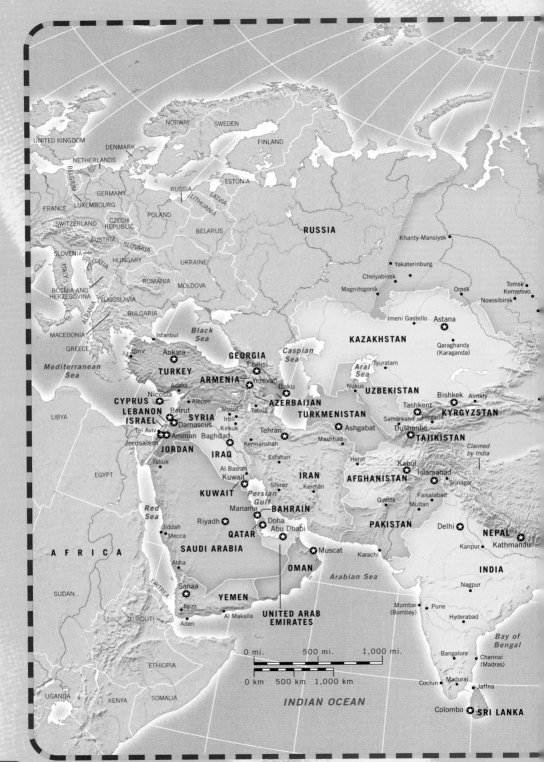

UNITED KINGDOM
NETHERLANDS
BELGIUM
LUXEMBOURG
FRANCE
SWITZERLAND
AUSTRIA
SLOVENIA
ITALY
BOSNIA AND
HERZEGOVINA
ALBANIA
MACEDONIA
GREECE

NORWAY
SWEDEN
FINLAND
DENMARK
GERMANY
POLAND
CZECH
REPUBLIC
SLOVAKIA
HUNGARY
CROATIA
ROMANIA
YUGOSLAVIA
BULGARIA

ESTONIA
LATVIA
LITHUANIA
RUSSIA
BELARUS
UKRAINE
MOLDOVA

RUSSIA

Khanty-Mansiysk
Yakaterinburg
Chelyabinsk
Magnitogorsk
Omsk
Tomsk
Kemerovo
Novosibirsk
Imeni Gastello
Astana
KAZAKHSTAN
Qaraghandy
(Karaganda)
Tyuratam
Aral
Sea
Nukus
UZBEKISTAN
Bishkek
Almaty
Tashkent
KYRGYZSTAN
Samarkand
Fergana
TAJIKISTAN
Dushanbe
Claimed
by India

Mediterranean
Sea
Black
Sea
Istanbul
Izmir
Ankara
TURKEY
Adana
Aleppo
Nicosia
CYPRUS
Caspian
Sea
GEORGIA
T'bilisi
ARMENIA
Yerevan
Baku
AZERBAIJAN
TURKMENISTAN
Ashgabat
Mashhad
Herat
Kabul
Islamabad
Srinagar
AFGHANISTAN
LEBANON
Beirut
SYRIA
ISRAEL
Damascus
Tel Aviv
Amman
Baghdad
JORDAN
IRAQ
Mosul
Irbil
Kirkuk
Tabriz
Tehran
Kermanshah
Esfahan
Quetta
Faisalabad
Multan
PAKISTAN
Jerusalem
Tabuk
EGYPT
Al Basrah
Kuwait
KUWAIT
Shiraz
IRAN
Kerman
Karachi
Delhi
Kanpur
NEPAL
Kathmandu
LIBYA
Red
Sea
Jiddah
Mecca
Riyadh
QATAR
Manama
BAHRAIN
Doha
Abu Dhabi
SAUDI ARABIA
Abha
Muscat
OMAN
Arabian
Sea
INDIA
Nagpur
AFRICA
SUDAN
Sanaa
Taizz
YEMEN
Al Makalla
Aden
UNITED ARAB
EMIRATES
Persian
Gulf
Hyderabad
Mumbai
(Bombay)
Pune
ERITREA
DJIBOUTI
ETHIOPIA
UGANDA
KENYA
SOMALIA
Bangalore
Chennai
(Madras)
Cochin
Madurai
Jaffna
Bay of
Bengal
Colombo
SRI LANKA
INDIAN OCEAN

0 mi.   500 mi.   1,000 mi.

0 km   500 km 1,000 km

226

ARCTIC OCEAN

Bering
Sea

Cherskiy

Tiksi

Verkhoyansk

oril'sk

RUSSIA

Magadan

Kamchatka
Peninsula

Yakutsk

Petropavlovsk-
Kamchatskiy

S I B E R I A

Sea of
Okhotsk

Krasnoyarsk

Sakhalin

okuznetsk

Irkutsk

Khabarovsk

Sapporo

Ulaanbaatar

Harbin

MONGOLIA

Gobi

Changchun

Vladivostok

qi

Shenyang

JAPAN

Jinxi

N. KOREA

Hohhot

Beijing

P'yongyang

Tokyo

Taiyuan

Tianjin

Seoul

Nagoya

Kyoto

Jinan

Taegu

Kobe Osaka

Lanzhou

S. KOREA

Pusan

Hiroshima

Xi'an

Qingdao

Fukuoka

CHINA

Nagasaki

PACIFIC
OCEAN

Hefei

Shanghai

Chengdu

Wuhan

Chongqing

Lhasa

Naha

mphu

Fuzhou

BHUTAN

Xiamen

Taipei

BANGLADESH

Liuzhou

Guangzhou

TAIWAN

Dhaka

Nanning

Kao-hsiung

tta Chittagong

Macao

Mandalay

Hanoi

Hong Kong

MYANMAR
(BURMA)

LAOS

Luzon

Chiang Mai

Vientiane

Baguio

Quezon City

Rangoon

Da Nang

Manila

THAILAND

Bangkok

VIETNAM

PHILIPPINES

CAMBODIA

Cebu

Phnom
Penh

Ho Chi Minh City

Phuket

Songkhla

Borneo

Asia and the
Middle East

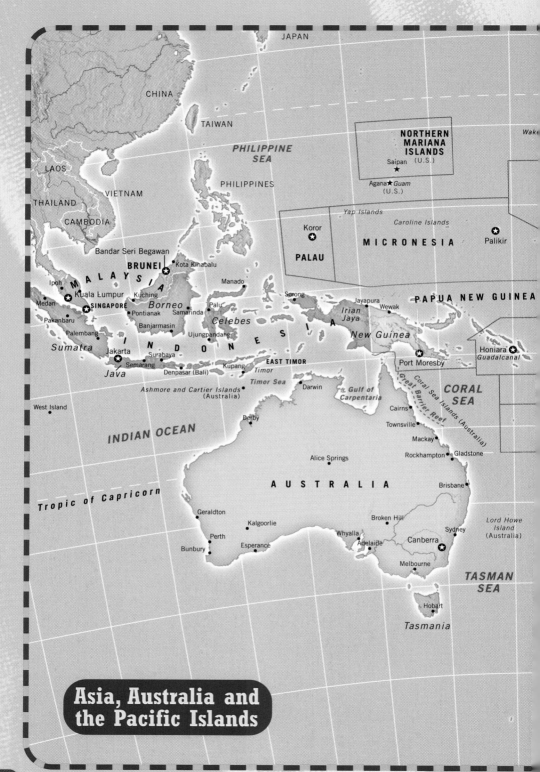

JAPAN

CHINA

TAIWAN

LAOS

VIETNAM

THAILAND

CAMBODIA

PHILIPPINE SEA

PHILIPPINES

NORTHERN MARIANA ISLANDS (U.S.)

Saipan ★

Wake

Agana ★ *Guam* (U.S.)

Yap Islands

Caroline Islands

Koror ⊛

M I C R O N E S I A

Palikir ⊛

PALAU

Bandar Seri Begawan

BRUNEI ⊛ Kota Kinabalu

M A L A Y S I A

Ipoh ●

Kuala Lumpur ⊛ Kuching

SINGAPORE ⊛

Medan ●

Pakanbaru ●

Palembang ●

Pontianak ●

Borneo

Samarinda ●

Banjarmasin ●

Manado ●

Palu ●

Celebes

Ujungpandang ●

Sorong ●

Jayapura ●

Irian Jaya

Wewak ●

P A P U A   N E W   G U I N E A

New Guinea

Honiara ⊛

Guadalcanal

Sumatra

I N D O N E S I A

Jakarta ⊛

Surabaya ●

Semarang ●

Java

Denpasar (Bali) ●

Kupang ●

Timor

EAST TIMOR

Port Moresby ⊛

Timor Sea

Darwin ●

Gulf of Carpentaria

Coral Sea Islands (Australia)

CORAL SEA

Ashmore and Cartier Islands (Australia)

West Island ●

INDIAN OCEAN

Derby ●

Cairns ●

Great Barrier Reef

Townsville ●

Mackay ●

Rockhampton ● ● Gladstone

Alice Springs ●

Tropic of Capricorn

A U S T R A L I A

Brisbane ●

Geraldton ●

Kalgoorlie ●

Broken Hill ●

Lord Howe Island (Australia)

Perth ●

Whyalla ●

Sydney ●

Bunbury ●

Esperance ●

Adelaide ●

Canberra ⊛

Melbourne ●

TASMAN SEA

Hobart ●

Tasmania

Asia, Australia and the Pacific Islands

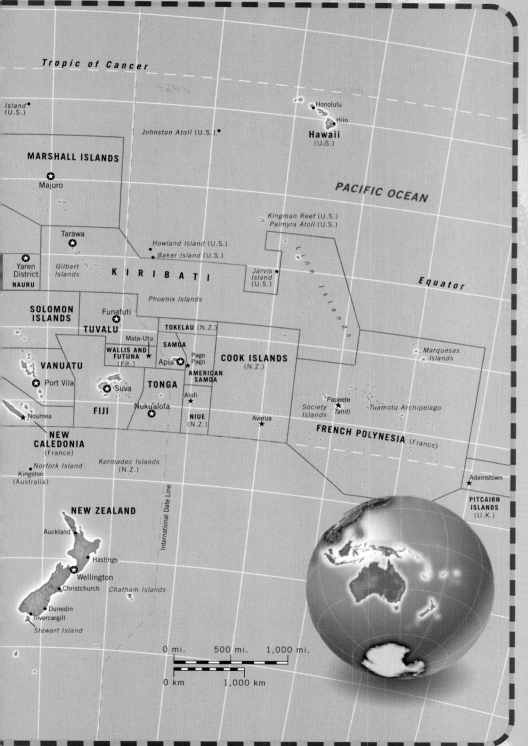

Tropic of Cancer

Island• (U.S.)

Johnston Atoll (U.S.)•

Honolulu
Hilo
Hawaii (U.S.)

MARSHALL ISLANDS

⊕ Majuro

PACIFIC OCEAN

Kingman Reef (U.S.)
Palmyra Atoll (U.S.)

Tarawa ⊕

Howland Island (U.S.)
• Baker Island (U.S.)

Gilbert Islands

K I R I B A T I

Jarvis Island (U.S.)

Line Islands

Equator

⊕ Yaren District
NAURU

SOLOMON ISLANDS

Phoenix Islands

Marquesas Islands

Funafuti
TUVALU ⊕

TOKELAU (N.Z.)

Mata-Utu
SAMOA

WALLIS AND FUTURA (FR.) ★
Apia ★

Pago Pago

COOK ISLANDS (N.Z.)

VANUATU

⊕ Port Vila

Suva ⊕

AMERICAN SAMOA

TONGA

Nuku'alofa ⊕

Alofi ★

NIUE (N.Z.)

Avarua ★

Papeete
Tahiti ★

Society Islands

Tuamotu Archipelago

★ Noumea

FIJI

NEW CALEDONIA (France)

FRENCH POLYNESIA (France)

• Norfork Island
Kingston (Australia)

Kermadec Islands (N.Z.)

Adamstown ★

PITCAIRN ISLANDS (U.K.)

International Date Line

NEW ZEALAND

Auckland •

Hastings •

Wellington •
• Christchurch
Chatham Islands

• Dunedin
Invercargill
Stewart Island

0 mi.   500 mi.   1,000 mi.

0 km   1,000 km

Europe

0 mi.   300 mi.   600 mi.

0 km   300 km   600 km

Reykjavik • **ICELAND**

Arctic Circle

FAROE ISLANDS
(Denmark)
• Torshavn

SHETLAND ISLANDS

• Trondheim

ORKNEY ISLANDS

HEBRIDES

NORWAY

Bergen •   Oslo ⭐   • Gävle

Stavanger •

• Aberdeen

Glasgow •

SWEDEN

• S

Edinburgh •

DENMARK

• Göteborg

Belfast •

UNITED KINGDOM

NORTH SEA

Ålborg •

Copenhagen ⭐

IRELAND

Dublin ⭐

• Liverpool   Leeds •

Manchester •

Malmö •

Ka

• Sheffield

NETHERLANDS

• Hamburg

• Bremen

Berlin •

• Poznan

Gda

Birmingham •

London •

Amsterdam ⭐

The Hague •

GERMANY

• Rotterdam

Calais •   Lille •

Antwerp •

Essen •

• Dusseldorf

• Cologne

Wroclaw •

GUERNSEY (U.K.)

JERSEY (U.K.)

Le Havre •

BELGIUM

Brussels •

Bonn •

Frankfurt •

LUXEMBOURG

Paris ⭐

Luxembourg ⭐

ATLANTIC OCEAN

Nantes •

Strasbourg •

Stuttgart •

⭐ Prague

CZECH REPUBLIC

• Brno

Dijon •

FRANCE

LIECHTENSTEIN

Munich •

Bratislava ⭐

S

Vienna ⭐

Zurich •

Vaduz ⭐

BAY OF BISCAY

Bern ⭐

Geneva •

SWITZERLAND

Ljubljana ⭐

AUSTRIA

Bu ⭐

H

• Bordeaux

Lyon •

SLOVENIA

Porto •

Bilbao •

Turin •

Milan •

Trieste •

Zagreb ⭐

PORTUGAL

Toulouse •

Genoa •

CROATIA

YUGOSLAVIA

Lisbon ⭐

Madrid ⭐

Andorra la Vella ⭐

Marseille •

⭐ **MONACO**

⭐ San Marino

SAN MARINO

BOSNIA AND HERZEGOVINA

ANDORRA

Florence •

• Sarajevo

SPAIN

Barcelona •

Bastia •

Corsica

ITALY

Podgorica •

Seville •

Valencia •

Majorca

Vatican City •

Rome •

ADRIATIC SEA

Tira

Faro •

Palma •

Sardinia

Bari •

Kor

Málaga •

Naples •

AL

Gibraltar •

MEDITERRANEAN SEA

Cagliari •

Kerkira •

MOROCCO

ALGERIA

Palermo •

Messina •

Sicily

AFRICA

TUNISIA

Valletta •

MALTA

Tromso

Kiruna

Murmansk

Pechora

A S I A

Lulea

Arkhangel'sk

Oulu

R U S S I A

FINLAND

Tampere

Izhevsk

Turku Helsinki

St. Petersburg

ckholm

Tallinn

Kazan

ESTONIA

Nizhniy Novgorod

ALTIC

Samara

EA

Riga LATVIA

Moscow

LITHUANIA

Smolensk

ingrad Vilnius

Minsk

Lipetsk

Saratov

RUSSIA

POLAND

BELARUS

Homyel'

Voronezh

KAZAKHSTAN

arsaw

Brest

Volgograd

iz

rakow

Kiev

Kharkiv

L'viv Derazhnya

Voroshilovgrad

VAKIA

UKRAINE

Gorlovka

Makeyevka

apest

Zhdanov Rostov

NGARY

Chisinau

Iasi Odessa Mykolavia

Arad

MOLDOVA

Kerch'

Groznyy

ROMANIA

Simferopol'

elgrade

Craiova Bucharest

Sevastopol'

erbia

Constanta

Montenegro

Varna

BLACK SEA

Nis Sofia

osovo

BULGARIA

MACEDONIA

Skopje

Istanbul

Thessaloniki

ANIA

T U R K E Y

Volos

GREECE

Izmir

Athens

SYRIA

IRAN

CYPRUS

IRAQ

LEBANON

Crete

ICELAND

Greenland Sea

Tasiilaq
(Ammassalik)

Narsarsuaq

GREENLAND
(Denmark)

Nuuk (Godthåb)

*Labrador
Sea*

Island of
Newfoundland

St. John's

Saint-Pierre

Charlottetown

Happy Valley
Goose Bay

Québec

Qaanaaq (Thule)

Baffin Bay

Davis Strait

Iqaluit

CANADA

Chisasibi
(Fort George)

Alert

Baffin Island

Moosonee

Queen Elizabeth Islands

Kaujuitoq (Resolute)

Arctic Circle

*HUDSON
BAY*

Churchill

**ARCTIC
OCEAN**

Banks Island

Victoria Island

Echo Bay

Yellowknife

Saskatoon

Regina

Bismarck

*Beaufort
Sea*

Inuvik

Edmonton

Calgary

Helena

Barrow

Prudhoe Bay

Whitehorse

Boise

Alaska (U.S.)

Fairbanks

Juneau

Vancouver

Seattle

Olympia

Portland

RUSSIA

Nome

Anchorage

Valdez

Victoria

Salem

Sacramento

Bethel

Kodiak

*Bering
Sea*

Aleutian Islands

North America and Central America

ATLANTIC OCEAN

BERMUDA (U.K.)
★ Hamilton

PACIFIC OCEAN

GULF OF MEXICO

CARIBBEAN SEA

UNITED STATES

MEXICO

Gulf of California

Tropic of Cancer

Halifax
Montréal
Ottawa
Montpelier
Concord
Augusta
Albany
Boston
Hartford
Providence
Buffalo
New York
Toronto
Cleveland
Philadelphia
Harrisburg
Dover
Pittsburgh
Baltimore
Washington, DC
Detroit
Milwaukee
Cincinnati
Frankfort
Richmond
Toledo
Indianapolis
Louisville
Raleigh
Chicago
Columbia
St. Paul
Minneapolis
Madison
Springfield
Louis
Saint Louis
Nashville
Charleston
Jacksonville
Des Moines
Jefferson City
Memphis
Atlanta
Columbia
Omaha
Topeka
Kansas City
Birmingham
Savannah
Lincoln
Little Rock
Jackson
Montgomery
Tallahassee
Cheyenne
Denver
Oklahoma City
Baton Rouge
New Orleans
Santa Fe
Dallas
Austin
Houston
Salt Lake City
Phoenix
San Antonio
El Paso
Monterrey
Ciudad Juárez
Hermosillo
Los Angeles
San Diego
Tijuana
Mazatlán
La Paz
Puerto Vallarta
Guadalajara
León
Acapulco
Oaxaca
Puebla
Mexico City
Veracruz
Tampico
Mérida
Cancun

Freeport
Nassau
BAHAMAS
Miami
Havana
CUBA
Camagüey
TURKS AND CAICOS ISLANDS (U.K.)
★ Grand Turk
DOMINICAN REPUBLIC
Santiago
PUERTO RICO (U.S.)
San Juan
VIRGIN ISLANDS (U.S.) (U.K.)
Santo Domingo
HAITI
Port-au-Prince
Guantánamo Bay
Kingston
JAMAICA
Montego Bay
CAYMAN ISLANDS (U.K.)
George Town

BELIZE
Belmopan
Belize City
GUATEMALA
Guatemala City
HONDURAS
Tegucigalpa
San Salvador
EL SALVADOR
NICARAGUA
Managua
COSTA RICA
San José
PANAMA
Panama City

ANGUILLA (U.K.)
SAINT MAARTEN/ SAINT MARTIN (Neth. Antilles)/(Guad.)
SAINT BARTHÉLEMY (Guad.)
ANTIGUA AND BARBUDA
SAINT KITTS AND NEVIS
MONTSERRAT (U.K.)
GUADELOUPE (Fr.)
DOMINICA
MARTINIQUE (Fr.)
SAINT LUCIA
BARBADOS
SAINT VINCENT AND THE GRENADINES
GRENADA
TRINIDAD AND TOBAGO
NETHERLANDS ANTILLES (Neth.)
ARUBA (Neth.)

VENEZUELA
COLOMBIA
GUYANA

Scale:
0 mi.
500 mi.
1,000 mi.
0 km
500 km
1,000 km

233

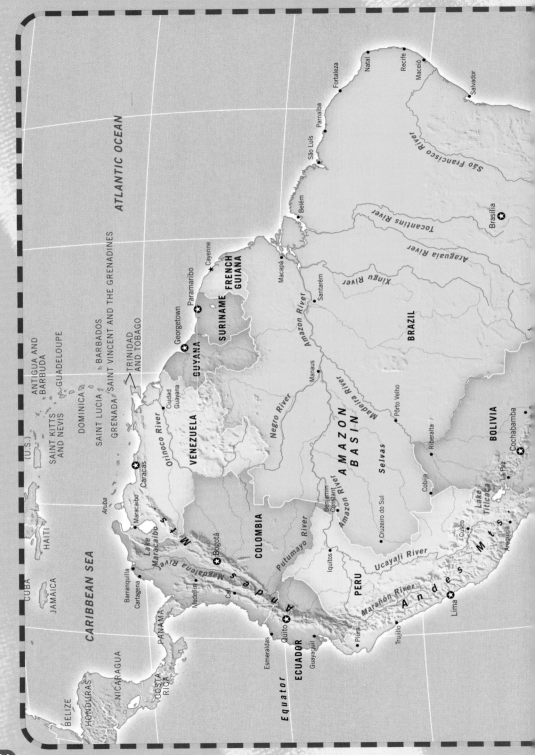

CUBA

JAMAICA

HAITI

BELIZE

HONDURAS

NICARAGUA

COSTA RICA

PANAMA

CARIBBEAN SEA

(U.S.)

SAINT KITTS AND NEVIS

ANTIGUA AND BARBUDA

GUADELOUPE

DOMINICA

SAINT LUCIA

BARBADOS

GRENADA

SAINT VINCENT AND THE GRENADINES

TRINIDAD AND TOBAGO

ATLANTIC OCEAN

Aruba

Barranquilla

Cartagena

Maracaibo

Lake Maracaibo

Medellín

Cali

Caracas

Ciudad Guayana

Georgetown

Paramaribo

Cayenne

SURINAME

FRENCH GUIANA

GUYANA

VENEZUELA

COLOMBIA

Bogotá

Orinoco River

Magdalena River

Putumayo River

Negro River

Macapá

Belém

São Luís

Parnaíba

Fortaleza

Natal

Recife

Maceió

Salvador

Amazon River

Santarém

Manaus

Benjamin Constant

Iquitos

Tabatinga

Amazon River

Madeira River

Xingú River

Tocantins River

Araguaia River

São Francisco River

BRAZIL

Brasília

AMAZON BASIN

Selvas

Pôrto Velho

Riberalta

Cobija

Cruzeiro do Sul

Ucayali River

Marañón River

Piura

Trujillo

Lima

PERU

Andes Mts

Cuzco

Arequipa

Lake Titicaca

La Paz

Cochabamba

BOLIVIA

Equator

ECUADOR

Quito

Esmeraldas

Guayaquil

A n d e s M t s

234

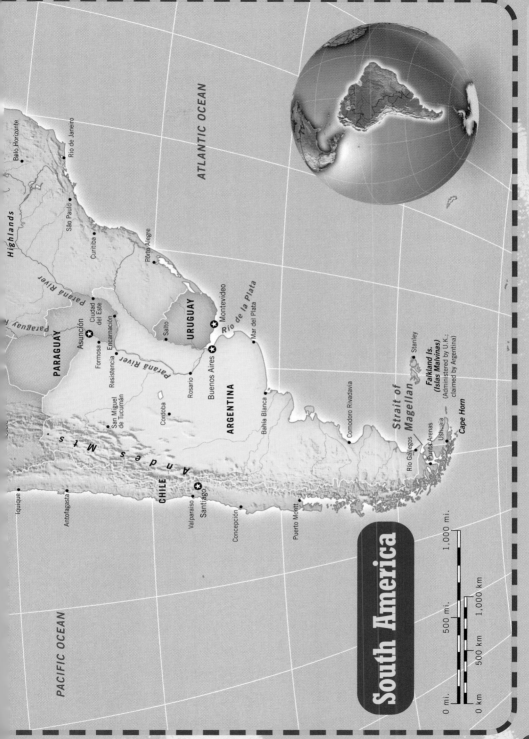

South America

ATLANTIC OCEAN

PACIFIC OCEAN

Highlands

Belo Horizonte
Rio de Janeiro
São Paulo
Curitiba
Pôrto Alegre

Paraná River

Paraguay River

PARAGUAY
Asunción
Ciudad del Este
Encarnación
Formosa
Resistencia
Parana River

URUGUAY
Salto
Montevideo
Río de la Plata
Mar del Plata

Buenos Aires
Rosario
San Miguel de Tucumán
Córdoba
ARGENTINA
Bahía Blanca

San tes Mts.
Andes

CHILE
Santiago
Valparaíso
Concepción
Iquique
Antofagasta
Puerto Montt

Comodoro Rivadavia

Strait of Magellan

Falkland Is.
(Islas Malvinas)
(Administered by U.K.;
claimed by Argentina)

Stanley

Río Gallegos
Punta Arenas
Ushuaia
Cape Horn

1,000 mi.

500 mi.

1,000 km

500 km

0 mi.

0 km

235

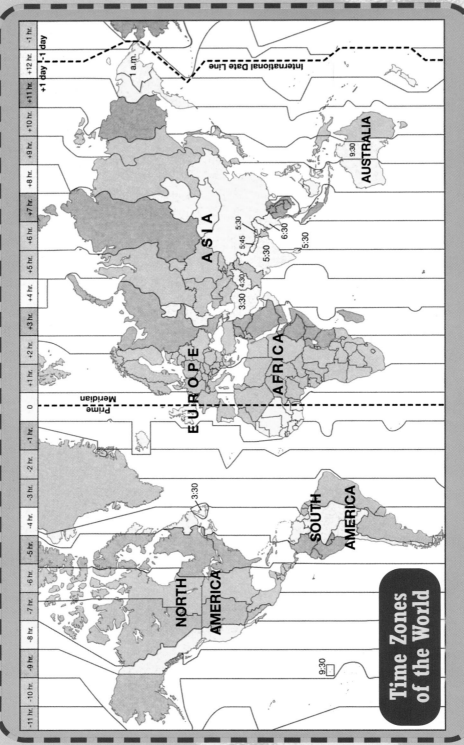

Time Zones of the World

-11 hr. -10 hr. -9 hr. -8 hr. -7 hr. -6 hr. -5 hr. -4 hr. -3 hr. -2 hr. -1 hr. 0 +1 hr. +2 hr. +3 hr. +4 hr. +5 hr. +6 hr. +7 hr. +8 hr. +9 hr. +10 hr. +11 hr. +12 hr. +1 day -1 hr. -1 day

Prime Meridian

International Date Line

1 a.m.

NORTH AMERICA

SOUTH AMERICA

EUROPE

AFRICA

ASIA

AUSTRALIA

3:30

9:30

3:30

4:30

5:30

5:45

5:30

6:30

5:30

9:30

If it's 1:00 P.M. Tuesday in New York ...

... it's 6:00 P.M. Tuesday in London, England

... it's 3:00 A.M. Wednesday in Tokyo, Japan

Time Zones

Source: National Institute of Standards and Technology Physics Laboratory

Time zones did not become necessary in the U.S. until trains made it possible to travel hundreds of miles in a day. Until the 1860s most cities relied upon their own local "sun" time, but this time changed by approximately one minute for every 12 miles traveled east or west. The problem of keeping track of over 300 local times was overcome by establishing railroad time zones. Until 1883 most railway companies relied on some 100 different time zones. That year, the U.S. was divided into four time zones. On November 1, 1884, the International Meridian Conference in Washington, D.C., applied the same procedure to zones all around the world. There are 24 time zones. (See page 236.)

TFK Mystery Person

Often compared to former U.S. President Bill Clinton, this British Prime Minister used to play guitar in a band called Ugly Rumours. But he is best known for his leadership of Britain's Labour Party, which he joined in 1975. The Labour Party is one of the two main political parties in Britain today.

Who is he?

TFK Puzzles & Games — Photo File

Get this traveler organized! Match each picture with the flag of the country where it was taken.

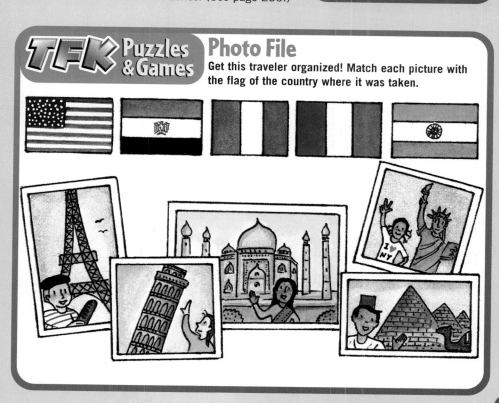

Presidents

1 GEORGE WASHINGTON (SERVED 1789-1797)
Born: February 22, 1732, in Westmoreland County, Virginia
Died: December 14, 1799
Political Party: None
Vice President: John Adams
DID YOU KNOW? Washington's first pair of false teeth was made of hippopotamus ivory.

2 JOHN ADAMS (SERVED 1797-1801)
Born: October 30, 1735, in Braintree, Massachusetts
Died: July 4, 1826
Political Party: Federalist
Vice President: Thomas Jefferson
DID YOU KNOW? Adams was the first President to live in the White House.

3 THOMAS JEFFERSON (SERVED 1801-1809)
Born: April 13, 1743, in Shadwell, Virginia
Died: July 4, 1826
Political Party: Democratic-Republican
Vice Presidents: Aaron Burr, George Clinton
DID YOU KNOW? In signing the 1803 Louisiana Purchase, Jefferson nearly doubled the size of the U.S.

4 JAMES MADISON (SERVED 1809-1817)
Born: March 16, 1751, in Port Conway, Virginia
Died: June 28, 1836
Political Party: Democratic-Republican
Vice Presidents: George Clinton, Elbridge Gerry
DID YOU KNOW? Madison was the first President who wore trousers, rather than knee breeches, on an everyday basis.

5 JAMES MONROE (SERVED 1817-1825)
Born: April 28, 1758, in Westmoreland County, Virginia
Died: July 4, 1831
Political Party: Democratic-Republican
Vice President: Daniel D. Tompkins
DID YOU KNOW? The Monroe Doctrine forbade foreign countries like Spain and Russia from expanding into North and South America.

6 JOHN QUINCY ADAMS (SERVED 1825-1829)
Born: July 11, 1767, in Braintree, Massachusetts
Died: February 23, 1848
Political Party: Democratic-Republican
Vice President: John C. Calhoun
DID YOU KNOW? In 1843, Adams became the first President to have his photograph taken.

7 ANDREW JACKSON (SERVED 1829-1837)
Born: March 15, 1767, in Waxhaw, South Carolina
Died: June 8, 1845
Political Party: Democratic
Vice Presidents: John C. Calhoun, Martin Van Buren
DID YOU KNOW? Jackson took several bullets while fighting in duels—an activity for which he was famous.

8 MARTIN VAN BUREN (SERVED 1837-1841)
Born: December 5, 1782, in Kinderhook, New York
Died: July 24, 1862
Political Party: Democratic
Vice President: Richard M. Johnson
DID YOU KNOW? Van Buren was the first President born a U.S. citizen rather than a British subject.

9 WILLIAM HENRY HARRISON (SERVED 1841)
Born: February 9, 1773, in Berkeley, Virginia
Died: April 4, 1841
Political Party: Whig
Vice President: John Tyler
DID YOU KNOW? Harrison had the shortest presidency: he died after only a month in office.

10 JOHN TYLER (SERVED 1841-1845)
Born: March 29, 1790, in Charles City County, Virginia
Died: January 18, 1862
Political Party: Whig
Vice President: None
DID YOU KNOW? Tyler was the first President to marry in office. He was also the President with the most children (15).

11 JAMES KNOX POLK (SERVED 1845-1849)
Born: November 2, 1795, in Mecklenburg County, North Carolina
Died: June 15, 1849
Political Party: Democratic
Vice President: George M. Dallas
DID YOU KNOW? Polk's inauguration was the first one to be reported by telegraph.

Presidents

12 ZACHARY TAYLOR (SERVED 1849-1850)

Born: November 24, 1784, in Montebello, Orange County, Virginia
Died: July 9, 1850
Political Party: Whig
Vice President: Millard Fillmore
DID YOU KNOW? Taylor's horse, "Whitey," grazed on the White House lawn.

13 MILLARD FILLMORE (SERVED 1850-1853)

Born: January 7, 1800, in Summerhill, New York
Died: March 8, 1874
Political Party: Whig
Vice President: None
DID YOU KNOW? Fillmore and his first wife, Abigail, started the White House Library.

14 FRANKLIN PIERCE (SERVED 1853-1857)

Born: November 23, 1804, in Hillsborough, New Hampshire
Died: October 8, 1869
Political Party: Democratic
Vice President: William R. King
DID YOU KNOW? Pierce was the first President to have a Christmas tree in the White House.

15 JAMES BUCHANAN (SERVED 1857-1861)

Born: April 23, 1791, in Cove Gap, Pennsylvania
Died: June 1, 1868
Political Party: Democratic
Vice President: John C. Breckinridge
DID YOU KNOW? Buchanan was the only President who never married.

16 ABRAHAM LINCOLN (SERVED 1861-1865)

Born: February 12, 1809, in Hodgenville, Kentucky
Died: April 15, 1865
Political Party: Republican
Vice Presidents: Hannibal Hamlin, Andrew Johnson
DID YOU KNOW? Lincoln was the only President to patent an invention: a device to help boats over shallow water.

17 ANDREW JOHNSON (SERVED 1865-1869)

Born: December 29, 1808, in Raleigh, North Carolina
Died: July 31, 1875
Political Party: Democratic
Vice President: None
DID YOU KNOW? Andrew Johnson never attended school. His wife taught him to read.

18 ULYSSES S. GRANT (SERVED 1869–1877)
Born: April 27, 1822, in Point Pleasant, Ohio
Died: July 23, 1885
Political Party: Republican
Vice Presidents: Schuyler Colfax, Henry Wilson
DID YOU KNOW? Grant's much-praised book *Memoirs* has been in print since 1885.

19 RUTHERFORD B. HAYES (SERVED 1877–1881)
Born: October 4, 1822, in Delaware, Ohio
Died: January 17, 1893
Political Party: Republican
Vice President: William A. Wheeler
DID YOU KNOW? The first telephone was installed in the White House while Hayes was President.

20 JAMES A. GARFIELD (SERVED 1881)
Born: November 19, 1831, in Orange, Ohio
Died: September 19, 1881
Political Party: Republican
Vice President: Chester A. Arthur
DID YOU KNOW? Garfield was the first President who campaigned in two languages—English and German.

21 CHESTER A. ARTHUR (SERVED 1881–1885)
Born: October 5, 1829, in Fairfield, Vermont
Died: November 18, 1886
Political Party: Republican
Vice President: None
DID YOU KNOW? A stylish dresser, Arthur was nicknamed "Gentleman Boss" and "Elegant Arthur."

22 GROVER CLEVELAND (SERVED 1885–1889)
Born: March 18, 1837, in Caldwell, New Jersey
Died: June 24, 1908
Political Party: Democratic
Vice President: Thomas A. Hendricks
DID YOU KNOW? Cleveland was the only President to be defeated and then re-elected, serving two nonconsecutive terms.

23 BENJAMIN HARRISON (SERVED 1889–1893)
Born: August 20, 1833, in North Bend, Ohio
Died: March 13, 1901
Political Party: Republican
Vice President: Levi P. Morton
DID YOU KNOW? Benjamin Harrison was the only President who was a grandson of a President (William Henry Harrison).

24 GROVER CLEVELAND (SERVED 1893–1897)

Born: March 18, 1837, in Caldwell, New Jersey
Died: June 24, 1908
Political Party: Democratic
Vice President: Adlai E. Stevenson

DID YOU KNOW? The "Baby Ruth" candy bar was named to honor Cleveland's daughter, Ruth.

25 WILLIAM MCKINLEY (SERVED 1897–1901)

Born: January 29, 1843, in Niles, Ohio
Died: September 14, 1901
Political Party: Republican
Vice Presidents: Garret A. Hobart, Theodore Roosevelt

DID YOU KNOW? McKinley was the first President to use a telephone to organize his campaign.

26 THEODORE ROOSEVELT (SERVED 1901–1909)

Born: October 27, 1858, in New York, New York
Died: January 6, 1919
Political Party: Republican
Vice President: Charles W. Fairbanks

DID YOU KNOW? Theodore Roosevelt was the first President to ride in an automobile, an airplane and a submarine.

27 WILLIAM H. TAFT (SERVED 1909–1913)

Born: September 15, 1857, in Cincinnati, Ohio
Died: March 8, 1930
Political Party: Republican
Vice President: James S. Sherman

DID YOU KNOW? Taft was the first President to throw out the first pitch at the start of baseball season.

28 WOODROW WILSON (SERVED 1913–1921)

Born: December 28, 1856, in Staunton, Virginia
Died: February 3, 1924
Political Party: Democratic
Vice President: Thomas R. Marshall

DID YOU KNOW? Wilson was the first President to speak on the radio.

29 WARREN G. HARDING (SERVED 1921–1923)

Born: November 2, 1865, in Corsica, Ohio
Died: August 2, 1923
Political Party: Republican
Vice President: Calvin Coolidge

DID YOU KNOW? Harding was a newspaper publisher before he was President.

30 CALVIN COOLIDGE (SERVED 1923–1929)
Born: July 4, 1872, in Plymouth, Vermont
Died: January 5, 1933
Political Party: Republican
Vice President: Charles G. Dawes
DID YOU KNOW? A man of few words, Coolidge was nicknamed "Silent Cal."

31 HERBERT C. HOOVER (SERVED 1929–1933)
Born: August 10, 1874, in West Branch, Iowa
Died: October 20, 1964
Political Party: Republican
Vice President: Charles Curtis
DID YOU KNOW? An asteroid, Hooveria, was named for Hoover.

32 FRANKLIN D. ROOSEVELT (SERVED 1933–1945)
Born: January 30, 1882, in Hyde Park, New York
Died: April 12, 1945
Political Party: Democratic
Vice Presidents: John Garner, Henry Wallace, Harry S Truman
DID YOU KNOW? Franklin D. Roosevelt was the only President elected to four terms.

33 HARRY S TRUMAN (SERVED 1945–1953)
Born: May 8, 1884, in Lamar, Missouri
Died: December 26, 1972
Political Party: Democratic
Vice President: Alben W. Barkley
DID YOU KNOW? Truman was a farmer, a hatmaker and a judge before entering politics.

34 DWIGHT D. EISENHOWER (SERVED 1953–1961)
Born: October 14, 1890, in Denison, Texas
Died: March 28, 1969
Political Party: Republican
Vice President: Richard M. Nixon
DID YOU KNOW? Eisenhower was the first President with an airplane pilot's license.

35 JOHN F. KENNEDY (SERVED 1961–1963)
Born: May 29, 1917, in Brookline, Massachusetts
Died: November 22, 1963
Political Party: Democratic
Vice President: Lyndon B. Johnson
DID YOU KNOW? Kennedy was the first Roman Catholic President.

36 LYNDON B. JOHNSON (SERVED 1963–1969)
Born: August 27, 1908, in Stonewall, Texas
Died: January 22, 1973
Political Party: Democratic
Vice President: Hubert H. Humphrey
DID YOU KNOW? Lyndon Johnson was the first Southerner since Andrew Johnson to become President.

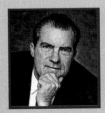

37 RICHARD M. NIXON (SERVED 1969–1974)
Born: January 9, 1913, in Yorba Linda, California
Died: April 22, 1994
Political Party: Republican
Vice Presidents: Spiro T. Agnew, Gerald R. Ford
DID YOU KNOW? Nixon was the first President to resign.

38 GERALD R. FORD (SERVED 1974–1977)
Born: July 14, 1913, in Omaha, Nebraska
Political Party: Republican
Vice President: Nelson A. Rockefeller
DID YOU KNOW? After college, Ford was a football coach, a park ranger and a male model.

39 JIMMY CARTER (SERVED 1977–1981)
Born: October 1, 1924, in Plains, Georgia
Political Party: Democratic
Vice President: Walter F. Mondale
DID YOU KNOW? Before he was President, Carter was a peanut farmer.

40 RONALD W. REAGAN (SERVED 1981–1989)
Born: February 6, 1911, in Tampico, Illinois
Political Party: Republican
Vice President: George H. W. Bush
DID YOU KNOW? Reagan worked for nearly 30 years as a Hollywood actor.

41 GEORGE H. W. BUSH (SERVED 1989–1993)
Born: June 12, 1924, in Milton, Massachusetts
Political Party: Republican
Vice President: J. Danforth Quayle
DID YOU KNOW? Bush was the first President to spend a holiday with troops overseas—Thanksgiving in Saudi Arabia.

42 WILLIAM J. CLINTON (SERVED 1993–2001)

Born: August 19, 1946, in Hope, Arkansas
Political Party: Democratic
Vice President: Albert Gore Jr.

DID YOU KNOW? Clinton was the first President who could play the saxophone.

43 GEORGE W. BUSH (SERVED 2001–)

Born: July 6, 1946, in New Haven, Connecticut
Political Party: Republican
Vice President: Richard B. Cheney

DID YOU KNOW? George W. Bush is the second President who is the son of a former President. (John Quincy Adams was the first.)

George W. Bush became the 43rd President of the United States on January 20, 2001. Bush grew up mostly in Midland, Texas, and became Governor of that state in 1994.

"... America is strong and determined and generous. I'm honored to lead such a country, and I know we are ready for the challenges ahead."

—George W. Bush
October 11, 2001

TFK Puzzles & Games

Presidential Match-Up

Can you match the President on the left with the fact that describes him? We've added some hints to help you out.

FACTS:	PRESIDENTS:
First president (U.S. capital city named after him)	George W. Bush
Youngest man elected president (comes from a family of politicians)	Bill Clinton
Former governor of Texas (his dad was a President, too)	John F. Kennedy
President for eight years until 2001 (real first name is William)	Abraham Lincoln
Issued Emancipation Proclamation to free slaves (President during Civil War)	George Washington

For biographies of all the Presidents
go to www.FACT MONSTER.COM

Most visitors don't get to see the **PRESIDENT'S MASTER BEDROOM,** but Zweifel got special permission to include it in the model. The **PRIVATE STUDY** has a one-inch-wide TV that really works!

The miniature books in the **LIBRARY** are the same ones that are kept in the real White House. Many of them even have the actual text and pictures inside, which can be read with a magnifying glass.

TFK **A little Tour of the White House**

The model has included details like the roller-skate marks left on the floor of the **EAST ROOM** by President Jimmy Carter's daughter Amy. Later, when the real floor was redone, Zweifel fixed his tiny floor too.

n November 1, 1800, President John Adams moved into the brand-new presidential home, the White House. America celebrated the great mansion's 200th birthday in November 2000.

John Zweifel, 64, has spent 40 years making this 60-foot by 20-foot model. His version is almost exactly like the real thing. The phones ring, and the tiny toilets flush. "If the President moves even a small painting, our model reflects that," he says.

Tour the mini White House room by room at **www.timeforkids.com/wh**

White House Facts

★ The White House has 132 rooms, including 32 bathrooms. The building features 412 doors, 147 windows, 28 fireplaces, 7 staircases and 3 elevators.

★ The White House has six floors—two basements, two floors for the First Family and two floors for offices and visitors.

★ About 6,000 people visit the White House every day.

★ It takes 570 gallons of white paint to paint the outside of the White House.

★ President Theodore Roosevelt gave the White House its official name in 1901. It has also been known as the President's Palace, the President's House and the Executive Mansion.

TFK TOP 5 Tallest Presidents

Presidents come in all different sizes. The shortest President was James Madison. He was 5 feet, 4 inches tall. But here are some leaders you could really look up to.

1. Abraham Lincoln . . . . .6 feet, 4 inches
2. Lyndon B. Johnson . . . . . . .6 feet, 3 inches
3. Thomas Jefferson . . . . . . .6 feet, 2 ½ inches
4. George Washington . . . . . .6 feet, 2 inches
5. Bill Clinton . . . . .6 feet, 2 inches

(Actually, three other Presidents were the exact same height as George Washington and Bill Clinton. Chester A. Arthur, Franklin D. Roosevelt and George H. W. Bush were each 6 feet, 2 inches.)

Presidential Pets

George W. Bush has a cat named India and two dogs named Spot and Barney.

First Families have had all kinds of pets— an alligator, a sheep, a pig, a rat, a raccoon, even a cow! Dogs are definitely the Commander-in-Chief's best friend. More than 50 pooches have lived in the White House. **Here are some of the best-loved First Pets in history:**

See Spot run! One of George W. Bush's dogs is named SPOT.

Calvin Coolidge had a raccoon, REBECCA, held here by his wife Grace. He walked Rebecca at the White House on a leash.

Benjamin Harrison's goat OLD WHISKERS pulled the Harrison grandchildren in a cart.

The Kennedys' pony MACARONI received thousands of fan letters.

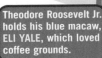

Theodore Roosevelt Jr. holds his blue macaw, ELI YALE, which loved coffee grounds.

TFK Mystery Person

This former peanut farmer from Georgia went on to become President of the United States. He tried to improve our respect for the environment by expanding the national park system and protecting more than 100 million acres of land in Alaska. He also created the Department of Education.

Who is he?

Religion

A Look at Islam

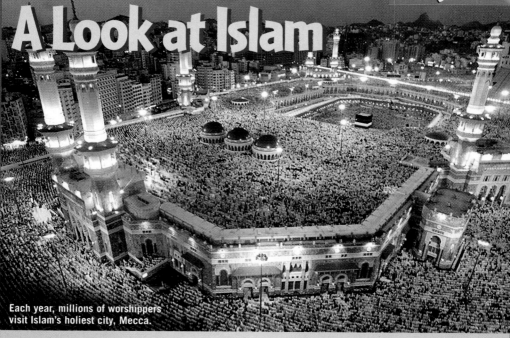

Each year, millions of worshippers visit Islam's holiest city, Mecca.

When President Bush visited a mosque in Washington, D.C., in 2001, he had this message: "Islam is peace." The President wanted Americans to know that while the terrorists who attacked the U.S. that same year follow the Islamic faith, their religion does not preach violence.

With more than 1 billion followers, Islam is the world's second largest religion after Christianity. Many countries in Asia, Africa and the Middle East have large populations of Muslims, the followers of Islam. More than 6 million Americans are Muslim.

Muslims, Christians and Jews share many beliefs. Most important is the belief in just one God. The city of Jerusalem is holy to all three religions. Abraham, Moses and Jesus are prophets to Muslims.

BY DINA EL NABLI

Islam was first preached by the prophet Muhammad. He was born in 570 in the city of Mecca in what is now Saudi Arabia. Muslims believe that the angel Gabriel gave Muhammad the words of God, which are contained in the Koran. The Koran is as important to Muslims as the Bible is to Christians and Jews.

Islam rests on five pillars, or rules. Muslims must declare their faith in God; pray five times a day; fast during the holy month of Ramadan; give to the poor; and try to journey to Mecca.

While the terrorists said they struck in the name of Islam, they represent only a small group of Muslims. Says Imam Ahmed Dewidar from an Islamic center in New York City: "The message of Islam is to live in peace and to love each other."

 Read more about Islam at
www.timeforkids.com/islam

Religious Dress

People from many religions use dress as a sign of their faith. Sometimes a special type of dress is required by religion, while other times it is a matter of custom.

- **Islam** requires both men and women to be modest not only in behavior but in dress. Some Muslim women wear modest dress, or *hijab*, that covers most of the head and body.

- **Sikhs**—followers of **Sikhism**, a religion from India—also keep their heads covered. Sikh men wrap their heads in cotton turbans, while Sikh women may wear turbans or headscarves.

- Most **Hasidic Jewish** men wear *payos*, curled forelocks, and *tzitzit*, fringed shawls, both of which were worn by some ancient Israelites. Jewish men of all backgrounds may wear yarmulkes (skullcaps).

- **Buddhist** nuns and monks wear robes in a variety of colors, from gray to orange, depending on their region and their tradition. In many cases, both nuns and monks in the Buddhist tradition shave their heads.

- **"Plain people"** such as the Amish and Mennonites dress in simple clothing that reflects a devotion to traditional ways. Men often wear plain hats and long coats, and women wear simple dresses and aprons.

Religion

Key Words in Islam

Allah The Arabic word for God

Hajj A Muslim person's religious journey to Mecca

Imam A religious scholar who leads Muslims in prayer

Jihad A religious struggle to better oneself, fight injustice or defend the teachings of Islam

Koran (or Qur'an) Islam's holy book, originally written in Arabic

Mosque A place of worship for Muslims

251

THE FIVE

	JUDAISM	CHRISTIANITY
FOUNDER	The Hebrew leader Abraham founded Judaism around 2000 B.C. Moses gave the Jews the Torah around 1250 B.C.	Jesus Christ, who was crucified around A.D. 30 in Jerusalem
HOW MANY GODS	One	One
HOLY WRITINGS	The most important is the Torah, or the five books of Moses. Others include Judaism's oral tradition, which is known as the Talmud when it is written down.	The Bible is the main sacred text of Christianity.
BELIEFS	Jews believe in the laws of God and the words of the prophets. In Judaism, however, actions are more important than beliefs.	Jesus taught love of God and neighbor, and a concern for justice.
TYPES	The three main types today are Orthodox, Conservative and Reform.	In 1054 Christians separated into the Eastern Orthodox Church and the Roman Catholic Church. In the early 1500s the major Protestant groups (Lutheran, Presbyterian and Episcopalian) came into being. A variety of other groups have since developed.
WHERE	There are large Jewish populations in Israel and the U.S.	Through its missionary activity Christianity has spread to most parts of the globe.

MAJOR FAITHS

Monotheism
Monotheism is the belief that there is only one god. **Judaism, Christianity** and **Islam** are all monotheistic faiths.

ISLAM	HINDUISM	BUDDHISM
Muhammad, who was born in A.D. 570 at Mecca, in Saudi Arabia	**Hinduism** has no founder. The oldest religion, it may date to prehistoric times.	**Siddhartha Gautama,** in the 4th or 5th century B.C. in India
One	**Many**	**None,** but there are enlightened beings (Buddhas)
The Koran is the sacred book of Islam.	**The most ancient are the four Vedas.**	**The most important are the Tripitaka, the Mahayana Sutras, Tantra and Zen texts.**
The Five Pillars, or main duties, are: profession of faith; prayer; charitable giving; fasting during the month of Ramadan; and pilgrimage to Mecca at least once.	**Reincarnation** states that all living things are caught in a cycle of death and rebirth. Life is ruled by the laws of **karma,** in which rebirth depends on moral behavior.	**The Four Noble Truths:** (1) all beings suffer; (2) desire—for possessions, power and so on—causes suffering; (3) desire can be overcome; and (4) there is a path that leads away from desire. This path is known as the Eightfold Path or the Middle Way.
Almost 90% of Muslims are **Sunnis. Shiites** are the second largest group.	No single belief system unites Hindus. A Hindu can believe in only one god, in many or in none.	**Theravada** and **Mahayana** are the two main types.
Islam is the main religion of the Middle East, Asia and the north of Africa.	Hinduism is practiced by more than 80% of India's population.	Buddhism is the main religion in many Asian countries.

Religion

For more on the world's religions, go to www.FACT MONSTER.com

253

Holy Places

Throughout the world are places of special significance to different religious groups. Here's just a sampling of the world's sacred spots.

★ **The Holy Land**—a collective name for areas of Israel, Jordan and Egypt—is a place of pilgrimage for Muslims, Jews and Christians.

★ **The Ganges River** in India is sacred to Hindus. They drink its water, bathe in it and scatter the ashes of their dead in it.

★ **Mount Fuji**, in Japan, is sacred to Buddhists, who believe it represents a gateway to another world.

★ The **Black Hills** of South Dakota are a holy place for some Native Americans, who travel there in vision quests—searches for peace and oneness with the universe.

★ The **Sacred Mosque in Mecca**, Saudi Arabia, is sacred to Muslims. Muslims around the world face in the direction of Mecca five times a day to pray.

★ **Mount Tai Shan** is China's most sacred mountain. It is thought to be a center of living energy—a holy place for Taoists and Buddhists.

★ **Lourdes, France,** is the home of a Roman Catholic shrine where the Virgin Mary was said to appear to St. Bernadette.

Mount Fuji is a volcano that last erupted in 1707. Its name means "everlasting life."

151

OTHER MAJOR RELIGIONS

There are many religions in the world. In addition to the five major faiths, religions with many followers include Shintoism, Taoism, Confucianism, Sikhism and Ba'hai.

10 Largest World Religions

Estimates of world religions are very rough. Aside from Christianity, few religions keep statistical records.
(in millions of people)

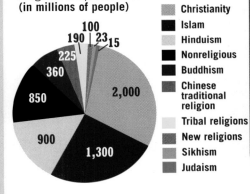

100
190 | 23 15
225
360
850
2,000
900
1,300

■ Christianity
■ Islam
■ Hinduism
■ Nonreligious
■ Buddhism
■ Chinese traditional religion
■ Tribal religions
■ New religions
■ Sikhism
■ Judaism

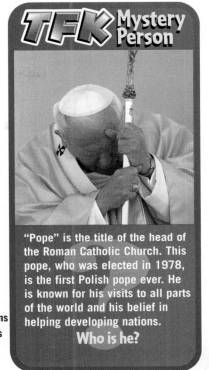

TFK Mystery Person

"Pope" is the title of the head of the Roman Catholic Church. This pope, who was elected in 1978, is the first Polish pope ever. He is known for his visits to all parts of the world and his belief in helping developing nations.
Who is he?

Religion in the U.S.

The U.S. has more religious groups than any other country in the world. Here are rough estimates of the five major faiths in the U.S.

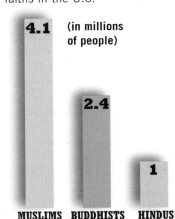

5.6
4.1 **(in millions of people)**
2.4
1

CHRISTIANS JEWS MUSLIMS BUDDHISTS HINDUS

Founded in the U.S.

Religious groups founded in the U.S. include **Christian Scientists, Latter-day Saints (Mormons), Seventh-day Adventists** and **Jehovah's Witnesses**.

Atheists and Agnostics

An **atheist** does not believe in God. An **agnostic** believes that it is not known whether God exists. About 7% of Americans say they are atheist or agnostic.

Religion

255

Safety

PLAY SMART!

Injuries sideline millions of kids. Learn how to stay healthy and in the game

More than 30 million U.S. kids play competitive sports. That's up from about 25 million in 1992. But as the number of kid athletes rises, so does the number of sports injuries.

In 2001, more than 3.5 million kids suffered an injury related to sports or recreation, says Angela Mickalide, program director of the National SAFE KIDS Campaign in Washington, D.C. The worst offenders: basketball, football and soccer.

Look before you leap! More than 100,000 kid baseball players land in the emergency room each year.

By Elizabeth Siris

The good news, says Mickalide, is that "nearly half of all kids' organized-sports-related injuries can be prevented." Experts agree that there's plenty a kid can do to keep healthy and stay in the game.

First tip: follow the rules. A poll of 539 people released by the American Academy of Orthopedic Surgeons reveals that 8 out of 10 injury-free kids know safety guidelines and use safety equipment all or most of the time.

It also helps to shape up before the season starts and to remember that even competitive sports are supposed to be fun. In 1989, Michelle Klein began the National Youth Sports Safety Foundation in Boston, Massachusetts. The foundation works with coaches, parents and athletes to reduce kids' sports injuries. Klein cautions athletes, "Don't be afraid to say something if you get hurt. Pain means something is wrong."

Test your safety smarts at
www.timeforkids.com/safesports

Safety Rules!

ONLINE SAFETY

The Internet is a great research tool. It can also be a fun, fascinating place to hang out. But just like the real world, the virtual world has important rules to follow. Keep a copy of these guidelines near your computer:

I will not give out personal information such as my address, telephone number, parents' work address or telephone number or the name and location of my school without my parents' permission.

I will tell my parents right away if I come across any information that makes me feel uncomfortable.

I will never agree to get together with someone I "meet" online without first checking with my parents. If my parents agree to the meeting, I will be sure that it is in a public place and bring my mother or father along.

I will never send anyone my picture or anything else without first checking with my parents.

I will not respond to any messages that are mean or in any way make me feel uncomfortable. It is not my fault if I get that sort of message. I will tell my parents right away about the message so that they can contact the online service.

My parents and I will agree to rules for going online. We will decide upon the time of day, the length of time and appropriate areas for me to visit. I will not break these rules without their permission.

Source: National Center for Missing and Exploited Children

Tips from a Pro

Want to jump higher, run faster, throw harder and stay healthy? Here are some tips from Dr. Jordan D. Metzl, director of the Sports Medicine Institute for Young Athletes in New York City.

PRESEASON

Start getting in shape five to six weeks before the season starts. Try doing something new: If you're a skater, play some basketball; if you're a football player, hit the pool. Choose activities that will exercise your heart and lungs. Do them for 30 to 40 minutes, four to five times a week.

Get strong: Do as many push-ups and pull-ups as you can manage, two to three times a week. You won't look like Arnold Schwarzenegger, but you will strengthen your muscles and bones.

DURING THE SEASON

Warm up before play. Stretch your muscles and practice with your team.

Always wear the proper gear and make sure it fits. Shin guards that are too small won't protect you. Wear a mouth guard for all contact sports.

ANYTIME

Don't overdo it! Too much exercise can lead to an overuse injury.

Listen to your body: Tell a parent and see a doctor when pain worsens with activity.

Have fun: Sports should be about fun, not only about winning. Try to keep a healthy perspective.

Safety

257

GIANT FUNGUS

What is probably the largest living organism on Earth has been discovered in the Malheur National Forest in eastern Oregon. A fungus living three feet underground is estimated to cover 2,200 acres. After testing samples from various locations, scientists say it is all one organism.

Officially known as *Armillaria ostoyae*, or the honey mushroom, the fungus is 3.5 miles across and takes up 1,665 football fields. The small mushrooms visible above ground are only the tip of the iceberg. Experts estimate that the giant mushroom is at least 2,400 years old, but could be 7,200 years old.

Dino Dash

British scientists believe they have proof that a *T. rex* ancestor sprinted across Oxfordshire, England, more than 160 million years ago. The well-preserved footprints, which extend nearly 600 feet, probably belonged to a two-ton *Megalosaurus*. At first, the giant beast seemed to be waddling at about 4 miles an hour. But suddenly, the spacing between its footprints doubled as it broke into a run of 18 miles an hour. Why the change in speed? Perhaps the massive meat-eater laid eyes on a tasty herbivore!

Although scientists have evidence that smaller dinosaurs could run, many thought that large dinosaurs were too heavy and clumsy to move quickly. These tracks may be the best proof yet that the big guys could gather speed.

Discoveries

Mars Meteorites

NASA scientists have confirmed that five recently discovered meteorites fell from the red planet. Like most of the other 19 known Mars meteorites, these were found in Antarctica and in the deserts of Oman and the Sahara, areas with little plant cover that could hide space rocks. Scientists hope the meteorites will offer clues about whether primitive life once existed on Mars.

Each year about 20,000 meteorites reach Earth, but few are from Mars. The new meteorites probably broke off from Mars billions of years ago, after an asteroid collision, and floated through space until landing on Earth.

Alien Germs

Scientists have been startled to learn that some 250 species of bacteria and fungi can live—and thrive—in outer space. After a recent mission of the Russian space program, Mir, officials were disturbed to discover a host of bacteria and fungi covering the craft.

To prevent the risk of contaminating outer space with Earth germs, spacecraft are thoroughly sanitized. But bacteria may hide under plastic parts where disinfectants cannot reach. Once in flight, they emerge into a sterile atmosphere with few competitors to stop them. By contrast, Earth's environment is so full of microorganisms that they usually keep each other in check.

Piggy Spinach

What do you get when you cross a pig with some spinach? Healthier pork—or so hopes a group of Japanese scientists, who have implanted spinach genes into pigs. After three years of experiments, they now have two generations of pigs that sport the spinach gene. This is the first time that plant genes have functioned normally in living animals.

The spinach gene, known as FAD2, transforms about 20% of the pigs' saturated fats into unsaturated fats, making for less fatty meat. But don't expect to see lean green bacon at a store near you—only about 1% of the pigs in the experiment inherited the spinach gene.

259

The Branches of Science

THE PHYSICAL SCIENCES	THE EARTH SCIENCES	THE LIFE SCIENCES (Biology)
include PHYSICS, CHEMISTRY and ASTRONOMY	include GEOLOGY, OCEANOGRAPHY, PALEONTOLOGY and METEOROLOGY	include BOTANY, ZOOLOGY, GENETICS and MEDICINE

What Makes a GOOD Science Project?

Maybe you already know what you want to do, or maybe you're clueless. Whatever you decide, here are steps you should consider when doing your project.

BE FRESH

Judges and teachers always look for original ideas. Your project could be original in the scientific concept, or maybe you've come up with a new way to solve an old problem or a new and better way to interpret the data.

PASSING THE "HUH?" TEST

It may be a super idea for a project but it won't impress others if you don't have a well-defined goal or objective of what you're doing. Just what scientific concept are you trying to prove or disprove with your project?

UNDERSTAND IT—IT'S YOUR PROJECT, NOT YOUR FOLKS'

Your project must show that YOU understand and know how to use scientific theory, terms, techniques and methodologies properly. Chances are if it doesn't make sense to you, it won't make sense to others.

PROVE YOUR POINT

Judges and teachers look for complete projects. As a scientist, it is your responsibility to provide all evidence to support whatever claims you are making. Without data or results that support your claims, it's not a completed work.

PUT IN SOME TIME (and FUN)

How much time and energy have you put into your project? Was it a one-hour wonder or did you actually put in some effort and time? Either way, it will show. Pick a topic you like. Science is found everywhere. Think "outside the box" and have some fun!

CLEAR AS GLASS

Your ideas should be clearly presented and easy to understand. Remember, the more you understand about the scientific principles, the easier it is for you to explain them in terms everyone understands.

Source: U.S. Government, California Energy Commission

How Well Do You Know YOUR Project?

Science-fair judges will ask lots of questions about a project.
Dazzle them with your brilliance by being
prepared to answer questions like these:

How did you come up with the idea for this project?

What did you learn from your background search?

How did you build the apparatus? How does it work?

How much time (how many days) did it take to run the experiments (or collect data properly)?

How many times did you run the experiment with a different set of parameters?

Do you think there is an application in industry for this knowledge (technique)?

Did you try something else that didn't work?

Can you explain to me how your project relates to (some scientific principle)?

What is the next experiment to do if you want to continue this study?

Were there any books that helped you do your analysis?

The BIG Picture:
Earth's Time Line

Life on Earth began about 2 billion years ago, but there are no good fossils from before the Cambrian Period (see below). The largely unknown past before then is called the Pre-Cambrian. It is divided into the Lower (or older) and Upper (or younger) Pre-Cambrian—also called the Archeozoic and Proterozoic Eras.

The history of Earth since the Cambrian Period began is divided into three giant chunks of time, or eras, each of which includes a number of shorter periods.

PALEOZOIC ERA

This era began 550 million years ago and lasted for 305 million years. It is sometimes called Early Life.

Period	Millions of Years Ago	Creatures that Appeared
CAMBRIAN	550-510	INVERTEBRATE SEA LIFE
ORDOVICIAN	510-439	FIRST FISH
SILURIAN	439-409	GIGANTIC SEA SCORPIONS
DEVONIAN	409-363	MORE FISH AND SEA LIFE
CARBONIFEROUS	363-290	EARLY INSECTS AND AMPHIBIANS
PERMIAN	290-245	EARLIEST TURTLES

MESOZOIC ERA

This era began 245 million years ago and lasted for 180 million years. It is sometimes called Middle Life or The Age of Reptiles.

Period	Millions of Years Ago	Creatures that Appeared
TRIASSIC	245-208	EARLY REPTILES AND MAMMALS
JURASSIC	208-146	EARLY DINOSAURS; FIRST BIRDS
CRETACEOUS	146-65	MORE DINOSAURS, BIRDS; FIRST MARSUPIALS

CENOZOIC ERA

This era began 64 million years ago and includes the geological present. It is sometimes called Recent Life or The Age of Mammals.

Period	Millions of Years Ago	Creatures that Appeared
TERTIARY	64-2	LARGER MAMMALS; MANY INSECTS; BATS
PLEISTOCENE (Ice Age)	2-0.01	EARLY HUMANS
HOLOCENE	0.01-now	THE LAST 3,000 YEARS ARE CALLED "HISTORY"

The LITTLE Picture: The Elements

Elements are the building blocks of nature. Water, for example, is built from two basic ingredients: hydrogen elements and oxygen elements. Each element is a pure substance—it cannot be split up into any simpler pure substances.

The smallest part of an element is an **atom**. An atom, however, is made up of even smaller particles. These are known as subatomic particles. The most important are:

- **protons, which have positive electrical charges**
- **electrons, which have negative electrical charges**
- **neutrons, which are electrically neutral**

The atomic number of an element is the number of protons in one atom of the element. Each element has a different atomic number. For example, the atomic number of hydrogen is 1, and the atomic number of oxygen is 8.

1
H
Hydrogen

2
He
Helium

7
N
Nitrogen

8
O
Oxygen

10
Ne
Neon

26
Fe
Iron

27
Co
Cobalt

28
Ni
Nickel

TYPES OF ELEMENTS

As of 2002, scientists have discovered at least 112 different elements.

- Elements with atomic numbers 1 (hydrogen) to 92 (uranium) are found naturally on Earth.

- Those with atomic numbers 93 (neptunium) or greater are artificial elements. They have to be synthesized, or created by combining two or more elements with lower atomic numbers.

- Elements with atomic numbers 101 and up are known as the transfermium elements. They are also known as heavy elements because their atoms have very large masses compared with atoms of hydrogen, the lightest of all elements.

HOW THE ELEMENTS ARE NAMED

Names for new elements are approved by the International Union of Pure and Applied Chemistry (IUPAC) in Geneva, Switzerland. They are often named for scientists, places or Greek or Latin words. For example, krypton (atomic number 36) is from the Greek word *kryptos*, meaning hidden, because it is colorless and odorless.

For information on all the elements
go www.FACT MONSTER.COM

Photosynthesis

Photosynthesis is a process in which green plants (and some bacteria) use **energy** from the sun, **carbon dioxide** from the air and **water** from the ground to make **oxygen** and **glucose**. Glucose is a sugar that plants use for energy.

Chlorophyll is what makes the process of photosynthesis work. Chlorophyll, a green pigment, traps the energy from the sun and helps change it into glucose.

Photosynthesis is one example of how people and plants depend on each other. It provides us with most of the oxygen we need in order to breathe. We, in turn, exhale the carbon dioxide needed by plants.

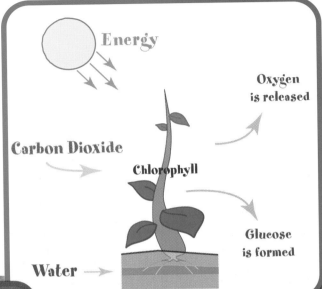

Energy

Oxygen
is released

Carbon Dioxide

Chlorophyll

Glucose
is formed

Water

Sean M. Dessureau

Did You Know?

Without photosynthesis, there would be no oxygen in our atmosphere. Almost all life on Earth would come to an end.

What Is a Plant?

A plant
- has chlorophyll
- is fixed in one place (doesn't move)
- has cell walls made sturdy by a material called cellulose

A plant can be as simple as algae or as complex as a tree. There are nearly 300,000 plant species in the world today.

How Long Some Plants Live

Some of the oldest known living things are trees. Plants that live for a long time have adaptations that help protect them from dangers in the environment. The thick, spongy bark of the giant sequoia protects it from being damaged by insects. Here are the oldest known plants:
- Bristlecone pine (5,000 years old)
- Giant sequoia (2,500 years old)
- Saguaro cactus (200 years)

ROCKS

Rocks are classified in **three** types based on how they are formed.

Igneous rocks are formed when molten rock (magma) from within Earth cools and solidifies. There are two types: intrusive igneous rocks solidify beneath Earth's surface; extrusive igneous rocks solidify at the surface.
Examples: Granite, basalt, obsidian

Sedimentary rocks are formed when sediment (bits of rock plus material such as shells and sand) gets packed together. They can take millions of years to form. Most rocks that you see on the ground are sedimentary.
Examples: Limestone, sandstone, shale

Metamorphic rocks are sedimentary or igneous rocks that have been transformed by heat, pressure or both. Metamorphic rocks are usually formed deep within Earth, during a process such as mountain building.
Examples: Schist, marble, **slate**

Some types of SCIENTISTS

An **agronomist** specializes in soil and crops.
An **astronomer** studies stars, planets and galaxies.
A **botanist** specializes in plants.
A **cytologist** specializes in the study of cells.
An **epidemiologist** studies the spread of diseases.
A **geologist** specializes in the history of Earth.
A **geographer** studies Earth's surface.
A **marine biologist** studies ocean plants and animals.
A **meteorologist** studies weather and climate.
A **microbiologist** studies microscopic plants and animals.
A **paleontologist** specializes in fossils.
A **seismologist** studies earthquakes.

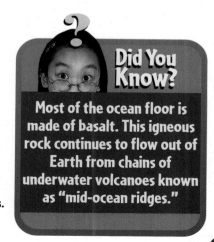

Did You Know?

Most of the ocean floor is made of basalt. This igneous rock continues to flow out of Earth from chains of underwater volcanoes known as "mid-ocean ridges."

Make Your Own LAVA Lamp!

Did you ever hear that "oil and water don't mix"? Here's groovy proof.

YOU WILL NEED:

vegetable oil
water
food coloring
glitter and sequins
a small, clean glass jar with a tight lid

1. Fill the jar about one-third full of oil. Next, sprinkle in the glitter and sequins.

2. Pour in water to the top of the jar. Add a few drops of food coloring. Screw the cap on the jar as tightly as you can.

3. Slowly turn the jar upside down, then up again. It's instant art!

MOLECULAR MAGIC

As you can see, oil and water don't mix. But why?

You may have heard water referred to as "H$_2$O." H$_2$O is the formula of the water molecule, the smallest building block of water. Molecules are made of even smaller building blocks called atoms. Every atom has an electrical charge. The charge can be positive, negative or neutral.

This charge is the secret to how water behaves with oil. In a water molecule, one part of the molecule has a mostly positive charge, and another part has a mostly negative charge. Molecules like this are called **polar molecules**. Have you heard that opposites attract? It's true of polar molecules. Because a positive charge is attracted to a negative charge, the positive end of one polar molecule will stick to the negative end of another polar molecule. As a result, polar molecules are good at sticking together.

In an oil molecule, however, positive and negative charges are spread out pretty evenly. Molecules like this are called **nonpolar molecules**. Trying to mix nonpolar molecules (like oil) with polar molecules (like water) leads nowhere. The polar molecules stick together so well that the nonpolar molecules get left out.

But why does the oil end up on top? Oil is lighter than water. A drop of water actually weighs more than a drop of oil that is exactly the same size. As a result, oil will float on top of water.

What makes POPCORN Pop?

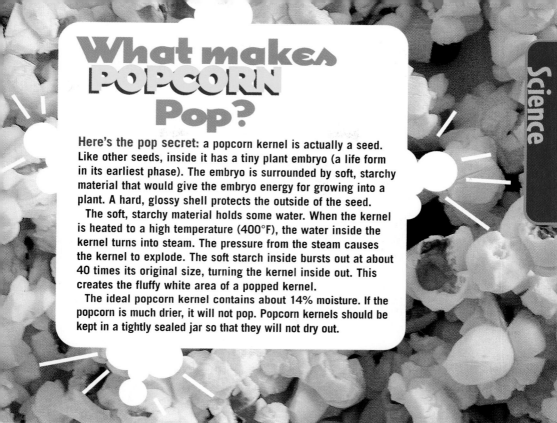

Here's the pop secret: a popcorn kernel is actually a seed. Like other seeds, inside it has a tiny plant embryo (a life form in its earliest phase). The embryo is surrounded by soft, starchy material that would give the embryo energy for growing into a plant. A hard, glossy shell protects the outside of the seed.

The soft, starchy material holds some water. When the kernel is heated to a high temperature (400°F), the water inside the kernel turns into steam. The pressure from the steam causes the kernel to explode. The soft starch inside bursts out at about 40 times its original size, turning the kernel inside out. This creates the fluffy white area of a popped kernel.

The ideal popcorn kernel contains about 14% moisture. If the popcorn is much drier, it will not pop. Popcorn kernels should be kept in a tightly sealed jar so that they will not dry out.

go Science Web Sites

National Science Foundation: *www.nsf.gov*

American Association for the Advancement of Science: *www.aaas.org*

Federation of American Scientists: *www.fas.org*

The Franklin Institute Science Museum: *sln.fi.edu*

Science News Online: *www.sciencenews.org*

Popular Science: *www.popsci.com*

Periodic Table of Elements: *www.webelements.com*

Discovery Channel Online: *www.discovery.com*

American Museum of Natural History (New York City): *www.amnh.org*

The Field Museum of Natural History (Chicago, Illinois): *www.fmnh.org*

Santa Barbara Museum of Natural History: *www.sbnature.org*

The Smithsonian Web: *www.si.edu*

TFK Mystery Person

This scientist helped inspire the modern environmental movement. In 1962, her popular book *Silent Spring* raised public awareness of the dangers of pollution and the harmful effects of chemical pesticides on the world's lakes, oceans—and humans.

Who is she?

MISSION TO MARS

BY KATHRYN HOFFMAN

THE ODYSSEY SEARCHES THE RED PLANET FOR SIGNS OF LIFE

SOLAR ARRAY
collects energy from the sun

ANTENNA
keeps contact with Earth

STAR CAMERAS
help orient the Odyssey

UHF ANTENNA
communicates with other crafts

MARTIAN RADIATION ENVIRONMENT EXPERIMENT
tests levels of radiation

IMAGING SYSTEM
locates minerals on Mars' surface

Scientists at NASA's Jet Propulsion Laboratory in Pasadena, California, had been working for more than two years to bring its Odyssey spacecraft to Mars. They had fine-tuned their instruments and triple-checked their calculations. Finally, in late 2001, they got the signal they were waiting for: Odyssey had arrived! The control room erupted into cheers. "We're back at Mars," shouted chief scientist Daniel McCleese.

But getting there was only the beginning of the mission. Once Odyssey's speed was slowed to its desired orbit—circling Mars every two hours—it began performing a series of tests designed to detect possible signs of life. The most important clue Odyssey is seeking: water.

One of the craft's super-sensitive instruments is studying the planet's surface for rocks and soils left behind by past water sources. Another searches the planet's soil for signs of water or ice below the surface. The spacecraft's camera system looks for "hot spots" on the dark side of Mars. Scientists think these spots may be a sign that water or some other liquid is bursting to the surface today.

Odyssey will also pave the way for a pair of compact rovers scheduled for touchdown on Mars by 2004. The spacecraft will then serve as a communications satellite, beaming data back to Earth.

go Learn about earlier Mars missions at *www.timeforkids.com/mars*

Our Solar System

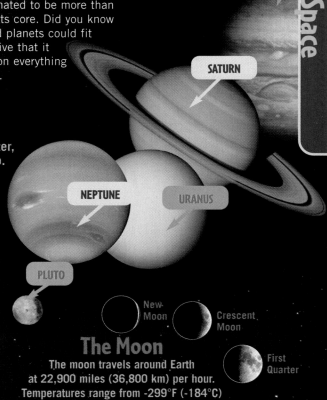

MERCURY → VENUS
EARTH
MARS
JUPITER
SATURN
NEPTUNE URANUS
PLUTO

The Sun

The solar system is made up of the the **sun** (*solar* means sun) at its center, the nine planets that orbit it and the various moons, asteroids, comets and meteorites controlled by the sun's gravitational pull.

Our closest star, the **sun**, is thought to be about 4.6 billion years old. This fiery ball is 870,000 miles (1,392,000 km) across and is estimated to be more than 27,000,000°F (15,000,000°C) at its core. Did you know that more than a million Earth-sized planets could fit inside the Sun? The **sun** is so massive that it exerts a powerful gravitational pull on everything in our solar system, including Earth.

The Planets

Our solar system has nine planets: **Mercury, Venus, Earth, Mars, Jupiter, Saturn, Uranus, Neptune** and **Pluto.** An easy way to remember their names in the correct order is to keep in mind the following sentence: My Very Educated Mother Just Served Us Nine Pizzas.

The Universe

Astronomers think that the universe could contain 40 to 50 billion galaxies—huge systems with billions of stars. Our own galaxy is the **Milky Way**. It contains about 200 billion stars.

The Moon

The moon travels around Earth at 22,900 miles (36,800 km) per hour. Temperatures range from -299°F (-184°C) during its night to 417°F (214°C) during its day, except at the poles, where the temperature is a constant -141°F (-96°C). The gravitational pull of the moon on Earth affects the ocean tides on Earth. The closer the moon is to Earth, the greater the effect. The time between high tides is about 12 hours and 25 minutes.

New Moon
Crescent Moon
First Quarter
Full Moon
Last Quarter
New Moon
Crescent Moon

Source: NASA

The Planets

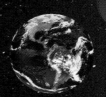

MERCURY

Named for a Roman god, a winged messenger, this planet zooms around the sun at 30 miles per second!

Size
Two-fifths the size of Earth

Diameter
3,032.4 miles (4,880 km)

Surface
Covered by a dusty layer of minerals, the surface is made up of plains, cliffs and craters

Atmosphere
A thin mixture of helium (95%) and hydrogen

Temperature
The sunlit side can reach 950°F (510°C). The dark side can drop to -346°F (-210°C)

Mean Distance from the Sun
36 million miles (57.9 million km)

Moons: 0 Rings: 0

VENUS

Named after the Roman goddess of love and beauty. Venus is also known as the "morning star" and "evening star" since it is visible at these times.

Size
About 650 miles smaller in diameter than Earth

Diameter
7,519 miles (12,100 km)

Surface
A rocky, dusty expanse of mountains, canyons, and plains, with a 200-mile river of hardened lava

Atmosphere
Carbon dioxide (95%), nitrogen, sulfuric acid, and traces of other elements

Temperature
Ranges from 55° F (13° C) to 396° F (202° C) at the surface

Mean Distance from the Sun
67.24 million miles (108.2 million km)

Moons: 0 Rings: 0

EARTH

Our planet is not perfectly round. It bulges at the equator and is flatter at the poles.

Size
Four planets in our solar system are larger and four are smaller than Earth

Diameter
7,926.2 miles (12,756 km)

Surface
Earth is made up of water (70%), air and solid ground

Atmosphere
Nitrogen (78%), oxygen (21%), other gases

Temperature
Averages 59°F (15°C) at sea level

Mean Distance from the Sun
92.9 million miles (149.6 million km)

Moons: 1 (the moon) Rings: 0

THE GREAT  SPOT

JUPITER'S "GREAT RED SPOT" IS A RAGING STORM OF GASES, MAINLY RED PHOSPHORUS. THE STORM IS LARGER IN SIZE THAN EARTH AND HAS CONTINUED FOR CENTURIES WITH NO SIGN OF DYING DOWN.

MARS

Because of its blood-red color (which comes from iron-rich dust), this planet was named for the Roman god of war.

Size

About one-quarter the size of Earth

Diameter

4,194 miles (6,794 km)

Surface

Canyons, dunes, volcanoes and polar caps of water ice and carbon dioxide ice

Atmosphere

Carbon dioxide (95%)

Temperature

As low as -305°F (-187°C)

Mean Distance from the Sun

141.71 million miles (227.9 million km)

Moons: 2
Rings: 0

JUPITER

The largest planet in our solar system was named for the most important Roman god.

Size

11 times the diameter of Earth

Diameter

88,736 miles (142,800 km)

Surface

A hot ball of gas and liquid

Atmosphere

Whirling clouds of colored dust, hydrogen, helium, methane, water and ammonia

Temperature

-234°F (-148°C) average

Mean Distance from the Sun

483.88 million miles (778.3 million km)

Moons: 16
Rings: 1

SATURN

Named for the Roman god of farming, the second-largest planet has many majestic rings surrounding it.

Size

About 10 times larger than Earth

Diameter

74,978 miles (120,660 km)

Surface

Liquid and gas

Atmosphere

Hydrogen and helium

Temperature

-288°F (-178°C) average

Mean Distance from the Sun

887.14 million miles (1,427 million km)

Moons: 19
Rings: 1,000?

Turn the page for more planets ➞

The Planets Continued

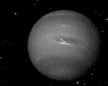

URANUS

This greenish-blue planet is named for an ancient Greek sky god.

Size

About 4 times larger than Earth

Diameter

Diameter: 32,193 miles (51,810 km)

Surface

Little is known

Atmosphere

Hydrogen, helium and methane

Temperature

Uniform temperature of -353°F (-214°C)

Mean Distance from the Sun

1,783.98 million miles (2,870 million km)

**Moons: 21
Rings: 11**

NEPTUNE

This stormy blue planet is named for an ancient Roman sea god.

Size

About 4 times the size of Earth

Diameter

30,775 miles (49,528 km)

Surface

A liquid layer covered with thick clouds and raging storms

Atmosphere

Hydrogen, helium, methane and ammonia

Temperature

Temperature: -353°F (-214°C)

Mean Distance from the Sun

2,796.46 million miles (4,497 million km)

**Moons: 8
Rings: 4**

PLUTO

Named for the Roman god of the underworld, Pluto is the coldest and smallest planet. Some astronomers now think it is actually a large comet orbiting the sun.

Size

Less than one-fifth the size of Earth

Diameter

1,423 miles? (2,290 km?)

Surface

A giant snowball of methane and water mixed with rock

Atmosphere

Methane

Temperature

Between -369° and -387°F (-223° and -233°C)

Mean Distance from the Sun

3,666 million miles (5,900 million km)

**Moons: 1
Rings: ?**

Your WEIGHT and AGE on Other Planets

On Earth I weigh 72 pounds. How much would I weigh on Mars?

To figure out what you would weigh on another planet, multiply your weight on Earth by the gravitational pull listed in the table.

Example: I weigh 90 pounds on Earth. On Mercury, I would weigh:

90 pounds X 0.38 = 34 pounds

To find your age according to another planet's year, divide your age on Earth by the period of revolution (in Earth years around the sun) of the planet listed in the table.

Example: I am 13 Earth years old. In Mercury's orbit, I would be:

13 years ÷ 0.241 = 54 years old

Celestial Object	Gravitational Pull Compared to Earth	Period of Revolution Compared to Earth
MERCURY	0.38	0.241 EARTH YEARS
VENUS	0.91	0.615 EARTH YEARS
EARTH	1.0	1 EARTH YEAR
MARS	0.38	1.88 EARTH YEARS
JUPITER	2.54	11.9 EARTH YEARS
SATURN	0.93	29.5 EARTH YEARS
URANUS	0.8	84 EARTH YEARS
NEPTUNE	1.2	164.8 EARTH YEARS
PLUTO	???	248.5 EARTH YEARS

Source: NASA

The Constellations

or more than 5,000 years, people have looked into the night sky and seen the same stars we see today. They noticed groups of stars and connected them with imaginary lines. These groups are known as "**constellations**." They help astronomers quickly locate other objects in the sky. There are 88 recognized constellations. Here are some of our favorites:

ORION
(The Great Hunter)

CANIS MAJOR
(The Greater Dog)

CENTAURUS
(The Centaur)

ANDROMEDA
(Princess of Ethiopia)

URSA MAJOR
(The Large Bear, including The Big Dipper)

URSA MINOR
(The Small Bear or The Little Dipper)

PEGASUS
(The Winged
Horse)

PERSEUS
(The Hero)

CANCER
(The Crab)

Space

TFK Puzzles & Games

Celebrate the discovery of Neptune 155 years ago! In the puzzle, circle the names of our solar system's nine planets. They run backward, forward and diagonally. The leftover letters spell the answer to the riddle.

NAME THAT NEPTUNE

MERCURY

VENUS

EARTH

MARS

JUPITER

SATURN

URANUS

NEPTUNE

PLUTO

N	S	U	N	A	R	U	M
E	R	S	R	A	M	E	A
P	R	E	O	O	R	U	H
T	N	D	T	C	L	V	T
U	A	U	U	I	N	E	R
N	C	R	L	H	P	N	A
E	Y	T	P	I	M	U	E
E	N	R	U	T	A	S	J

275

The Dawning of the Space Age

O n October 4, 1957, the Soviet Union put the first artificial satellite, **Sputnik I,** into Earth orbit and ushered in the modern space age. **Sputnik** (which means "traveling companion") was round in shape, 23 inches in diameter and weighed 183.4 pounds. It circled the globe every 96 minutes at a speed of 18,000 miles per hour. After 92 days, on January 4, 1958, it re-entered the atmosphere and burned up.

A month later, on November 3, 1957, the Soviet Union launched **Sputnik II,** the first satellite put into orbit with an animal on board, an 11-pound mongrel dog named **Laika** ("barker"). She died a week later after the oxygen supply ran out. The satellite carried more sophisticated instrumentation, weighed 1,120 pounds and circled Earth every 103.7 minutes. The satellite burned up after being in orbit for 162 days.

TFK TOP 5

Stars Closest to the Earth

Do you think we'll ever actually get to the stars? If we do, it's going to take a long time. In fact, it is estimated that it would take more than 70,000 years for a ship to make it to the closest star. That's a lot of in-flight movies! Here are the stars closest to us.

1. The sun
   (92.9 million miles away)

2. Proxima Centauri
   (4.2 light years)

3. Alpha Centauri A
   (4.3 light years)

4. Alpha Centauri B
   (4.3 light years)

5. Barnard's Star (5.96 light years)

Space Exploration
TIME LINE

1957 The Soviet Union launches Sputnik, the first satellite.

1961 Soviet Yuri Gagarin is the first space traveler.

1962 John Glenn is the first American to orbit Earth.

1969 Apollo 11 astronaut Neil Armstrong becomes the first human to walk on the moon.

1976 Viking I is the first spacecraft to land on Mars.

1981 U.S. space shuttle Columbia, the world's first reusable spacecraft, is launched.

1990 The Hubble Space Telescope is put into orbit.

1995 Cosmonaut Valery Polyakov completes a record 439 days in space onboard Russian space station Mir.

2006 The International Space Station is scheduled to be completed.

For more on space, go www.FACT MONSTER.com

Famous
Star Gazers

PTOLEMY
(A.D. 120-189)
The ancient Greek astronomer Ptolemy theorized that Earth was the center of the universe, and the sun, moon, planets and stars revolved around it.

ERATOSTHENES
(276-195 B.C.)
This Greek astronomer was the first to accurately measure the size of Earth.

NICOLAUS COPERNICUS
(1473-1543)
Polish astronomer Copernicus was the first to theorize that the sun, not Earth, was the center of our universe—a controversial idea that was strongly denounced.

JOHANNES KEPLER
(1571-1630)
The German astronomer Kepler discovered that the orbits of the planets are elliptical (oval) rather than round.

GALILEO GALILEI
(1564-1642)
The Italian astronomer Galileo is considered the first to use the telescope. With it he discovered craters on our moon and proved that the planets circle the sun.

EDWIN HUBBLE
(1889-1953)
This American astronomer classified the different types of galaxies in the universe and developed the theory that the universe is expanding. This theory is called Hubble's Law.

SIR ISAAC NEWTON
(1643-1727)
The British astronomer Newton discovered the principle of gravity. He used the theory of gravity to explain how the moon is held in its orbit around Earth.

EDMOND HALLEY
(1656-1742)
This British astronomer was the first to calculate the orbit of a comet. The comet named for him, Halley's comet, passes close enough to Earth to be seen about every 76 years.

TFK Mystery Person

This former Navy pilot went on to fly an aircraft that goes much farther than any airplane has ever gone. In 1969, he and two other astronauts took off on Apollo 11. He is best known for becoming the first person to walk on the moon.

Who is he?

Field of His Dreams

Work is a ball for umpire Larry Young

Fans boo him. Players call him names. Managers question his calls. But Major League Baseball umpire Larry Young is always ready to go to work. Young loves his job—even if it means getting yelled at! Young is one of only 68 umpires working in the major leagues. During his 17 years in the majors, he has umpired many big games, including an All-Star Game and a World Series.

Young's journey to the big leagues began when he was 13. That's when the baseball fan first began umpiring games in his hometown of Oregon, Illinois. In 1978, Young graduated from the Bill Kinnamon Umpire School in Florida and scored with a job in the Midwest League. He toiled for six years in the minors before getting called up to the majors.

Young attributes his success to the lessons he learned at home: "My parents instilled in me the [belief] that you work hard." The challenges of his job include lots of travel, spending long hours standing in the hot sun and, of course, patiently dealing with criticism.

Still, Young says the payoff has been huge: "The best part is fulfilling a childhood dream, and being able to provide for my family while doing something I enjoy."

"You're out!" Young calls a Giants-Athletics game.

Every year hundreds attend umpire schools, but most graduates never even land a job in the minor leagues. Young has been in the majors for 17 years.

By Laura G. Girardi

Baseball

It is believed that baseball is based on an old English game called rounders. The first baseball games in the U.S. occurred in the 1840s.

Major League Stadium Fun Facts

Bank One Ballpark in Phoenix features a swimming pool for fans in the outfield stands.

The oldest Major League Baseball stadium is Fenway Park in Boston. It opened on April 20, 1912.

Qualcomm Stadium in San Diego holds the most people: 66,307.

Comerica Park in Detroit features a merry-go-round and Ferris wheel under the stands.

The Negro Leagues

From the 1920s through the 1940s, black professional ballplayers played for the segregated teams of the legendary Negro Leagues. The leagues included such Hall of Famers as Josh Gibson, Cool Papa Bell and Satchel Paige. The color barrier was finally broken when African-American baseball player **Jackie Robinson** joined the Brooklyn Dodgers in 1947.

The Little League World Series

The Little League World Series, which is the sport's annual world championship tournament, has been played in Williamsport, Pennsylvania, every year since 1947. Taiwan has won 16 times, more than any other foreign country.

Teams representing towns in the U.S. have won 26 times. Which U.S. state can brag of having the most winners? California tops the list with five championship wins; Connecticut, New Jersey and Pennsylvania each have four wins and New York and Texas have two each.

Did You Know?

San Francisco Giants outfielder Barry Bonds broke Mark McGwire's record for home runs hit in a season by smacking 73 round-trippers in 2001.

Taking Stock of Barry Bonds' 73 Home Runs

- 1 was hit outside of the United States (Montreal, Canada)
- 2 were hit with the bases loaded (otherwise known as grand slams)
- 11 were hit off San Diego Padres pitchers (more than any other team)
- 17 were hit off left-handed pitchers
- 37 were hit at his home stadium (PacBell Park)
- 43 were hit in the state of California (more than any other state)
- 480 feet is how far his longest home run traveled

Top Players of 2001

Most Valuable Player
A.L.—Ichiro Suzuki, **OF, Seattle Mariners**
N.L.—Barry Bonds, **OF, San Francisco Giants**

Cy Young Award (Best Pitcher)
A.L.—Roger Clemens, **New York Yankees**
N.L.—Randy Johnson, **Arizona Diamondbacks**

Rookie of the Year
A.L.—Ichiro Suzuki, **OF, Seattle Mariners**
N.L.—Albert Pujols, **3B-OF, St. Louis Cardinals**

279

Basketball

Trivia Time:

Who is the tallest player ever to play in the NBA?

Actually there's a tie. Gheorghe Muresan and Manute Bol are both 7 feet, 7 inches tall. Muresan, who starred in the aptly titled movie My Giant in 1998, is from Romania and last played in 2000. Bol was drafted by the Washington Bullets in 1985 and led the league in blocked shots in 1986 and again in 1989. Bol is a Dinka tribesman who was born in Sudan and comes from a family of very tall people. His sister is 6 feet, 10 inches.

At the other end of the spectrum stands a former teammate of Bol's, Tyrone "Muggsy" Bogues. Bogues, at 5 feet, 3 inches, is the shortest player in NBA history and ironically has had more success than either Muresan or Bol. His incredible quickness is his greatest asset. His success proves that basketball is not just a sport for tall people.

Muresan towers over actor Billy Crystal.

NBA TOP FIVE CAREER NBA SCORERS	
	POINTS PER GAME
MICHAEL JORDAN	31.5
WILT CHAMBERLAIN	30.1
SHAQUILLE O'NEAL	27.7
ELGIN BAYLOR	27.4
JERRY WEST	27.0

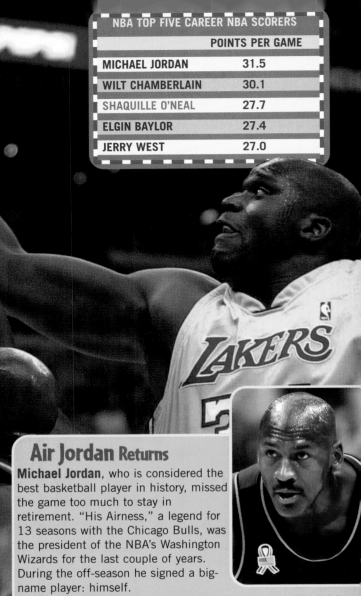

Air Jordan Returns

Michael Jordan, who is considered the best basketball player in history, missed the game too much to stay in retirement. "His Airness," a legend for 13 seasons with the Chicago Bulls, was the president of the NBA's Washington Wizards for the last couple of years. During the off-season he signed a big-name player: himself.

Jordan retired on top of the world following the 1997-98 season in which the Bulls won their sixth championship. The big question upon his surprising return to the league was whether he would be able to keep up with the new generation of basketball superstars like Kobe Bryant and Allen Iverson. He answered the question pretty decisively when he scored 51 points early in the season.

In 2001, Jordan made another bold move. He made 19-year-old Kwame Brown the first pick in the NBA Draft. Brown, from Brunswick, Georgia, became the first high school kid ever drafted first overall. The 6-foot, 11-inch Brown follows other high schoolers who have had success in the league, such as Kobe Bryant, Kevin Garnett and Moses Malone.

Football

Originally a game played by colleges, professional football gained popularity in America in the 1920s. The National Football League (NFL) was established in 1922 and merged with the American Football League in 1970 to form a 26-team league. With the addition of the Houston Texans in 2002, the NFL now consists of 32 teams.

2001 Top Players

Passing Leader
Kurt Warner, St. Louis Rams (4,830 yards)
Rushing Leader
Priest Holmes, Kansas City Chiefs (1,555 yards)
Receiving Leader
David Boston, Arizona Cardinals (1,598 yards)
Touchdowns
Marshall Faulk, St. Louis Rams (21)
Interceptions
Anthony Henry, Cleveland Browns (10)
Ronde Barber, Tampa Bay Buccaneers (10)
Sacks
Michael Strahan, New York Giants (22.5, NFL record)

FUTURE SUPER BOWL SITES			
2003 SUPER BOWL XXXVII	(37)	San Diego, California
2004 SUPER BOWL XXXVIII	(38)	Houston, Texas
2005 SUPER BOWL XXXIX	(39)	Jacksonville, Florida
2006 SUPER BOWL XL	(40)	Detroit, Michigan

Patriots Shock The World

The New England Patriots were huge underdogs against the mighty St. Louis Rams in Super Bowl XXXVI. The Rams were led by superstars Kurt Warner and Marshall Faulk. The Patriots, under head coach **Bill Belichick**, had no recognizable superstars. With just seven seconds remaining, kicker Adam Vinatieri booted a 48-yard field goal to give the Patriots a 20–17 win in one of the most thrilling Super Bowls ever. They truly showed that if you work well as a team, you can overcome any odds.

Boy Wonder

When Patriots' star quarterback Drew Bledsoe was injured in the second week of the season, little-known **Tom Brady** came in as his replacement. The previous year (2000), he had been the team's fourth-string quarterback. Brady miraculously piloted the Patriots to their first Super Bowl win in team history. With the score in Super Bowl XXXVI tied 17-17, he calmly steered his team downfield to set up the game-winning field goal. Brady was voted the game's MVP and at just 24 years old became the youngest quarterback to lead his team to a Super Bowl victory.

Sports

281

College Basketball

Here are the NCAA Division I men's basketball teams with the best records for each decade.

Decade	Team	W-L	Pct.
1950s	Kentucky	224-33	.872
1960s	UCLA	234-52	.818
1970s	UCLA	273-27	.910
1980s	North Carolina	281-63	.817
1990s	Kansas	286-60	.827
2000s	Duke	95-13	.880

More Than Just Lions, Tigers and Bears

A lot of college sports teams have nicknames like Tigers, Wildcats and Huskies. But have you ever wondered how some of your favorite college teams got their unusual nicknames? Here are a few explanations:

Blue Devils—Duke University

Determined by a contest run by the student paper in 1921, the nickname is borrowed from a group of legendary French World War I mountain soldiers, "les Diables Bleus."

Jayhawks—University of Kansas

Believed to be a combination of two familiar birds—the hawk and the blue jay—the Jayhawk has been associated with the school since 1866. It was once a nickname used by lawless pioneers, but it took on new meaning during the Civil War, when Kansas's first cavalry was founded as the "Independent Mounted Kansas Jayhawkers."

Trojans—University of Southern California

In need of a new nickname, the school's athletic director looked to Los Angeles Times sports editor Owen Bird. Bird wanted a nickname that embodied the school's fighting spirit against usually bigger and better-equipped teams. He called them

the Trojans for the first time in 1912. It's a reference to the legendary people of Troy, who were famous for taking on the mighty Greek empire.

Buckeyes—Ohio State University

A tree native to Ohio, the buckeye produces small, shiny, dark-brown nuts with a lighter tan patch that resembles the eye of a deer. Legend has it that carrying one in your pocket brings good luck. The nickname has been used since 1950.

Hokies—Virginia Tech

When the school changed its name to the Virginia Polytechnic Institute in 1896, the student body held a competition to write a new school cheer. Senior O.M. Stull's "Hokie Yell" won the contest, and it has been used ever since. Stull said the word had no special meaning when he wrote it. He just wanted something that got peoples' attention.

March Madness

Fans describe the end of college basketball season as "March Madness." That's because the men's and women's championship tournaments are held in March and feature the best teams in the country. Many of the games have dramatic finishes. The biggest tournament is the NCAA tournament, which began in 1939. UCLA has won the most men's titles (11) and Tennessee has won the most women's titles (6). In 2002, Maryland won the men's national championship, and the University of Connecticut won the women's.

College Football

A Perfect Storm

The **University of Miami Hurricanes** ended their 12-0 season by beating the University of Nebraska Cornhuskers, 37-14, in the Rose Bowl on January 3, 2002. The Hurricanes were named Division I-A national champion by the media and by opposing football coaches.

Other 2002 Bowl Game Results

Orange Bowl (Miami, Florida)
Florida 56, Maryland 23
Sugar Bowl (New Orleans, Louisiana)
LSU 47, Illinois 34
Fiesta Bowl (Tempe, Arizona)
Oregon 38, Colorado 16

Trophy Case

The Heisman Trophy is an annual award given since 1935 to the most outstanding college football player in the country. Several Heisman winners have gone on to success in the NFL and have been elected to the Pro Football Hall of Fame after retiring. Current NFL stars **Eddie George** (1995), **Charles Woodson** (1997) and **Ricky Williams** (1998) are recent winners. In 2001, University of Nebraska quarterback **Eric Crouch** won the award.

You'll Get a Kick Out of This

When Jacksonville State's placekicker ran onto the field to attempt an extra point on August 30, 2001, fans noticed something unusual about the kicker's helmet—a brown ponytail hanging out the back. Sophomore Ashley Martin kicked three extra points that day, becoming the first woman to play and score during an NCAA Division I football game. Martin, who is also a member of the school's women's soccer team, has been a two-sport star since high school. When she was named homecoming queen in her senior year, Martin accepted her crown in her football uniform!

Sports

COLLEGE CODE FOR FOOTBALL NUMBERS	
1-49	Quarterbacks, running backs, defensive backs, some wide receivers and linebackers
50-59	Offensive and defensive linemen and linebackers
60-69	Offensive and defensive linemen
70-79	Offensive and defensive linemen
80-89	Wide receivers and tight ends
90-99	Defensive ends, tackles and linemen

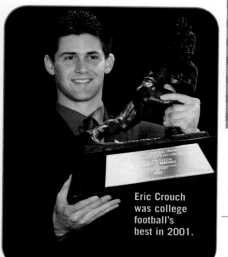

Eric Crouch was college football's best in 2001.

Hockey

Who Was That Masked Man?

The first goaltender to regularly wear a face mask was Montreal's Jacques Plante. A shot broke his nose in 1959 and he wore a mask after that. He was ridiculed at first, but now every goaltender wears a mask. Thanks to Plante, many broken bones and stitches have been avoided.

Boom Boom

One of the most feared (and certainly the most powerful) shots used by hockey players is the slap shot. Some players can unleash accurate blasts of more than 100 miles an hour. The slap shot was invented and popularized by hall of famer **Bernie "Boom Boom" Geoffrion** in the 1950s. With his booming shot, Geoffrion (along with teammate Maurice "Rocket" Richard) led the Montreal Canadiens to six Stanley Cup titles.

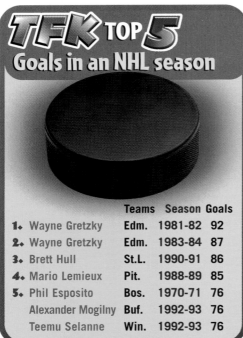

TFK TOP 5
Goals in an NHL season

		Teams	Season	Goals
1.	Wayne Gretzky	Edm.	1981-82	92
2.	Wayne Gretzky	Edm.	1983-84	87
3.	Brett Hull	St.L.	1990-91	86
4.	Mario Lemieux	Pit.	1988-89	85
5.	Phil Esposito	Bos.	1970-71	76
	Alexander Mogilny	Buf.	1992-93	76
	Teemu Selanne	Win.	1992-93	76

Original Six

Between 1942 and 1967, the NHL consisted of just six teams—Boston Bruins, Chicago Blackhawks, Detroit Red Wings, Montreal Canadiens, New York Rangers and Toronto Maple Leafs. As you might expect, the teams got to know each other pretty well. They had to play each other 14 times during the regular season. Today there are 30 teams in the NHL.

The Stanley Cup

Each player that wins the NHL championship gets his name engraved on the **Stanley Cup** along with all the previous winners. The original cup was only seven inches high; now it stands about three feet tall. The Montreal Canadiens have won the most titles with 23.

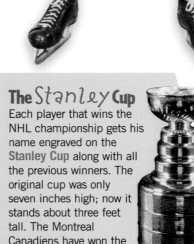

Golf

Tiger Woods Time Line

1975 Born Eldrick T. Woods on December 30 and given the nickname "Tiger" after his father Earl's friend, a Vietnamese soldier with the same nickname

1984 Age 8 Wins the Optimist International Junior Championship

1994 Age 18 Wins the U.S. Amateur Championship, becoming the youngest winner ever; enrolls at Stanford University and wins his first collegiate event

1997 Age 21 Wins his first major championship, the Masters, by an amazing 12 strokes. He is the youngest Masters winner ever and the first of African or Asian descent

2001 Age 25 Becomes the first golfer to be reigning champion of all four majors at once

Tee Time

The four major events in men's professional golf (the Grand Slam) are
- Masters
- British Open
- U.S. Open
- PGA Championship

The four major events in women's professional golf (the Women's Grand Slam) are
- LPGA Championship
- U.S. Women's Open
- Nabisco Championship
- Women's British Open

The **Ryder Cup** is the most prestigious team golf event in the world. It is played every two years between a team of American golfers and a team of European golfers.

World Wide Webb

In 2001, 26-year-old Australian Karrie Webb became the youngest golfer in LPGA history to win the "career grand slam" (all four major tournaments).

Did You Know?

Odds of hitting a hole-in-one — 8,400 to 1

Oldest golfer to hit a hole-in-one — Harold Stilson, 101 years old, Deerfield Beach, Florida, 108 yards, May 2001

Youngest golfer to hit a hole-in-one — Jake Paine, 3 years old, Lake Forest, California, 66 yards, July 2001

Longest hole-in-one (non-dogleg) — 447 yards, Robert Mitera, Omaha, Nebraska, October 1965

Longest hole-in-one (dogleg) — 496 yards, Shawn Lynch, Exeter, England, July 1995

Olympics

What Do the Olympic Rings Symbolize?

The rings represent the world's five continents: Africa, Asia, Australia, Europe and the Americas.

And You Thought They Just Used a Match

The Olympic flame in Olympia, Greece, is rekindled every two years using a mirror and the sun's rays.

Weary Warriors

A 1912 wrestling match between Alfred Asikainen and Martin Klein lasted 11 hours. Klein won but was too tired to participate in the next round.

The Olympics will return to its roots in 2004. The very first Olympics was held in Greece in 776 B.C. In 1896, more than 2,000 years later, Athens was the site of the first Modern Olympics as 245 athletes from 14 nations came together to compete. Athens is currently the site of massive building preparations for the 2004 Games. Unlike other recent Olympics, no new sports will be added for the 2004 Games, but you can be sure that there will be a lot more than 245 competitors this time. More than 10,000 athletes from more than 200 nations will assemble in Athens August 13 to 29, 2004, to compete for gold.

Upcoming Olympic Gar

2004	(SUMMER)	Athens, Gr
2006	(WINTER)	Turin, Italy
2008	(SUMMER)	Beijing, Ch

Countries with the Al Most Medals

Summer	Gold	Silver	Br
1. U.S.A.	872	658	58
2. U.S.S.R.* (1952-88)	395	319	29
3. Great Britain	180	233	22

Winter	Gold	Silver	Br
1. Norway	94	94	75
2. U.S.S.R.* (1956-88)	78	57	59
3. U.S.A.	69	72	52

*In 1991 the U.S.S.R. (Union of Soviet Socia broke up into several countries, including Rus

 Test your Olympic triv with the Trivia Track www.timeforkids.com

Extreme Sports

"Extreme sports" refers to sports as different as skateboarding and ice climbing. Probably the most famous "extreme" athlete is skateboarder Tony Hawk. Hawk is the Michael Jordan of skateboarding. At the 1999 Summer X Games, Hawk became the first skateboarder to successfully land a 900 trick in the half-pipe competition. A 900 is 2½ complete midair rotations while on the skateboard. It's called a 900 because one complete spin is 360 degrees around (like a circle), and $2\frac{1}{2} \times 360 = 900$.

Which of the following sports do you consider "extreme": surfing, skateboarding, snowboarding, fishing, tennis, rock climbing, golf, baseball, bowling, skeleton, auto racing, mountain biking, sky diving, basketball, soccer, football, archery?

Americans made an "extreme" statement with their success in the snowboarding halfpipe at the 2002 Winter Olympics in Salt Lake City, Utah. Kelly Clark won gold in the women's event while Ross Powers, Danny Kass and J.J. Thomas took gold, silver and bronze in the men's halfpipe.

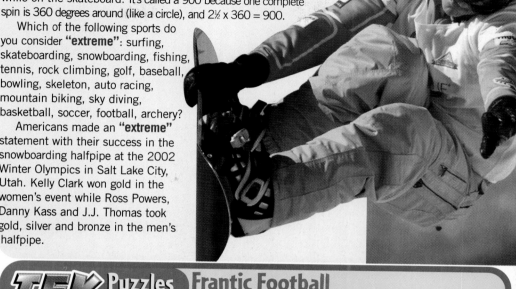

 **Puzzles & Games**

Frantic Football

There's a fox on a field-goal post in this frantic football folly. Can you find a total of **22** things that begin with the letter "**F**"?

1. football
2. fish
3. fork
4. funnel
5. field
6. fence
7. fruit
8. five
9. forty-seven
10. flashlight
11. fire
12. flying saucer
13. fraction
14. face mask
15. flamingo
16. flags
17. frog
18. fox
19. field goal post
20. feathers
21. flower
22. Frankenstein

Track and Field

Did you ever wonder...

. . . why the distance of a marathon is 26 miles, 385 yards? At the 1908 Olympic marathon in London, the royal family wanted a better view of the finish line. Organizers added 385 yards to the 26-mile race so the finish would be in front of the royal box. It's been that way ever since.

Vaulting to the Top

One of the most popular and successful American track-and-field stars is pole vaulter **Stacy Dragila.** She won the pole vaulting competition at the 1999 and 2001 World Championships. When the sport made its Olympic debut at Sydney in 2000, Dragila won the gold there, too. Just in 2001, she broke eight world records!

Give Him a Speeding Ticket

The world record holder of the 100-meter dash is widely considered the "World's Fastest Man." Currently that title belongs to American sprinter **Maurice Greene.** In Athens, Greece, in 1999, Greene ran a sizzling 9.79 seconds, shattering the previous mark. Over the entire race, Greene averaged almost 23 miles per hour.

Cycling
Three in a Row for Lance

In 2001, **Lance Armstrong** again showed the world that he was "King of the Mountains," as he roared past his rivals in the grueling mountain climbs to win his third consecutive Tour de France. His closest competitor finished six minutes and 44 seconds behind him. Amazingly, in October 1996 Armstrong had been diagnosed with cancer and was given only a 50% chance to live.

Swimming

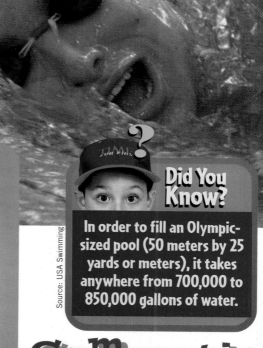

The Thorpedo

Australia's **Ian Thorpe** is one of the most dominant male swimmers in recent memory. He was just 17 when he won five medals at the 2000 Olympics in Sydney. Then, at the 2001 World Swimming Championships, Thorpe broke three world records and won an unprecedented six gold medals. At 6 feet, 4 inches with huge hands and size 17 feet, Thorpe has a body made for the pool.

Style Points

The five swimming styles used in competition are:

- **Breaststroke**
- **Backstroke**
- **Butterfly**
- **Freestyle**
- **Medley (combination of all)**

Seven Up

Mark Spitz won a record seven gold medals at the 1972 Olympics in Munich—and he set world records in each event! He has nine Olympic gold medals in all, more than any other swimmer.

The Magnificent Seven

Kerri Strug provided us with one of the most exciting events of the 1996 Olympics and gymnastics history when she nailed her vault on an injured ankle to ensure the gold medal for the United States team. Strug was just one member of the gold-medal-winning team that is known as the "Magnificent Seven." The others are **Amanda Borden, Amy Chow, Dominique Dawes, Shannon Miller, Dominique Moceanu** and **Jaycee Phelps.**

Source: USA Swimming

Did You Know?

In order to fill an Olympic-sized pool (50 meters by 25 yards or meters), it takes anywhere from 700,000 to 850,000 gallons of water.

Gymnastics

Gymnastics is one of the world's most physically demanding sports, not to mention one of the most popular sports at the Summer Olympics.

There are several different events within the sport of gymnastics.

- **Women** compete in the floor exercise, balance beam, uneven bars and vault.

- **Men** participate in the floor exercise, vault, horizontal bar, parallel bars, pommel horse and rings.

- **All of the events** in gymnastics take incredible coordination, strength, balance and stamina.

go For more on all the sports in this chapter, go to **www.FACT MONSTER.com**

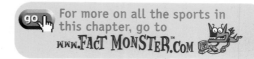

Sports

Soccer

Soccer is the world's most popular sport. Known widely as football throughout the rest of the world, soccer is played by boys and girls and men and women of nearly all ages. In all, hundreds of millions of people play around the world.

The World Cup

The world's biggest soccer tournament is called the World Cup. It's played every four years by teams made up of each country's best players.

The U.S. won the women's World Cup in 1999, while France was the winner of the men's World Cup in 1998. In 2002, the men's World Cup tournament was held in Japan and South Korea. The next women's World Cup is scheduled for 2003.

World Cup Champions

Men	Women
1930 **Uruguay**	1991 **U.S.A.**
1934 **Italy**	1995 **Norway**
1938 **Italy**	1999 **U.S.A.**
1942-46 **not held**	
1950 **Uruguay**	
1954 **West Germany**	
1958 **Brazil**	
1962 **Brazil**	
1966 **England**	
1970 **Brazil**	
1974 **West Germany**	
1978 **Argentina**	
1982 **Italy**	
1986 **Argentina**	
1990 **West Germany**	
1994 **Brazil**	
1998 **France**	

Hamm It Up

Mia Hamm, the captain of the U.S. national soccer team, is the best female soccer player in the world. And she has the trophy to prove it. Hamm won the inaugural FIFA World Women's Player of the Year award in 2001. She added the award to the long list of honors she's already received, including a 1996 Olympic gold medal, a 1999 Women's World Cup title and four consecutive NCAA national championships at the University of North Carolina. Hamm was also one of the big-name players in the brand-new Women's United Soccer Association, or WUSA, in 2001.

Tennis

Four tournaments make up the tennis Grand Slam

Australian Open   Wimbledon
French Open   U.S. Open

Love Means Zero

Learn how to speak and score like a tennis pro.

Love is zero points.

15, 30, 40 are tennis terms for one point, two points and three points.

Game point is the fourth point. The first player to win the fourth point (and lead by two) wins the game.

Deuce is the term for when the game is tied 40-40. Play continues until one player wins by two points.

Set: To win a set a player must win six games and lead by at least two. If each player wins five sets the players play a seventh game. If each player wins six games there is a seven-point tiebreaker game to decide the winner.

Match: The match usually ends when one player wins two out of three sets.

The Meaning of Love

In tennis, when someone has zero points it's called love, but historians aren't exactly sure why. The best explanation takes us to France, where the sport was invented. The French word for egg is *l'oeuf*, which if pronounced correctly sounds like the word *love*. A zero was given this name because on a scoreboard it resembles an egg.

This Australian Rules

In 2001, Australian tennis star **Lleyton Hewitt** (pronounced LAY-ton HYOO-it) became the youngest male tennis player to finish the year ranked Number 1 in the world. Just 20 years old, Hewitt began playing tennis in 1994. When he was younger he played Australian Rules Football, a game that his dad played professionally and is somewhat similar to rugby. Hewitt was also named the men's pro tennis tour's player of the year.

Some of Tennis' Best Rivalries			
M E N	Pete Sampras vs. Andre Agassi	1980s–	Sampras leads, 18-14
	Jim Courier vs. Michael Chang	1990s	Tied, 12-12
	Ivan Lendl vs. John McEnroe	1980s	Lendl, 21-15
	John McEnroe vs. Jimmy Connors	1970s–90s	McEnroe, 20-13
	Jimmy Connors vs. Bjorn Borg	1970s–80s	Borg, 10-8
W O M E N	Venus Williams vs. Serena Williams	1990s–	Venus leads, 5-2
	Martina Hingis vs. Lindsay Davenport	1990s–	Davenport, 14-11
	Steffi Graf vs. Monica Seles	1980s–90s	Graf, 10-5
	Martina Navratilova vs. Chris Evert	1970s–80s	Navratilova, 43-37
	Margaret Smith Court vs. Billie Jean King	1960s–70s	Smith Court, 22-10

RACING

Automobile racing originated in France in 1894 and appeared in the U.S. the next year.

Racing Anyone?

The National Association for Stock Car Racing's (NASCAR) **Winston Cup Series** is the most popular auto racing series in the U.S. The biggest Winston Cup race of the year is the **Daytona 500,** and it's also the first race of the year.

Our Need for Speed

The biggest and oldest race held in the U.S. is the **Indianapolis 500.** It's held every year at the oval-shaped Indianapolis Motor Speedway in Indiana. The track is nicknamed the Brickyard because it was originally made of brick. Cars race around the track at average speeds of up to 225 miles per hour.

Who's Who in Pit Row

When a car pulls off the track for a "pit stop" what might look like chaos is actually a precise routine. Here's a list of the key pit-crew men and women.

jack man—the crew "quarterback" is in charge of jacking up the car so its tires can be changed

gas-can man—refills the gas tank with a giant gas can that can weigh 90 pounds when full; most pit stops require two cans

catch-can man—catches overflow of gas in a special canister; lets jack man know when fueling is complete

front/rear tire carrier—carries new tires to the car; carries old ones back over the wall; tires can weigh 75 pounds and are extremely hot

front/rear tire changer—takes off the five lug nuts holding each tire in place with an air gun in less than two seconds and secures the new tires

What Do the Flags Mean?

Race officials use flags to instruct drivers during a race. Here's what the flags mean:

Green – Go!

Yellow – Caution. There is a problem on the track, and drivers must go slow and not pass.

Red – Stop. Something has made the track unusable (maybe an accident or bad weather).

White – Last lap.

Checkered – Finish. The race is over.

World Champions

Germany's **Michael Schumacher** won his fourth Formula One driver's world championship in 2001, moving him into a tie for second on the all-time list. Here are the drivers with the most world titles listed with their home countries.

5– **Juan-Manuel Fangio (Argentina)**

4– **Michael Schumacher (Germany) and Alain Prost (France)**

3– **Jack Brabham (Australia), Niki Lauda (Austria), Nelson Piquet (Brazil), Ayrton Senna (Brazil) and Jackie Stewart (Great Britain)**

Animal Sports

Horse Racing

Animals are a big part of the sports world, and horses in particular play a large role. The history of horse racing can be traced to ancient Egypt and Greece, where horse-and-chariot races were part of the Olympic Games. It is often called "the sport of kings" because breeding and racing horses was a popular hobby of the royal family in England during the 12th century.

Sled-Dog Racing

The popular 2002 film **Snow Dogs** is based on one man's real-life experience in the world's most famous dog race. In the annual Iditarod Trail Sled Dog Race, an average team uses 16 dogs. Each team pulls a large sled (and driver!) more than 1,100 miles through the snowy Alaskan wilderness. The race from Anchorage to Nome, first run in 1973, commemorates a 1925 lifesaving delivery of medicine to the village of Nome by sled dogs.

Triple Crown

Horse racing reaches its pinnacle each spring with the running of the **Triple Crown.** The Triple Crown is a series of three prestigious races starting with the Kentucky Derby, which is held each year on the first Saturday in May at Churchill Downs in Louisville, Kentucky. The next race is the Preakness Stakes, followed by the Belmont Stakes.

Here is a list of the 11 horses that have won the Triple Crown—that is, won all three races in the same year. Notice that it hasn't been done in more than 20 years!

1919 **Sir Barton**	1946 **Assault**
1930 **Gallant Fox**	1948 **Citation**
1935 **Omaha**	1973 **Secretariat**
1937 **War Admiral**	1977 **Seattle Slew**
1941 **Whirlaway**	1978 **Affirmed**
1943 **Count Fleet**	

33 USA

Secretariat Wins Triple Crown

TFK Mystery Person

In 1891, this Presbyterian minister, doctor and gym teacher invented basketball in Springfield, Massachusetts. Of his 13 original rules, 12 still stand. The first game involved 18 players, a soccer ball and two peach baskets, which had to be emptied after each "basket."

Who is he?

go Sports Web Sites

ANIMAL SPORTS
www.iditarod.com

BASEBALL
www.baseballhalloffame.org
www.littleleague.org
www.mlb.com

BASKETBALL
www.nba.com
www.wnba.com

COLLEGE SPORTS
www.ncaa.org

CYCLING
www.letour.fr

FOOTBALL
www.nfl.com
www.profootballhof.com
www.superbowl.com

GOLF
www.masters.org
www.pgatour.com

HOCKEY
www.nhl.com

OLYMPICS
www.olympic.org

RACING
www.nascar.com

SOCCER
www.mlsnet.com
www.worldcup.com

TENNIS
www.atptour.com
www.tennisfame.com
www.wtatour.com

Sports

United States

State Regions

New England Connecticut, Maine, Massachusetts, New Hampshire, Rhode Island, Vermont

From the 17th century until well into the 19th, New England was the country's cultural and economic center. The mainstays of the region became shipbuilding, fishing and trade.

Middle Atlantic Delaware, Maryland, New Jersey, New York, Pennsylvania

Philadelphia was the birthplace of the Declaration of Independence in 1776 and the U.S. Constitution in 1787. New York is the nation's most populous city and its financial hub.

South Alabama, Arkansas, Florida, Georgia, Kentucky, Louisiana, Mississippi, Missouri, North Carolina, South Carolina, Tennessee, Virginia, West Virginia

The South was first settled by English Protestants. Especially in coastal areas, settlers grew wealthy by raising and selling cotton and tobacco on large farms called plantations.

Midwest Illinois, Indiana, Iowa, Kansas, Michigan, Minnesota, Nebraska, North Dakota, Ohio, South Dakota, Wisconsin

Starting in the early 1800s, easterners moved to the Midwest in search of better farm-land. The fertile soil made it possible for farmers to produce harvests of cereal crops.

Southwest Arizona, New Mexico, Oklahoma, Texas

The Southwest differs from the adjoining Midwest in weather (drier), population (less dense) and ethnicity (strong Spanish-American and Native-American components).

West Alaska, California, Colorado, Hawaii, Idaho, Montana, Nevada, Oregon, Utah, Washington, Wyoming

The West is a region of scenic beauty on a grand scale. All of its states are partly mountainous, and the ranges are the sources of startling contrasts.

Source: The U.S. Department of State

The *Great Seal* of the U.S.

Benjamin Franklin, John Adams and Thomas Jefferson began designing the Great Seal in 1776. The Great Seal is printed on the back of the one-dollar bill and is used on certain government documents, such as foreign treaties.

The bald eagle, our national bird, is at the center of the seal. It holds a banner in its beak. The motto says *E pluribus unum*, which is Latin for "out of many, one." This refers to the colonies that united to make a nation. In one claw, the eagle holds an olive branch for peace; in the other claw, arrows for war.

Many things in the Great Seal add up to 13, for the 13 colonies:
- **13 letters in the motto**
- **13 stripes**
- **13 stars**
- **13 olives**
- **13 olive leaves**
- **13 arrows**

Other Symbols of the United States

The bald eagle has been our national bird since 1872. The Founding Fathers had been unable to agree on which native bird should have the honor— Benjamin Franklin strongly preferred the turkey! Besides appearing on the Great Seal, the bald eagle is pictured on coins, the dollar bill, all official U.S. seals and the President's flag.

The image of Uncle Sam, with his white hair and top hat, first became famous on World War I recruiting posters. The artist, James Montgomery Flagg, used himself as a model. But the term dates back to the War of 1812, when a meat packer nicknamed "Uncle Sam" supplied beef to the troops. You'll notice that the initials for his nickname were quite appropriate!

The **U.S.** Flag

In 1777 the Continental Congress decided that the flag would have 13 alternating red and white stripes, for the 13 colonies, and 13 white stars on a blue background. A new star has been added for every new state. Today the flag has 50 stars.

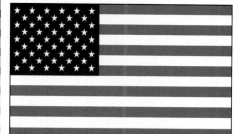

Some Nicknames for the U.S. Flag

⭐ The Stars and Stripes
⭐ The Red, White and Blue
⭐ Old Glory

A LOOK AT THE U.S. POPULATION

MEDIAN AGE

All: 35.5
Men: 34.3
Women: 36.6

About 40 million Americans are nine years old or younger.

About 70,000 are 100 years old or older! It is estimated that by the year 2050, some 834,000 Americans will be at least 100 years old.

LIFE EXPECTANCY

When the nation was founded, the average American could expect to live to the age of 35. By 1900, life expectancy had increased to 47.3. In 1999, the life expectancy was 77.3. It's a little bit higher for women—80.0 years, as opposed to 74.4 for men.

SEX AND RACE

The U.S. population is about 51% female and 49% male. According to the 2000 Census:

75.1% of Americans are white
12.3% are black
3.7% are Asian, Native Hawaiian or Pacific Islander
0.9% are Native American or Alaskan Native
5.5% are of some other race
2.4 % belong to two or more races

In addition, 12.5% of Americans say they are of Hispanic origin (they may be of any race).

KIDS AT HOME

About 71% of kids live with two parents. About 25% live with one parent, while nearly 4% live with neither parent. About 5.5% of kids live in a home maintained by a grandparent.

BABY NAMES

About 4,000,000 babies are born in the U.S. each year! The most popular names for American boys born in 2001 were Jacob, Michael, Joshua, Matthew and Andrew. The most popular names for American girls born in 2001 were Emily, Hannah, Madison, Samantha and Ashley.

MOST COMMON LAST NAMES IN THE U.S.

1. Smith
2. Johnson
3. Williams
4. Jones
5. Brown
6. Davis
7. Miller
8. Wilson
9. Moore
10. Taylor
11. Anderson
12. Thomas
13. Jackson
14. White
15. Harris
16. Martin
17. Thompson
18. Garcia
19. Martinez
20. Robinson
21. Clark
22. Rodriguez
23. Lewis
24. Lee
25. Walker

Foreign-Born Americans

The term "foreign born" refers to Americans who were not U.S. citizens when they were born. More than one-third of foreign-born Americans came from Mexico or from Central or South America.

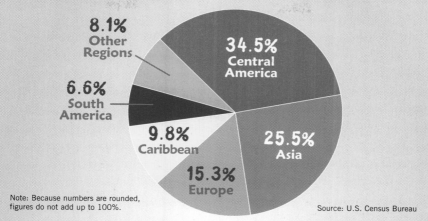

8.1% Other Regions

6.6% South America

9.8% Caribbean

34.5% Central America

25.5% Asia

15.3% Europe

Note: Because numbers are rounded, figures do not add up to 100%.

Source: U.S. Census Bureau

Where Immigrants Come From

The U.S. admitted a total of 646,568 immigrants in 1999. Of these, 47,573 —nearly one in four—came from Mexico. Here are the top countries for U.S. immigration.

1. Mexico
2. China
3. Philippines
4. India
5. Vietnam
6. Dominican Republic
7. Haiti
8. Jamaica
9. El Salvador
10. Cuba
11. Pakistan
12. Nicaragua
13. Korea
14. Russia
15. Ukraine
16. Colombia
17. Ecuador
18. Canada
19. Poland
20. Peru

Source: Immigration and Naturalization Service (INS)

Naturalization

When immigrants enter the United States, they are not American citizens. In order to enjoy many of the privileges of being an American, such as the right to vote and hold public office, a person must gain citizenship. The process for becoming a citizen is called naturalization. To become a naturalized citizen, a person must fill out an application with the Immigration and Naturalization Service and meet language and residency requirements, among other conditions.

Immigrants in Miami, Florida, take an oath to become citizens.

United States

297

AMERICAN INDIANS

There are more than 550 federally recognized Indian tribes in the United States, including 223 village groups in Alaska. "Federally recognized" means these tribes and groups have a special legal relationship with the U.S. government.

Largest American Indian Tribes

1. Cherokee
2. Navajo
3. Chippewa
4. Sioux
5. Choctaw
6. Pueblo
7. Apache
8. Iroquois
9. Lumbee
10. Creek
11. Blackfoot
12. Canadian and Latin American tribes
13. Chickasaw
14. Potawatomi
15. Tohono O'Odham
16. Pima
17. Tlingit
18. Seminole
19. Alaskan Athabaskans
20. Cheyenne

Indian Reservations

The largest reservation is the Navajo Reservation, which has about 16 million acres of land in Arizona, New Mexico and Utah. Many of the smaller reservations are less than 1,000 acres with the smallest less than 100 acres. Here are the reservations with the largest populations:

1. Navajo (Arizona, New Mexico and Utah)
2. Pine Ridge (Nebraska and South Dakota)
3. Fort Apache (Arizona)
4. Gila River (Arizona)
5. Papago (Arizona)
6. Rosebud (South Dakota)
7. San Carlos (Arizona)
8. Zuni Pueblo (Arizona and New Mexico)
9. Hopi (Arizona)
10. Blackfeet (Montana)

November is National Native American Heritage Month

Schools, the government and various organizations sponsor events that honor the history and culture of the first Americans.

Did You Know?

California has the highest number of American Indians and Alaska Natives—627,600 according to Census 2000. Oklahoma is next, with 391,900.

INDIAN PLACE NAMES

Many American places have been named after Indian words. In fact, about half of the states got their names from Indian words. The name of Kentucky comes from an Iroquoian word (Kentahten), which means "land of tomorrow." And the word "Podunk," which is used to describe an insignificant town in the middle of nowhere, comes from a Natick Indian word meaning "swampy place." **Here are some other Indian place names:**

Chicago (Illinois): Algonquian for "garlic field"

Mississippi (river): Indian word in several languages for "great water"

Manhattan (New York): Algonquian, believed to mean "isolated thing in water"

Milwaukee (Wisconsin): Algonquian, believed to mean "a good spot or place"

Niagara (falls): named after an Iroquoian town, Ongiaahra

Pensacola (Florida): Choctaw words for "hair" and "people"

Roanoke (Virginia): Algonquian for "shell money" (Indian tribes often used shells that were made into beads called wampum as money)

Saratoga (New York) believed to be Mohawk for "springs (of water) from the hillside"

Sunapee (lake in New Hampshire): Pennacook for "rocky pond"

Tahoe (lake in California/Nevada): Washo for "big water"

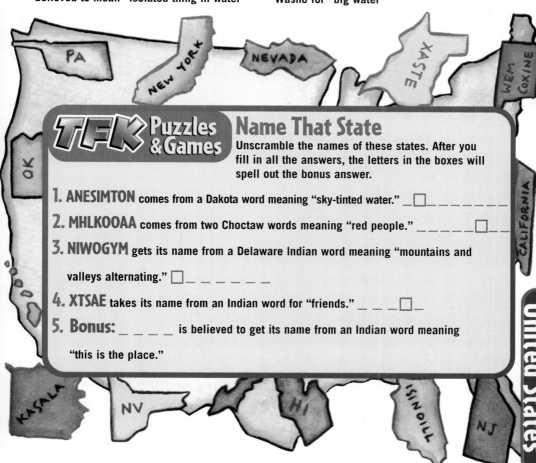

TFK Puzzles & Games — Name That State

Unscramble the names of these states. After you fill in all the answers, the letters in the boxes will spell out the bonus answer.

1. **ANESIMTON** comes from a Dakota word meaning "sky-tinted water." _ ☐ _ _ _ _ _ _ _

2. **MHLKOOAA** comes from two Choctaw words meaning "red people." _ _ _ _ _ ☐ _ _

3. **NIWOGYM** gets its name from a Delaware Indian word meaning "mountains and valleys alternating." ☐ _ _ _ _ _ _

4. **XTSAE** takes its name from an Indian word for "friends." _ _ _ ☐ _

5. **Bonus:** _ _ _ _ _ is believed to get its name from an Indian word meaning "this is the place."

United States

299

The National Park System

The National Park System of the U.S. is run by the National Park Service, a bureau of the Department of the Interior. Yellowstone, which was opened in 1872, was the first national park in the world. The system includes not only the most extraordinary and spectacular scenic exhibits in the U.S. but also a large number of sites distinguished either for their historic importance, prehistoric importance, scientific interest or for their superior recreational assets.

Beehive Geyser, one of the gushing geysers in Yellowstone National Park

The National Park System is made up of 378 areas covering more than 83 million acres in every state except Delaware. It also includes areas in the District of Columbia, American Samoa, Guam, Puerto Rico and the Virgin Islands. For a complete listing of National Park areas, visit the web site of the Park Service: www.nps.gov

TFK TOP 5
Most Visited National Parks

Yellowstone is now the sixth most visited national park in the U.S. But in 1872 it was the only national park! Today there are hundreds. These five attract the most visitors:

1. **Great Smoky Mountains National Park** (North Carolina and Tennessee)

2. **Grand Canyon National Park** (Arizona)

3. **Yosemite National Park** (California)

4. **Olympic National Park** (Washington)

5. **Rocky Mountain National Park** (Colorado)

World Heritage Sites in the UNITED STATES

The United Nations Educational, Scientific and Cultural Organization (UNESCO) has identified 582 World Heritage sites that it considers of "outstanding universal value." In the United States, there are 22 of these sites; the 17 that are natural sites are listed below.

Cahokia Mounds State Historic Site, Illinois Between A.D. 900 and A.D. 1500 the Cahokia site was the regional center for the Mississippian Indian culture. It features the largest prehistoric earthen constructions in the Americas. **(continued)**

World Heritage Sites in the
UNITED STATES (continued)

Carlsbad Caverns National Park, New Mexico Carlsbad Caverns National Park is a network of more than 80 limestone caves.

Chaco Culture National Historical Park, New Mexico Between A.D. 900 and A.D. 1100, the Anasazi Indians built large multistory stone villages and an impressive 400-mile road system in Chaco canyon.

Everglades National Park, Florida The Everglades is formed by a shallow river 50 miles wide that flows through marshes, pine forests and mangrove islands.

Glacier Bay National Park and Preserve, Alaska The park is made up of a huge chain of glaciers and a dramatic range of landscapes.

Grand Canyon National Park, Arizona For the past 6 to 10 million years, the Colorado River has been carving its way through the Grand Canyon, exposing the many colorful layers of rock.

Great Smoky Mountains National Park, North Carolina/Tennessee The forest here exudes water vapor and oily residues that create a smokelike haze.

Hawaii Volcanoes National Park, Hawaii The Hawaiian islands were created when molten rock pushed through Earth's crust, forming volcanoes.

Mammoth Cave National Park, Kentucky Mammoth Cave is the world's most extensive cave system, with 345 miles of passages.

Mesa Verde National Park, Colorado In the sixth century, the Anasazi built villages on this high, flat land. In the late 1100s they began constructing stone apartment houses, or pueblos, on ledges and under overhangs.

Even the tallest person seems short compared to California's giant redwoods.

Olympic National Park, Washington The park encompasses Mount Olympus, glaciers and one of the few temperate rain forests in the world.

Redwood National Park, California Redwood National Park contains the tallest living things on Earth, trees that grow to 350 feet.

Taos Pueblo, New Mexico Pueblo de Taos appeared before A.D. 1400 and is the best preserved of the pueblos (communal housing) north of the Mexico border.

Waterton–Glacier International Peace Park, Montana The two parks sustain a diverse habitat, including wolves, bears and mountain lions.

Wrangell–St. Elias National Park and Preserve, Alaska The park is made up of ice-fields and glaciers that have created a sculpted landscape of valleys, peaks and lakes.

Yosemite National Park, California Yosemite contains breathtaking scenery and a huge variety of plant and animal life.

U.S. Cities

LARGEST CITIES

1. New York, New York
2. Los Angeles, California
3. Chicago, Illinois
4. Houston, Texas
5. Philadelphia, Pennsylvania
6. Phoenix, Arizona
7. San Diego, California
8. Dallas, Texas
9. San Antonio, Texas
10. Detroit, Michigan
11. San Jose, California
12. Indianapolis, Indiana
13. San Francisco, California
14. Jacksonville, Florida
15. Columbus, Ohio
16. Austin, Texas
17. Baltimore, Maryland
18. Memphis, Tennessee
19. Milwaukee, Wisconsin
20. Boston, Massachusetts

Did You Know?

St. Augustine, Florida, is the oldest continuously settled city in the United States. It was founded by Spanish explorers in 1565.

Some City Nicknames

Boston	Beantown
Chicago	The Windy City
Denver	The Mile-High City
New York	The Big Apple
Philadelphia	The City of Brotherly Love
San Francisco	The City by the Bay
Seattle	The Emerald City

Some Firsts in U.S. Cities

Aquarium: Chicago, Illinois, 1893
Department Store: Salt Lake City, Utah, 1868
Elevator: New York, New York, 1850
Ferris wheel: Chicago, Illinois, 1893
Hospital: Philadelphia, Pennsylvania, 1752
Lighthouse: Boston, Massachusetts, 1716
Subway: Boston, Massachusetts, 1897
Zoo: Philadelphia, Pennsylvania, 1874

Great AMERICAN
Claims to Fame

Sure, you've probably heard Hollywood called the "movie capital of the world," or Detroit the "automotive capital of the world." But here are some "self-proclaimed capitals" you may not know about.

Cow Chip Throwing Capital of the World
Beaver, Oklahoma
Established as a tribute to the natural fuel source of the town's early settlers, the World Cow Chip Throwing Championship has been held in Beaver every April since 1969.

Troll Capital of the World
Mount Horeb, Wisconsin
Mount Horeb offers a "Troll Stroll" down the Trollway, site of the country's largest collection of life-sized troll sculptures, which are carved into trees along the town's main drag.

Sock Capital of the World
Fort Payne, Alabama
According to The Hosiery Association, the industry's leading trade association, one out of every eight Americans who put on socks this morning will be wearing a pair made in Fort Payne/DeKalb County.

Breakfast Capital of the World
Battle Creek, Michigan
Battle Creek produces most of the breakfast cereal consumed in the U.S. There you can visit Kellogg's Cereal City USA, an interactive museum that honors cereal and its impact on our culture.

Mushroom Capital of the World
Kennett Square, Pennsylvania
No U.S. state produces more mushrooms than Pennsylvania. In the heart of mushroom country, the Phillips Mushroom Museum celebrates three generations of mushroom farmers.

Decoy Capital of the World
Havre de Grace, Maryland
This Maryland community on the Susquehanna River is home to the Havre de Grace Decoy Museum, which features the country's largest collection of wooden duck decoys.

Bratwurst Capital of the World
Sheboygan, Wisconsin
Sheboygan hosts Bratwurst Days, an annual two-day festival of music and bratwurst. Sausage lovers come to try new bratwurst in flavors such as taco and Cajun.

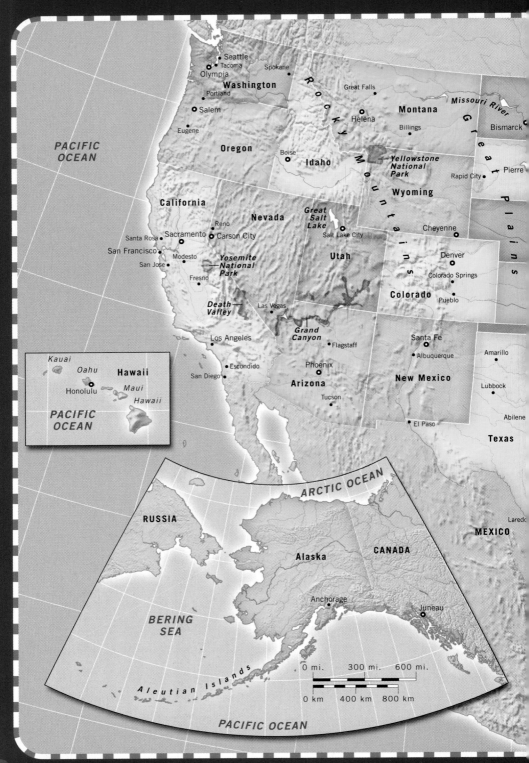

PACIFIC
OCEAN

Seattle
Tacoma
Olympia   Spokane
Washington
Portland
Salem

Eugene

Oregon
Boise
Idaho

California

Reno
Santa Rosa   Sacramento
San Francisco   Carson City   Nevada
Modesto
San Jose   Fresno   Yosemite
National
Park

Death—
Valley   Las Vegas

Grand
Canyon   Flagstaff
Los Angeles
Phoenix
Escondido
San Diego   Arizona
Tucson
El Paso

Great Falls

Montana
Helena
Billings

Missouri River
Bismarck

Yellowstone
National
Park   Rapid City   Pierre
Wyoming
Cheyenne

Great
Salt
Lake
Salt Lake City
Denver
Utah
Colorado Springs
Colorado
Pueblo

Santa Fe
Albuquerque   Amarillo

New Mexico   Lubbock

Abilene

Texas

Rocky Mountains

Great Plains

Kauai
Oahu   Hawaii
Honolulu   Maui
Hawaii
PACIFIC
OCEAN

ARCTIC OCEAN

RUSSIA

Alaska   CANADA

Laredo
MEXICO

Anchorage
Juneau

BERING
SEA

Aleutian Islands

0 mi.   300 mi.   600 mi.

0 km   400 km   800 km

PACIFIC OCEAN

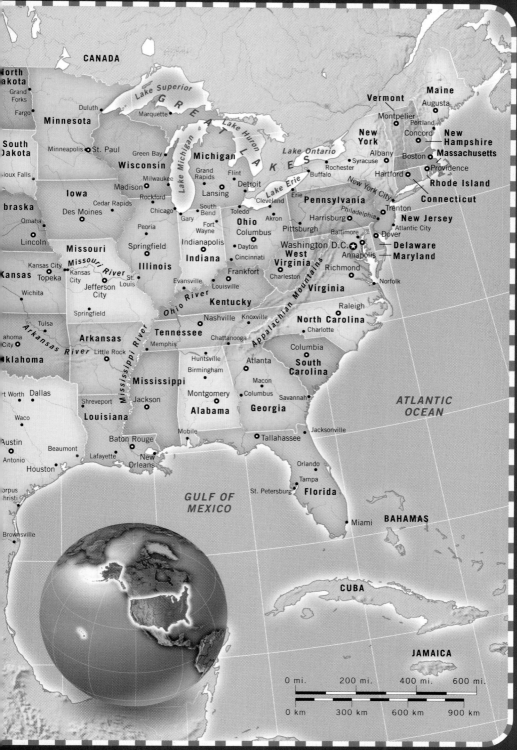

CANADA

North Dakota
Grand Forks
Fargo

Minnesota

Lake Superior

Duluth
Marquette

G R E A T

Lake Michigan

Lake Huron

L A K E S

Lake Ontario

Lake Erie

Vermont
Montpelier

Maine
Augusta

Portland
Concord

New Hampshire

South Dakota
Sioux Falls

Minneapolis
St. Paul

Green Bay

Wisconsin

Michigan

Grand Rapids
Flint

New York

Albany
Syracuse

Rochester

Boston

Massachusetts

Providence

nebraska

Iowa

Madison

Milwaukee

Lansing

Detroit

Buffalo

Hartford

Rhode Island

Omaha

Cedar Rapids

Rockford

Des Moines

Chicago

South Bend

Cleveland

Erie

Pennsylvania

New York City

Trenton

Connecticut

New Jersey

Lincoln

Peoria

Gary

Fort Wayne

Ohio

Toledo

Akron

Harrisburg

Philadelphia

Atlantic City

Missouri

Springfield

Indianapolis

Columbus

Pittsburgh

Baltimore

Dover

Delaware

Kansas City

Missouri River

Kansas
Topeka

Wichita

Kansas City

Jefferson City

St. Louis

Illinois

Indiana

Frankfort

Dayton

Cincinnati

Washington D.C.

West Virginia

Annapolis

Maryland

Richmond

ahoma
City

Springfield

Evansville

Louisville

Kentucky

Charleston

Virginia

Norfolk

Tulsa

Arkansas River

klahoma

Arkansas

Little Rock

Ohio River

Nashville

Tennessee

Memphis

Chattanooga

Knoxville

Raleigh

North Carolina

Charlotte

Appalachian Mountains

rt Worth
Dallas

Waco

Mississippi

Mississippi River

Jackson

Huntsville

Birmingham

Atlanta

Columbia

South Carolina

Austin

Shreveport

Louisiana

Alabama

Montgomery

Columbus

Macon

Georgia

Savannah

ATLANTIC OCEAN

Antonio

Houston

Beaumont

Lafayette

Baton Rouge

New Orleans

Mobile

Jacksonville

orpus
hristi

GULF OF MEXICO

St. Petersburg

Tallahassee

Florida

Orlando

Tampa

Brownsville

BAHAMAS

Miami

CUBA

JAMAICA

0 mi.   200 mi.   400 mi.   600 mi.

0 km   300 km   600 km   900 km

ALABAMA

Origin of name: May come from a Choctaw word meaning "thicket-clearers"

Entered union (rank): December 14, 1819 (22)

Motto: *Audemus jura nostra defendere* (We dare defend our rights)

Tree: southern longleaf pine

Flower: camellia

Bird: yellowhammer

Other: dance, square dance; nut, pecan

Song: *Alabama*

Nickname: Yellowhammer State

Residents: Alabamian, Alabaman

Land area: 50,750 square miles (131,443 sq km)

Population (2000): 4,447,100

Home of: George Washington Carver, who discovered more than 300 uses for peanuts

Capital: Montgomery
Largest city: Birmingham

ALASKA

Origin of name: From an Aleut word meaning "great land" or "that which the sea breaks against"

Entered union (rank): January 3, 1959 (49)

Motto: North to the future

Tree: sitka spruce

Flower: forget-me-not

Bird: willow ptarmigan

Other: fossil, woolly mammoth; sport, dog mushing

Song: *Alaska's Flag*

Nicknames: The Last Frontier and Land of the Midnight Sun

Residents: Alaskan

Land area: 570,374 square miles (1,477,267 sq km)

Population (2000): 626,932

Home of: The longest coastline in the U.S., 6,640 miles, which is greater than that of all other states combined

Capital: Juneau
Largest city: Anchorage

Origin of name: **From the Native American *Arizonac,* meaning "little spring"**

Entered union (rank): **February 14, 1912 (48)**

Motto: ***Ditat deus* (God enriches)**

Tree: **palo verde**

Flower: **flower of saguaro cactus**

Bird: **cactus wren**

Other: **gemstone, turquoise; neckwear, bola tie**

Song: ***Arizona***

Nickname: **Grand Canyon State**

Residents: **Arizonan, Arizonian**

Land area: **113,642 square miles (296,400 sq km)**

Population (2000): **5,130,632**

Home of: **The most telescopes in the world, in Tucson**

Capital: **Phoenix**
Largest city: **Phoenix**

Origin of name: **From the Quapaw Indians**

Entered union (rank): **June 15, 1836 (25)**

Motto: ***Regnat populus* (The people rule)**

Tree: **pine**

Flower: **apple blossom**

Bird: **mockingbird**

Other: **fruit and vegetable, pink tomato; insect, honeybee**

Song: ***Arkansas***

Nickname: **The Natural State**

Residents: **Arkansan**

Land area: **52,075 square miles (134,874 sq km)**

Population (2000): **2,673,400**

Home of: **The only active diamond mine in the U.S.**

Capital: **Little Rock**
Largest city: **Little Rock**

United States

CALIFORNIA

Origin of name: From a book, *Las Sergas de Esplandián*, by Garcia Ordóñez de Montalvo, ca. 1500

Entered union (rank): September 9, 1850 (31)

Motto: *Eureka* (I have found it)

Tree: California redwood

Flower: golden poppy

Bird: California valley quail

Other: dance, West Coast Swing Dance; prehistoric artifact, chipped stone bear

Song: *I Love You, California*

Nickname: Golden State

Residents: Californian

Land area: 155,973 square miles (403,970 sq km)

Population (2000): 33,871,648

Home of: "General Sherman," a 2,500-year-old sequoia

Capital: Sacramento
Largest city: Los Angeles

COLORADO

Origin of name: From the Spanish, "ruddy" or "red"

Entered union (rank): August 1, 1876 (38)

Motto: *Nil sine numine* (Nothing without providence)

Tree: Colorado blue spruce

Flower: Rocky Mountain columbine

Bird: lark bunting

Other: fossil, Stegosaurus; gemstone, aquamarine

Song: *Where the Columbines Grow*

Nickname: Centennial State

Residents: Coloradan, Coloradoan

Land area: 103,730 square miles (268,660 sq km)

Population (2000): 4,301,261

Home of: The world's largest silver nugget (1,840 pounds), found in 1894 near Aspen

Capital: Denver
Largest city: Denver

CONNECTICUT

Origin of name: From a Quinnehtukqut Indian word meaning "beside the long tidal river"

Entered union (rank): January 9, 1788 (5)

Motto: *Qui transtulit sustinet* (He who transplanted still sustains)

Tree: white oak

Flower: mountain laurel

Bird: American robin

Other: hero, Nathan Hale; heroine, Prudence Crandall

Song: *Yankee Doodle*

Nickname: Nutmeg State

Residents: Nutmegger

Land area: 4,845 square miles (12,550 sq km)

Population (2000): 3,405,565

Home of: The first American cookbook, *American Cookery* by Amelia Simmons, published in Hartford in 1796

Hartford

Bridgeport

Capital: Hartford
Largest city: Bridgeport

DELAWARE

Origin of name: From Delaware River and Bay, named for Sir Thomas West, Baron De La Warr

Entered union (rank): December 7, 1787 (1)

Motto: Liberty and independence

Tree: American holly

Flower: peach blossom

Bird: blue hen chicken

Other: colors, colonial blue and buff; insect, ladybug

Song: *Our Delaware*

Nicknames: Diamond State, First State and Small Wonder

Residents: Delawarean

Land area: 1,955 square miles (5,153 sq km)

Population (2000): 783,600

Home of: The first log cabins in North America, built in 1683 by Swedish immigrants

Wilmington

Dover

Capital: Dover
Largest city: Wilmington

FLORIDA

Origin of name: From the Spanish, meaning "feast of flowers"

Entered union (rank): March 3, 1845 (27)

Motto: In God we trust

Tree: sabal palm

Flower: orange blossom

Bird: mockingbird

Other: shell, horse conch; soil, Myakka fine sand

Song: *The Swanee River*

Nickname: Sunshine State

Residents: Floridian, Floridan

Land area: 54,153 square miles (140,256 sq km)

Population (2000): 15,982,378

Capital: Tallahassee
Largest city: Jacksonville

Home of: U.S. spacecraft launches from Cape Canaveral, formerly Cape Kennedy

GEORGIA

Origin of name: In honor of George II of England

Entered union (rank): January 2, 1788 (4)

Motto: Wisdom, justice, and moderation

Tree: live oak

Flower: Cherokee rose

Bird: brown thrasher

Other: crop, peanut; fossil, shark tooth

Song: *Georgia on My Mind*

Nicknames: Peach State and Empire State of the South

Residents: Georgian

Land area: 57,919 square miles (150,010 sq km)

Population (2000): 8,186,453

Capital: Atlanta
Largest city: Atlanta

Home of: The Girl Scouts, founded in Savannah by Juliette Gordon Low in 1912

HAWAII

Origin of name: Probably from a Polynesian word meaning "ancestral home"

Entered union (rank): August 21, 1959 (50)

Motto: *Ua mau ke ea o ka aina i ka pono* (The life of the land is perpetuated in righteousness)

Tree: kukui (candlenut)

Flower: yellow hibiscus

Bird: nene (Hawaiian goose)

Other: gem, black coral; marine mammal, humpback whale

Song: *Hawaii Ponoi*

Nickname: Aloha State

Residents: Hawaiian

Land area: 6,423 square miles (16,637 sq km)

Population (2000): 1,211,537

Home of: The only royal palace in the U.S. (Iolani)

Capital: Honolulu (on Oahu)
Largest city: Honolulu

IDAHO

Origin of name: Though popularly believed to be a Native American word, it is an invented name whose meaning is unknown.

Entered union (rank): July 3, 1890 (43)

Motto: *Esto perpetua* (It is forever)

Tree: white pine

Flower: syringa

Bird: mountain bluebird

Other: fish, cutthroat trout; horse, Appaloosa

Song: *Here We Have Idaho*

Nickname: Gem State

Residents: Idahoan

Land area: 82,751 square miles (214,325 sq km)

Population (2000): 1,293,953

Home of: The longest main street in America, 33 miles, in Island Park

Capital: Boise
Largest city: Boise

ILLINOIS

Origin of name: Algonquian for "tribe of superior men"

Entered union (rank): December 3, 1818 (21)

Motto: State sovereignty, national union

Tree: white oak

Flower: violet

Bird: cardinal

Other: animal, white-tailed deer; prairie grass, big bluestem

Song: *Illinois*

Nickname: Prairie State

Residents: Illinoisan

Land area: 55,593 square miles (143,987 sq km)

Population (2000): 12,419,293

Home of: The tallest building in the country, Sears Tower, in Chicago

Capital: Springfield
Largest city: Chicago

INDIANA

Origin of name: Means "land of Indians"

Entered union (rank): December 11, 1816 (19)

Motto: The crossroads of America

Tree: tulip tree

Flower: peony

Bird: cardinal

Other: river, Wabash; stone, limestone

Song: *On the Banks of the Wabash, Far Away*

Nickname: Hoosier State

Residents: Indianan, Indianian

Land area: 35,870 square miles (92,904 sq km)

Population (2000): 6,080,485

Home of: The famous car race, the Indianapolis 500

Capital: Indianapolis
Largest city: Indianapolis

IOWA

Origin of name: Probably from an Indian word meaning "this is the place"

Entered union (rank): December 28, 1846 (29)

Motto: Our liberties we prize and our rights we will maintain

Tree: oak

Flower: wild rose

Bird: eastern goldfinch

Other: fossil, crinoid; rock, geode

Song: *Song of Iowa*

Nickname: Hawkeye State

Residents: Iowan

Land area: 55,875 square miles (144,716 sq km)

Population (2000): 2,926,324

Home of: The shortest and steepest railroad in the U.S., in Dubuque, 60° incline, 296 feet

Capital: Des Moines
Largest city: Des Moines

KANSAS

Origin of name: From a Sioux word meaning "people of the south wind"

Entered union (rank): January 29, 1861 (34)

Motto: *Ad astra per aspera*
(To the stars through difficulties)

Tree: cottonwood

Flower: sunflower

Bird: western meadowlark

Other: animal, buffalo; reptile, ornate box turtle

Song: *Home on the Range*

Nicknames: Sunflower State and Jayhawk State

Residents: Kansan

Land area: 81,823 square miles (211,922 sq km)

Population (2000): 2,688,418

Home of: Helium, discovered in 1905 at the University of Kansas

Capital: Topeka
Largest city: Wichita

KENTUCKY

Origin of name: From an Iroquoian word (Kentahten) meaning "land of tomorrow"

Entered union (rank): June 1, 1792 (15)

Motto: United we stand, divided we fall

Tree: tulip poplar

Flower: goldenrod

Bird: Kentucky cardinal

Other: bluegrass song, "Blue Moon of Kentucky"; horse, Thoroughbred

Song: *My Old Kentucky Home*

Nickname: Bluegrass State

Residents: Kentuckian

Land area: 39,732 square miles (102,907 sq km)

Population (2000): 4,041,769

Home of: The largest underground cave in the world, the Mammoth-Flint Cave system, over 300 miles long

Louisville ● ★ Frankfort

Capital: Frankfort
Largest city: Louisville

LOUISIANA

Origin of name: In honor of Louis XIV of France

Entered union (rank): April 30, 1812 (18)

Motto: Union, justice, and confidence

Tree: bald cypress

Flower: magnolia

Bird: eastern brown pelican

Other: crustacean, crawfish; dog, Catahoula leopard hound

Songs: *Give Me Louisiana* and *You Are My Sunshine*

Nickname: Pelican State

Residents: Louisianan, Louisianian

Land area: 43,566 square miles (112,836 sq km)

Population (2000): 4,468,976

Home of: About 98% of the world's crawfish

New Orleans

Baton Rouge ★

Capital: Baton Rouge
Largest city: New Orleans

MAINE

Origin of name: First used to distinguish the mainland from the offshore islands

Entered union (rank): March 15, 1820 (23)

Motto: *Dirigo* (I lead)

Tree: white pine tree

Flower: white pine cone and tassel

Bird: chickadee

Other: animal, moose; cat, Maine coon cat

Song: *State of Maine Song*

Nickname: Pine Tree State

Residents: Mainer

Land area: 30,865 square miles (79,939 sq km)

Population (2000): 1,274,923

Home of: The most easterly point in the U.S., West Quoddy Head

Capital: Augusta
Largest city: Portland

MARYLAND

Origin of name: In honor of Henrietta Maria (queen of Charles I of England)

Entered union (rank): April 28, 1788 (7)

Motto: *Fatti maschii, parole femine* (Manly deeds, womanly words)

Tree: white oak

Flower: black-eyed Susan

Bird: Baltimore oriole

Other: crustacean, Maryland blue crab; sport, jousting

Song: *Maryland! My Maryland!*

Nicknames: Free State and Old Line State

Residents: Marylander

Land area: 9,775 square miles (25,316 sq km)

Population (2000): 5,296,486

Home of: The first umbrella factory in the U.S., opened 1928, in Baltimore

Capital: Annapolis
Largest city: Baltimore

MASSACHUSETTS

Origin of name: From the Massachusett Indian tribe, meaning "at or about the great hill"

Entered union (rank): February 6, 1788 (6)

Motto: *Ense petit placidam sub libertate quietem* (By the sword we seek peace, but peace only under liberty)

Tree: American elm

Flower: mayflower

Bird: chickadee

Other: beverage, cranberry juice; dessert, Boston cream pie

Song: *All Hail to Massachusetts*

Nicknames: Bay State and Old Colony State

Residents: Bay Stater

Land area: 7,838 square miles (20,300 sq km)

Population (2000): 6,349,097

Home of: The first World Series, played between the Boston Pilgrims and the Pittsburgh Pirates in 1903

Boston ✪

Capital: Boston
Largest city: Boston

MICHIGAN

Origin of name: From an Indian word (Michigana) meaning "great or large lake"

Entered union (rank): January 26, 1837 (26)

Motto: *Si quaeris peninsulam amoenam circumspice* (If you seek a pleasant peninsula, look around you)

Tree: white pine

Flower: apple blossom

Bird: robin

Other: reptile, painted turtle; wildflower, Dwarf Lake iris

Song: *Michigan, My Michigan*

Nickname: Wolverine State

Residents: Michigander, Michiganite

Land area: 56,809 square miles (147,135 sq km)

Population (2000): 9,938,444

Home of: Battle Creek, "Cereal City," produces most of the breakfast cereal in the U.S.

Capital: Lansing
Largest city: Detroit

Lansing ✪

Detroit ●

Origin of name: From a Dakota Indian word meaning "sky-tinted water"

Entered union (rank): May 11, 1858 (32)

Motto: *L'Étoile du nord* (The north star)

Tree: red (or Norway) pine

Flower: lady slipper

Bird: common loon

Other: drink, milk; mushroom, morel

Song: *Hail Minnesota*

Nicknames: North Star State, Gopher State and Land of 10,000 Lakes

Residents: Minnesotan

Land area: 79,617 square miles (206,207 sq km)

Population (2000): 4,919,479

Minneapolis
St. Paul

Capital: St. Paul
Largest city: Minneapolis

Home of: The oldest rock in the world, 3.8 billion years old, found in the Minnesota River valley

Origin of name: From an Indian word meaning "great water"

Entered union (rank): December 10, 1817 (20)

Motto: *Virtute et armis* (By valor and arms)

Tree: magnolia

Flower: flower or bloom of the magnolia or evergreen magnolia

Bird: mockingbird

Other: stone, petrified wood; water mammal, bottlenosed dolphin

Song: *Go, Mississippi*

Nickname: Magnolia State

Residents: Mississippian

Land area: 46,914 square miles (121,506 sq km)

Population (2000): 2,844,658

Home of: Coca-Cola, first bottled in 1894 in Vicksburg

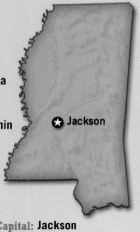

Jackson

Capital: Jackson
Largest city: Jackson

United States

MISSOURI

Origin of name: Named after the Missouri Indian tribe; "Missouri" means "town of the large canoes."

Entered union (rank): August 10, 1821 (24)

Motto: *Salus populi suprema lex esto*
(The welfare of the people shall be the supreme law)

Tree: flowering dogwood

Flower: hawthorn

Bird: bluebird

Other: musical instrument, fiddle; tree nut, eastern black walnut

Song: *Missouri Waltz*

Nickname: Show-Me State

Residents: Missourian

Land area: 68,898 square miles (178,446 sq km)

Population (2000): 5,595,211

Capital: Jefferson City
Largest city: Kansas City

Home of: Mark Twain and some of his characters, such as Tom Sawyer and Huckleberry Finn

MONTANA

Origin of name: The Latin form of a Spanish word meaning "mountainous"

Entered union (rank): November 8, 1889 (41)

Motto: *Oro y plata* (Gold and silver)

Tree: ponderosa pine

Flower: bitterroot

Bird: western meadowlark

Other: animal, grizzly bear; stones, sapphire and agate

Song: *Montana*

Nickname: Treasure State

Residents: Montanan

Land area: 145,556 square miles (376,991 sq km)

Population (2000): 902,195

Capital: Helena
Largest city: Billings

Home of: Grasshopper Glacier, named for the grasshoppers that can still be seen frozen in ice

NEBRASKA

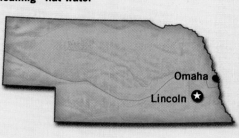

Origin of name: From an Oto Indian word meaning "flat water"

Entered union (rank): March 1, 1867 (37)

Motto: Equality before the law

Tree: cottonwood

Flower: goldenrod

Bird: western meadowlark

Other: ballad, "A Place Like Nebraska"; soft drink, Kool-Aid

Song: *Beautiful Nebraska*

Nicknames: Cornhusker State and Beef State

Residents: Nebraskan

Land area: 76,878 square miles (199,113 sq km)

Population (2000): 1,711,263

Home of: The only roller-skating museum in the world, in Lincoln

Capital: Lincoln
Largest city: Omaha

NEVADA

Origin of name: From the Spanish, "snowcapped"

Entered union (rank): October 31, 1864 (36)

Motto: All for our country

Trees: single-leaf piñon and bristlecone pine

Flower: sagebrush

Bird: mountain bluebird

Other: metal, silver; reptile, desert tortoise

Song: *Home Means Nevada*

Nicknames: Sagebrush State, Silver State and Battle Born State

Residents: Nevadan, Nevadian

Land area: 109,806 square miles (284,397 sq km)

Population (2000): 1,998,257

Home of: The Devils Hole pupfish, found only in Devils Hole, and other rare fish from prehistoric lakes

Capital: Carson City
Largest city: Las Vegas

NEW HAMPSHIRE

Origin of name: **From the English county of Hampshire**

Entered union (rank): **June 21, 1788 (9)**

Motto: **Live free or die**

Tree: **white birch**

Flower: **purple lilac**

Bird: **purple finch**

Other: **amphibian, spotted newt; sport, skiing**

Songs: *Old New Hampshire* and *New Hampshire, My New Hampshire*

Nickname: **Granite State**

Residents: **New Hampshirite**

Land area: **8,969 square miles (23,231 sq km)**

Population (2000): **1,235,786**

Home of: **Artificial rain, first used near Concord in 1947 to fight a forest fire**

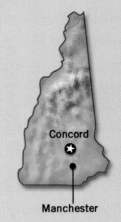

Concord

Manchester

Capital: **Concord**
Largest city: **Manchester**

NEW JERSEY

Origin of name: **From the Channel Isle of Jersey**

Entered union (rank): **December 18, 1787 (3)**

Motto: **Liberty and prosperity**

Tree: **red oak**

Flower: **purple violet**

Bird: **eastern goldfinch**

Other: **folk dance, square dance; shell, knobbed whelk**

Song: *I'm from New Jersey*

Nickname: **Garden State**

Residents: **New Jerseyite, New Jerseyan**

Land area: **7,419 square miles (19,215 sq km)**

Population (2000): **8,414,350**

Home of: **The world's first drive-in movie theater, built in 1933 near Camden**

Newark

Trenton

Capital: **Trenton**
Largest city: **Newark**

NEW MEXICO

Origin of name: **From the country of Mexico**

Entered union (rank): **January 6, 1912 (47)**

Motto: *Crescit eundo* **(It grows as it goes)**

Tree: **piñon**

Flower: **yucca**

Bird: **roadrunner**

Other: **cookie, biscochito; vegetables, chili and frijole**

Song: *O Fair New Mexico*

Nickname: **Land of Enchantment**

Residents: **New Mexican**

Land area: **121,365 square miles (314,334 sq km)**

Population (2000): **1,819,046**

Capital: **Santa Fe**
Largest city: **Albuquerque**

Home of: **Smokey Bear, a cub orphaned by fire in 1950, buried in Smokey Bear Historical State Park in 1976**

NEW YORK

Origin of name: **In honor of the Duke of York**

Entered union (rank): **July 26, 1788 (11)**

Motto: *Excelsior* **(Ever upward)**

Tree: **sugar maple**

Flower: **rose**

Bird: **bluebird**

Other: **animal, beaver; muffin, apple**

Song: *I Love New York*

Nickname: **Empire State**

Residents: **New Yorker**

Land area: **47,224 square miles (122,310 sq km)**

Population (2000): **18,976,457**

Capital: **Albany**
Largest city: **New York**

Home of: **The first presidential inauguration. George Washington took the oath of office in New York City on April 30, 1789.**

NORTH CAROLINA

Origin of name: In honor of Charles I of England

Entered union (rank): November 21, 1789 (12)

Motto: *Esse quam videri* (To be rather than to seem)

Tree: pine

Flower: dogwood

Bird: cardinal

Other: dog, plott hound; historic boat, shad boat

Song: *The Old North State*

Nickname: Tar Heel State

Residents: North Carolinian

Land area: 48,718 square miles (126,180 sq km)

Population (2000): 8,049,313

Capital: Raleigh
Largest city: Charlotte

Home of: Virginia Dare, the first English child born in America, on Roanoke Island in 1587

NORTH DAKOTA

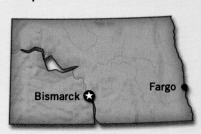

Origin of name: From the Sioux tribe, meaning "allies"

Entered union (rank): November 2, 1889 (39)

Motto: Liberty and union, now and forever: one and inseparable

Tree: American elm

Flower: wild prairie rose

Bird: western meadowlark

Other: equine, Nokota horse; grass, western wheatgrass

Song: *North Dakota Hymn*

Nicknames: Sioux State, Flickertail State, Peace Garden State and Rough Rider State

Residents: North Dakotan

Land area: 70,704 square miles (183,123 sq km)

Population (2000): 642,200

Capital: Bismarck
Largest city: Fargo

Home of: The "World's Largest Buffalo," a 26-foot-high, 46-foot-long, 60-ton concrete monument

OHIO

Origin of name: From an Iroquoian word meaning "great river"

Entered union (rank): March 1, 1803 (17)

Motto: With God all things are possible

Tree: buckeye

Flower: scarlet carnation

Bird: cardinal

Other: beverage, tomato juice; fossil, trilobite

Song: *Beautiful Ohio*

Nickname: Buckeye State

Residents: Ohioan

Land area: 40,953 square miles (106,067 sq km)

Population (2000): 11,353,140

Home of: The first electric traffic lights, invented and installed in Cleveland in 1914

Capital: Columbus
Largest city: Columbus

OKLAHOMA

Origin of name: From two Choctaw Indian words meaning "red people"

Entered union (rank): November 16, 1907 (46)

Motto: *Labor omnia vincit* (Labor conquers all things)

Tree: redbud

Flower: mistletoe

Bird: scissor-tailed flycatcher

Other: furbearer, raccoon; waltz, "Oklahoma Wind"

Song: *Oklahoma*

Nickname: Sooner State

Residents: Oklahoman

Land area: 68,679 square miles (177,877 sq km)

Population (2000): 3,450,654

Home of: The first parking meter, installed in Oklahoma City in 1935

Capital: Oklahoma City
Largest city: Oklahoma City

United States

OREGON

Origin of name: **Unknown**

Entered union (rank): **February 14, 1859 (33)**

Motto: ***Alis volat propriis* (She flies with her own wings)**

Tree: **douglas fir**

Flower: **Oregon grape**

Bird: **western meadowlark**

Other: **fish, Chinook salmon; nut, hazelnut**

Song: ***Oregon, My Oregon***

Nickname: **Beaver State**

Residents: **Oregonian**

Land area: **96,003 square miles (248,647 sq km)**

Population (2000): **3,421,399**

Capital: **Salem**
Largest city: **Portland**

Home of: **The world's smallest park, totaling 452 square inches, created in Portland on St. Patrick's Day in 1948 for leprechauns and snail races**

PENNSYLVANIA

Origin of name: **In honor of Sir William Penn, father of state founder William Penn. It means "Penn's Woodland."**

Entered union (rank): **December 12, 1787 (2)**

Motto: **Virtue, liberty, and independence**

Tree: **hemlock**

Flower: **mountain laurel**

Bird: **ruffed grouse**

Other: **dog, Great Dane; insect, firefly**

Song: ***Pennsylvania***

Nickname: **Keystone State**

Residents: **Pennsylvanian**

Land area: **44,820 square miles (116,083 sq km)**

Population (2000): **12,281,054**

Capital: **Harrisburg**
Largest city: **Philadelphia**

Home of: **The first magazine in America, the *American Magazine*, published in Philadelphia for three months in 1741**

RHODE ISLAND

Origin of name: From the Greek Island of Rhodes

Entered union (rank): May 29, 1790 (13)

Motto: Hope

Tree: red maple

Flower: violet

Bird: Rhode Island Red hen

Other: shell, quahog; stone, cumberlandite

Song: *Rhode Island*

Nickname: Ocean State

Residents: Rhode Islander

Land area: 1,045 square miles (2,706 sq km)

Population (2000): 1,048,319

Home of: Rhode Island Red chickens, first bred in 1854; the start of poultry as a major American industry

Providence

Capital: Providence
Largest city: Providence

SOUTH CAROLINA

Origin of name: In honor of Charles I of England

Entered union (rank): May 23, 1788 (8)

Mottoes: *Animis opibusque parati* (Prepared in mind and resources) and *Dum spiro spero* (While I breathe, I hope)

Tree: palmetto

Flower: yellow jessamine

Bird: Carolina wren

Other: hospitality beverage, tea; music, the spiritual

Song: *Carolina*

Nickname: Palmetto State

Residents: South Carolinian

Land area: 30,111 square miles (77,988 sq km)

Population (2000): 4,012,012

Home of: The first tea farm in the U.S., created in 1890 near Summerville

Columbia

Capital: Columbia
Largest city: Columbia

United States

SOUTH DAKOTA

Origin of name: From the Sioux tribe, meaning "allies"

Entered union (rank): November 2, 1889 (40)

Motto: Under God the people rule

Tree: black hills spruce

Flower: American pasqueflower

Bird: ring-necked pheasant

Other: dessert, kuchen; jewelry, Black Hills gold

Song: *Hail! South Dakota*

Nicknames: Mount Rushmore State and Coyote State

Residents: South Dakotan

Land area: 75,898 square miles (196,575 sq km)

Population (2000): 754,844

Home of: The world's largest natural indoor warm-water pool, Evans' Plunge in Hot Springs

Capital: Pierre
Largest city: Sioux Falls

TENNESSEE

Origin of name: Of Cherokee origin; the exact meaning is unknown

Entered union (rank): June 1, 1796 (16)

Motto: Agriculture and commerce

Tree: tulip poplar

Flower: iris

Bird: mockingbird

Other: amphibian, Tennessee cave salamander; animal, raccoon

Songs: *Tennessee Waltz; My Homeland, Tennessee; When It's Iris Time in Tennessee; My Tennessee; Rocky Top* and *Tennessee*

Nickname: Volunteer State

Residents: Tennessean, Tennesseean

Land area: 41,220 square miles (106,759 sq km)

Population (2000): 5,689,283

Home of: Graceland, the estate and gravesite of Elvis Presley

Capital: Nashville
Largest city: Memphis

TEXAS

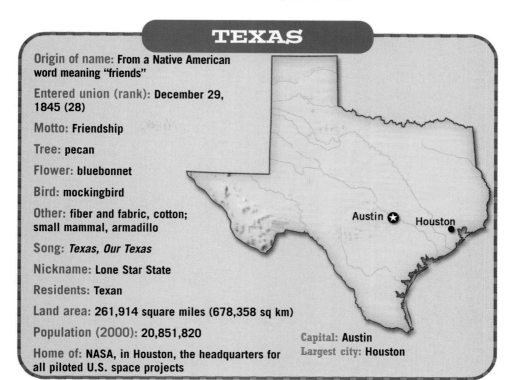

Origin of name: From a Native American word meaning "friends"

Entered union (rank): December 29, 1845 (28)

Motto: Friendship

Tree: pecan

Flower: bluebonnet

Bird: mockingbird

Other: fiber and fabric, cotton; small mammal, armadillo

Song: *Texas, Our Texas*

Nickname: Lone Star State

Residents: Texan

Land area: 261,914 square miles (678,358 sq km)

Population (2000): 20,851,820

Home of: NASA, in Houston, the headquarters for all piloted U.S. space projects

Capital: Austin
Largest city: Houston

Austin · Houston

UTAH

Origin of name: From the Ute tribe, meaning "people of the mountains"

Entered union (rank): January 4, 1896 (45)

Motto: Industry

Tree: blue spruce

Flower: sego lily

Bird: California gull

Other: cooking pot, dutch oven; fruit, cherry

Song: *Utah, We Love Thee*

Nickname: Beehive State

Residents: Utahan, Utahn

Land area: 82,168 square miles (212,816 sq km)

Population (2000): 2,233,169

Home of: Rainbow Bridge, the largest natural stone bridge in the world, 290 feet high, 275 feet across

Capital: Salt Lake City
Largest city: Salt Lake City

Salt Lake City

VERMONT

Origin of name: From the French *vert mont,* meaning "green mountain"

Entered union (rank): March 4, 1791 (14)

Motto: Vermont, freedom and unity

Tree: sugar maple

Flower: red clover

Bird: hermit thrush

Other: animal, Morgan horse; insect, honeybee

Song: *Hail, Vermont!*

Nickname: Green Mountain State

Residents: Vermonter

Land area: 9,249 square miles (23,956 sq km)

Population (2000): 608,827

Home of: The largest production of maple syrup in the U.S.

Capital: Montpelier
Largest city: Burlington

VIRGINIA

Origin of name: In honor of Elizabeth I, "Virgin Queen" of England

Entered union (rank): June 25, 1788 (10)

Motto: *Sic semper tyrannis* (Thus always to tyrants)

Tree: dogwood

Flower: American dogwood

Bird: cardinal

Other: dog, American foxhound; shell, oyster shell

Song: *Carry Me Back to Old Virginia*

Nicknames: The Old Dominion and Mother of Presidents

Residents: Virginian

Land area: 39,598 square miles (102,558 sq km)

Population (2000): 7,078,515

Home of: The only full-length statue of George Washington

Capital: Richmond
Largest city: Virginia Beach

WASHINGTON

Origin of name: In honor of George Washington

Entered union (rank): November 11, 1889 (42)

Motto: *Al-ki* (Indian word meaning "by and by")

Tree: western hemlock

Flower: coast rhododendron

Bird: willow goldfinch

Other: fossil, Columbian mammoth; fruit, apple

Song: *Washington, My Home*

Nickname: Evergreen State

Residents: Washingtonian

Land area: 66,582 square miles (172,447 sq km)

Population (2000): 5,894,121

Home of: The Lunar Rover, the vehicle used by astronauts on the moon. Boeing, in Seattle, makes aircraft and spacecraft.

Seattle
Olympia

Capital: Olympia
Largest city: Seattle

WEST VIRGINIA

Origin of name: In honor of Elizabeth I, "Virgin Queen" of England

Entered union (rank): June 20, 1863 (35)

Motto: *Montani semper liberi* (Mountaineers are always free)

Tree: sugar maple

Flower: rhododendron

Bird: cardinal

Other: animal, black bear; fruit, golden delicious apple

Songs: *West Virginia, My Home Sweet Home, The West Virginia Hills* and *This Is My West Virginia*

Nickname: Mountain State

Residents: West Virginian

Land area: 24,087 square miles (62,384 sq km)

Population (2000): 1,808,344

Home of: Marbles. Most of the country's glass marbles are made around Parkersburg.

Charleston

Capital: Charleston
Largest city: Charleston

United States

WISCONSIN

Origin of name: **French corruption of an Indian word whose meaning is disputed**

Entered union (rank): **May 29, 1848 (30)**

Motto: **Forward**

Tree: **sugar maple**

Flower: **wood violet**

Bird: **robin**

Other: **dance, polka; symbol of peace, mourning dove**

Song: *On Wisconsin*

Nickname: **Badger State**

Residents: **Wisconsinite**

Land area: **54,314 square miles (140,673 sq km)**

Population (2000): **5,363,675**

Home of: **The typewriter, invented in Milwaukee in 1867**

Capital: **Madison**
Largest city: **Milwaukee**

WYOMING

Origin of name: **From a Delaware Indian word, meaning "mountains and valleys alternating"**

Entered union (rank): **July 10, 1890 (44)**

Motto: **Equal rights**

Tree: **cottonwood**

Flower: **Indian paintbrush**

Bird: **meadowlark**

Other: **dinosaur, Triceratops; gemstone, jade**

Song: *Wyoming*

Nickname: **Equality State**

Residents: **Wyomingite**

Land area: **97,105 square miles (251,501 sq km)**

Population (2000): **493,782**

Home of: **The Register of the Desert, a huge granite boulder that covers 27 acres and has 5,000 early pioneer names carved on it**

Capital: **Cheyenne**
Largest city: **Cheyenne**

Sizing Up the States

LARGEST:
Alaska, 570,374 square miles (1,477,267 sq km)

SMALLEST:
Rhode Island, 1,045 square miles (2,706 sq km)

MOST POPULOUS:
California, 33,871,648 residents

LEAST POPULOUS:
Wyoming, 493,782 residents

WASHINGTON, D.C.

The District of Columbia, which covers the same area as the city of Washington, is the capital of the United States. It is located between Virginia and Maryland on the Potomac River. The district is named after Columbus. The Federal Government and tourism are the mainstays of its economy. Many unions as well as business, professional and nonprofit organizations are also headquartered there.

D.C. history began in 1790 when Congress took charge of organizing a new site for the capital. George Washington chose the spot, midway between the northern and southern states on the Potomac River. The seat of government was transferred from Philadelphia, Pennsylvania, to Washington, D.C., on December 1, 1800, and President John Adams became the first resident of the White House.

A petition asking for the district's admission to the Union as the 51st state was filed in Congress on September 9, 1983. The district is continuing this drive for statehood.

Motto: *Justitia omnibus* (Justice to all)

Flower: American beauty rose

Tree: scarlet oak

Land area: 68.25 square miles (177 sq km)

Population (2000): 572,059

The Lincoln Memorial, Washington Monument and Capitol attract millions of visitors each year.

For fun facts and trivia on all the states, go to
go **www.FACT MONSTER.com**

United States

The U.S. Territories

A territory is a region that belongs to the U.S., but which is not one of the 50 states. Although territories govern themselves to a limited extent, they are really governed by the U.S. Territories sometimes become states—Alaska and Hawaii were the last two territories admitted to the Union as states.

The Commonwealth of Puerto Rico

Puerto Rico is located in the Caribbean Sea, about 1,000 miles east-southeast of Miami, Florida. A U.S. possession since 1898, it consists of the island of Puerto Rico plus the adjacent islets of Vieques, Culebra and Mona.

Capital: **San Juan**
Land area: **3,459 square miles (8,959 sq km)**
Population estimate (2000): **3,915,798**
Languages: **Spanish and English**

Guam

Guam, the largest and southernmost island in the Marianas island chain (see "Northern Mariana Islands," right), became a U.S. territory in 1898.

Capital: **Agaña**
Land area: **212 square miles (549 sq km)**
Population estimate (2000): **154,623**
Languages: **English and Chamorro; Japanese is also widely spoken**

The U.S. Virgin Islands

The Virgin Islands consist of nine main islands and some 75 islets. Since 1666, Britain has ruled six of the main islands; the remaining three (St. Croix, St. Thomas and St. John), as well as about 50 of the islets, were acquired by Denmark, and then purchased by the U.S in 1917.

Capital: **Charlotte Amalie (on St. Thomas)**
Land area: **140 square miles (363 sq km):**
St. Croix, 84 square miles (218 sq km);
St. Thomas, 32 square miles (83 sq km);
St. John, 20 square miles (52 sq km)
Population estimate (2000): **120,917**
Languages: **English, but Spanish and French are also spoken**

American Samoa

American Samoa is a group of five volcanic islands and two coral atolls. It is located some 2,600 miles south of Hawaii in the South Pacific. It includes the eastern Samoan islands of Tutuila, Aunu'u and Rose; three islands (Ta'u, Olosega and Ofu) of the Manu'a group; and Swains Island. The territory became part of the U.S. in 1900, except for Swains Island, which was acquired in 1925.

Capital: **Pago Pago**
Land area: **77 square miles (199 sq km)**
Population estimate (2000): **65,446**
Languages: **Samoan (closely related to Hawaiian) and English**

The Commonwealth of the Northern Mariana Islands (CNMI)

The Northern Mariana Islands, east of the Philippines and south of Japan, have been part of the U.S. since 1986. They include the islands of Rota, Saipan, Tinian, Pagan, Guguan, Agrihan and Aguijan.

Capital: **Chalan Kanoa (on Saipan)**
Total area: **184.17 square miles (477 sq km)**
Population estimate (2000): **71,912**
Languages: **English, Chamorro, Carolinian**

The Midway Islands

The Midway Islands lie about 1,150 miles west-northwest of Hawaii. They became part of the U.S. in 1867.

Total area: 2 square miles (5.2 sq km)
Population estimate (1995): no indigenous inhabitants; 453 U.S. military personnel

Wake Island

Wake Island, between Midway and Guam, is an atoll consisting of the three islets of Wilkes, Peale and Wake. It was annexed by Hawaii in 1899.

Total area: 2.5 square miles (6.5 sq km)
Population estimate (1995): no indigenous inhabitants; 302 U.S. military personnel and civilian contractors

Johnston Atoll

Johnston is a coral atoll about 700 miles southwest of Hawaii. It consists of four small islands—Johnston Island, Sand Island, Hikina Island and Akau Island—which lie on a 9-mile-long reef. It was claimed by Hawaii in 1858.

Land area: 1.08 square miles (2.8 sq km)
Population estimate (1997): no indigenous inhabitants; 1,200 U.S. military and civilian personnel

Baker, Howland and Jarvis Islands

These Pacific islands were claimed by the U.S. in 1936. **Baker Island** is an atoll of approximately 1 square mile (2.6 sq km) located about 1,650 miles from Hawaii. **Howland Island,** 36 miles to the northwest, is 1 mile long. Tiny **Jarvis Island** is several hundred miles to the east.

Kingman Reef

Kingman Reef, located about 1,000 miles south of Hawaii, has been a U.S. possession since 1922. Triangular in shape, it is about 9.5 miles long.

Did You Know?

An atoll is a coral island.

Navassa Island

Navassa Island is located in the Caribbean Sea, between Cuba, Haiti and Jamaica. It has an area of 2 square miles (5.2 sq km) and was claimed for the U.S. in 1857.

Palmyra Atoll

Palmyra Atoll has a total area of 4.6 square miles (11.9 sq km) and is located 994 miles (1,600 km) southwest of Honolulu.

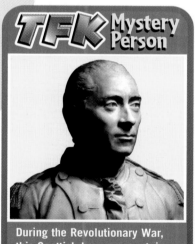

TFK Mystery Person

During the Revolutionary War, this Scottish-born sea captain fought for American independence. The British called him a pirate for taking up arms against his mother country. Americans remember his courage. Rather than surrender, he once said, "I have not yet begun to fight!"

Who is he?

Weather

SEND IN THE CLOUDS

Clouds are little drops of water hanging in the atmosphere. A ceilometer measures the height of clouds.

Cloud	Nickname	Height	Appearance
CIRRUS	Mare's tails	4 miles or more	thin, feathery
CIRROCUMULUS	Mackerel sky	4 miles or more	small patches of white
CIRROSTRATUS	Bedsheet clouds	4 miles	thin, white sheets
STRATUS*	High fogs	0-1 mile	low, gray blanket
CUMULUS	Cauliflowers	¼-4 miles	flat-bottomed, white puffy
CUMULONIMBUS*	Thunderheads	¼-4 miles	mountains of heavy, dark clouds

*Rain or snow clouds

Rain, Snow and Hail

When clouds become heavy with humidity, water falls from them. This is called precipitation. In warmer clouds, precipitation falls as rain. In colder clouds, precipitation falls as snow. Thunderstorm clouds can bring another kind of precipitation—hail. When ice crystals in a cloud get tossed around by strong air currents, and then become stuck together by water that freezes on them, hail forms.

How's the WEATHER?

Temperature

Air temperature is measured by a mercury thermometer. When the temperature rises, the mercury expands and rises in the thermometer tube. When the temperature falls, the mercury contracts and falls.

In the U.S., the **Fahrenheit** scale is used most often. On this scale, 32° is the freezing point of water, and 212° is the boiling point.

The **Celsius**, or centigrade, scale is used by the World Meteorological Organization and most countries in the world. On this scale, 0° is freezing, and 100° is boiling.

> To convert Fahrenheit to Celsius, subtract 32, multiply by 5, and divide the result by 9.
> Example: To convert 50°F to °C: 50 – 32 = 18; 18 x 5 = 90; 90 ÷ 9 = 10

> To convert Celsius to Fahrenheit, multiply by 9, divide by 5, and add 32.
> Example: To convert 10°C to °F: 10 x 9 = 90; 90 ÷ 5 = 18; 18 + 32 = 50

°Celsius	°Fahrenheit
–50	–58
–40	–40
–30	–22
–20	–4
–10	14
0	32
5	41
10	50
15	59
20	68
25	77
30	86
35	95
40	104
45	113
50	122

Air Pressure and Humidity

Air pressure is the weight of the atmosphere pressing down on Earth. It is measured by a barometer in units called millibars. Most barometers use mercury in a glass column, like a thermometer, to measure the change in air pressure.

Air pressure changes with altitude. When you move to a higher place, say a tall mountain, air pressure decreases because there are fewer air molecules as you move higher up.

Relative humidity is the amount of moisture the air can hold before it rains. The most it can hold is 100 percent. Humidity is measured by a psychrometer, which indicates the amount of water in the air at any one temperature.

Yes, Mom, I'm wearing my hat.

go
Convert some temperatures and crunch all kinds of other numbers at
www.timeforkids.com/numbers

THUNDERSTORMS

Nearly 1,800 thunderstorms are happening at any moment around the world. That's 16 million a year!

You can estimate how many miles away a storm is by counting the number of seconds between the flash of lightning and the clap of thunder. Divide the number of seconds by five to get the distance in miles. The lightning is seen before the thunder is heard because light travels faster than sound.

Thunderstorms need three things:
* **Moisture**—to form clouds and rain
* **Unstable Air**—relatively warm air that can rise rapidly
* **Lift**—fronts, sea breezes and mountains that are capable of lifting air to help form thunderstorms

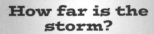

How far is the storm?

Did You Know?

Contrary to popular belief, lightning can strike the same place twice! It has "favorite" sites that it may hit many times during one storm.

LIGHTNING

The action of rising and descending air within a thunderstorm separates positive and negative electric charges. Water and ice particles also affect the distribution of electrical charge. Lightning results from the buildup and discharge of electrical energy between positively and negatively charged areas.

The average flash of lightning could turn on a 100-watt light bulb for more than three months. The air near a lightning strike is hotter than the surface of the sun!

The rapid heating and cooling of air near the lightning channel causes a shock wave that results in thunder.

336

TFK TOP 5

Most Intense Hurricanes in the United States

Name/Location	Year
1. **Florida Keys**	1935
2. **Camille** (Mississippi/Louisiana/Virginia)	1969
3. **Andrew** (Florida/Louisiana)	1992
4. **Florida Keys/Texas**	1919
5. **Lake Okeechobee, Florida**	1928

(Hurricanes were not named before 1953.)
Source: National Oceanic and Atmospheric Administration

Hang on to Your Hat! It's a HURRICANE!

Here comes the wind—at speeds of more than 74 miles per hour. In the U.S., the official hurricane season lasts from June 1 to November 30, but hurricanes can happen at any time of the year.

3 Tropical storms and hurricanes form
If the storm holds together, a column-shaped "eye" forms at its center. Winds spin around it faster and faster. When winds reach 40 miles an hour, the system is a tropical storm. When they reach 74 miles an hour, it's a hurricane!

4 After the storm
Hurricanes weaken after they hit land. Some never reach land but turn northeast and die out over the Atlantic Ocean.

2 Travels across the Atlantic
Some storms remain small. But a few gather warm ocean moisture and speed up as they travel west. When bands of these thunderstorms form a swirl pattern, the system is called a tropical depression.

A HURRICANE'S LIFE

Hurricanes get their start in Africa. The swirling storms are fueled by wet weather, winds and warm ocean water. Start at number one to follow a hurricane's path.

Hurricane

Atlantic Ocean

Storm systems

AFRICA

SAHARA

SAHEL

Pacific Ocean

Winds above the equator
Upper-level and lower-level winds blowing in the same direction help hurricanes gather strength. Winds blowing in different directions or at different speeds can blow the storm apart.

Upper-level wind (7.4 miles above Earth)

Lower-level wind (0.6 miles above Earth)

SOUTH AMERICA

1 Born in West Africa
When hot, dry air from the Sahara desert meets cooler, moist air from the Sahel region to the south, little storms form.

337

IT'S A TWISTER!

A tornado is a dark, funnel-shaped cloud made up of violently churning winds that can reach speeds of up to 300 miles an hour. A tornado can be from a few feet wide to a mile wide, and its track can extend from less than a mile to several hundred miles. Tornadoes generally travel in a northeast direction at speeds ranging from 20 to 60 miles an hour.

Did You Know?

Tornadoes can occur in all U.S. states. But they occur most often in the South and the Midwest. Typically, Texas has the most tornadoes and Alaska has the fewest. From 1950 to 1994, Texas averaged 125 tornadoes per year! During the same period, Alaska averaged just one tornado per year.

For more about all kinds of weather, go to www.FACT MONSTER.com

TFK Puzzles & Games — Through Rain, Sleet or Snow

No matter what the weather's like, you have to get to school! Can you make it through this maze of flip-flops, umbrellas and sunglasses?

EXTREMES of Climate

Highest Recorded Temperatures

Place	Date	°F	°C
World: El Azizia, Libya, Africa	September 13, 1922	136	58
U.S.: Death Valley, California	July 10, 1913	134	57

Lowest Recorded Temperatures

Place	Date	°F	°C
World: Vostok, Antarctica	July 21, 1983	−129	−89
U.S.: Prospect Creek, Alaska	January 23, 1971	−80	−62

Greatest Rainfalls

Place	Date	Inches	Centimeters
1 day, World: Foc-Foc, La Réunion (African island)	January 7-8, 1966	72	182.5
1 day, U.S.: Alvin, Texas	July 25-26, 1979	43	109
1 year, World: Cherrapunji, India	August 1860-August 1861	1,042	2,647
1 year, U.S.: Kukui, Maui, Hawaii	December 1981-December 1982	739	1,878

Snowed In

The town of **Tamarack, California,** had 390 inches (991 cm) of snowfall during the month of January 1911. That's more than 32 feet of snow!

A Change in Weather

On January 22, 1943, in **Spearfish, South Dakota,** the temperature rose 49°F (9.4°C) in two minutes! At 7:30 A.M., the temperature was -4°F. By 7:32 A.M., it had risen to 45°F.

Now That's What They Call a Dry Spell

Arica, Chile, may be the driest place in the world. For more than half a century it averaged 0.03 inches (0.08 cm) of rain each year.

Thwonk!

On September 3, 1970, a record-making hailstone fell in **Coffeyville, Kansas.** It measured 17.5 inches (44.5 cm) around.

TFK Mystery Person

This German physicist dedicated much of his life to designing instruments used to study different aspects of weather. His most famous invention was a mercury thermometer that relied on the measuring scale most often used in the United States today.

Who is he?

Answer Key

ANIMALS
Page 35, The ducks are speaking Japanese and French.
Page 37, Mystery Person: Louis Pasteur

ART
Page 41, You Ought to Be in Plaster!:

Page 41, Mystery Person: Pablo Picasso

BOOKS
Page 43, Harry at Hogwarts: 1) c; 2) c; 3) a; 4) b; 5) a; 6); b
Page 47, Mystery Person: J. R. R. Tolkien

BUILDINGS & LANDMARKS
Page 53, Mystery Person: Emma Lazarus

CALENDARS
Page 57, The Chinese Calendar Fill-in-the-blanks: 1. goat; 2. artistic; 3. monkey
BONUS: The next Year of the Dragon is 2012.
Page 59, Mystery Person: Augustus

COMPUTERS AND THE INTERNET
Page 63, Smiley Faces: 1. Harry Potter; 2. Pac-Man; 3. Marilyn Monroe
Page 63, Mystery Person: Steve Jobs

DANCE
Page 65, Mystery Person: Gregory Hines

DINOSAURS
Page 71, Mystery Person: Woodrow Wilson

DISASTERS
Page 77, Mystery Person: Gale Norton

ENVIRONMENT
Page 83, Mystery Person: Christine Todd Whitman

FASHION
Pages 86-87, Fashionable Trendsetters: 1900s—Camille Clifford (the original "Gibson Girl"); 1930s—Shirley Temple (left); 1940s—The Andrews Sisters; 1950s—Elvis Presley, Lucille Ball; 1960s—The Beatles; 1970s—The Brady Bunch; 1980s—Madonna; 1990s—TLC; 2000s—Alicia Keys
Page 87, Mystery Person: Gabrielle "Coco" Chanel

GEOGRAPHY
Page 93, Animal Safari!: Mount Kenya (Bonus—Leopard)
Page 95, Mystery Person: Christopher Columbus

GOVERNMENT
Page 101, What's My Branch: George W. Bush—Executive; Edward M. Kennedy—Legislative; Nydia Velázquez—Legislative; Richard B. Cheney—Executive; Ruth Bader Ginsburg—Judicial; Colin Powell—Executive
Page 107, Presidential Succession: Elaine Chao (born in China) and Melquiades Martinez (born in Cuba)
Page 107, Mystery Person: Samuel Adams

HEALTH
Page 114, Food Pyramid: egg—protein; hot dog—fat, meat, grain; ice-cream cone—fat, sweets, grain, dairy; French fries—oil and vegetable; peas—vegetable; strawberry—fruit; cheese—dairy; orange juice—fruit
Page 115, Mystery Person: Hippocrates

HISTORY
Page 117, Mystery Person: Julius Caesar

HOLIDAYS
Page 125, Turkey Time:

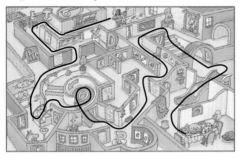

Page 127, Mystery Person: Coretta Scott King

HOMEWORK HELPER
Page 145, Order in the Classroom:

BONUS 12-3=9
Page 147, Mystery Person: Al Gore

INVENTIONS
Page 150, Great Ideas: Granville T. Woods—third rail; Madame C. J. Walker—hair and beauty products; George Washington Carver—peanut butter; Lewis Latimer—improved light bulb; Garrett A. Morgan—automatic traffic signal
Page 153, Mystery Person: Alfred Nobel

LANGUAGE
Page 159, The Analogy Game: 1) fruit; 2) joy; 3) book; 4) furry; 5) fix
Page 159, Mystery Person: Jacob Grimm

MATH
Page 167, Number Stumper: 3 x 3 = 9; 9 + 31 = 40; 40 ÷ 5 = 8; 8 - 7 = 1
Page 171, Mystery Person: Pythagoras

MONEY
Page 176, Money Man Match-Up: 1—Woodrow Wilson; 2—Grover Cleveland; 3—Andrew Jackson; 4—Thomas Jefferson; 5—William McKinley
Page 177, Mystery Person: Susan B. Anthony

MOVIES AND TV
Page 183, Mystery Person: Lucille Ball

MUSIC
Page 186, Play That Funky Music: 1) c; 2) a; 3) b; 4) e; 5) d
Page 187, Mystery Person: Miles Davis

NATIONS
Page 237, Photo File:

Page 237, Mystery Person: Tony Blair

PRESIDENTS
Page 245, Presidential Match-Up: first president—George Washington; youngest man elected president—John F. Kennedy; former Governor of Texas—George W. Bush; President for eight years until 2001—Bill Clinton; issued Emancipation Proclamation to free slaves—Abraham Lincoln
Page 249, Mystery Person: Jimmy Carter

RELIGION
Page 255, Mystery Person: Pope John Paul II

SCIENCE
Page 267, Mystery Person: Rachel Carson

SPACE
Page 273: A 72-pound earthling would weigh 27 pounds on Mars.
Page 275, Name that Neptune: Around launch time
Page 277, Mystery Person: Neil Armstrong

SPORTS
Page 287, Frantic Football:

Page 293, Mystery Person: James Naismith

UNITED STATES
Page 299, Name That State: 1. Minnesota; 2. Oklahoma; 3. Wyoming; 4. Texas; 5. Iowa
Page 333, Mystery Person: John Paul Jones

WEATHER
Page 338, Through Rain, Sleet or Snow:

Page 339, Mystery Person: Daniel Fahrenheit

INNER FRONT COVER
Newsmakers: Hughes, Clones, copy cat, Clinton, Grammys, Concorde, Ice Age, Winter, Transporter, Romeo, Enron, Skittles, Alicia, Squid, Secrets.

T	Y	I	X	E	D	R	O	C	N	O	C
E	R	M	K	H	V	G	W	O	C	K	O
G	R	A	M	M	Y	S	T	B	L	M	P
A	W	Q	N	O	J	N	G	E	O	D	Y
E	S	U	A	S	I	I	N	E	N	I	C
C	E	E	I	L	P	O	M	R	E	U	A
I	L	Y	C	R	T	O	E	W	S	Q	T
O	T	N	I	J	R	T	R	D	W	S	N
P	T	K	L	E	N	Y	H	T	Y	H	O
C	I	W	A	I	H	U	G	H	E	S	R
N	K	W	W	G	V	U	S	M	L	R	N
V	S	E	C	R	E	T	S	J	I	U	E

INNER BACK COVER
Trivia Time!: Across, 1—East Timor; 2—immune; 3—birds; 4—Roman; 5—Constitution; 6—Snicket; 7—Antarctica; 8—fungus.
Down, 1—Ethologist; 2—Independence; 3—New York; 4—Cenozoic; 5—bug; 6—*Titanic*; 7—Abraham; 8—Bonds; 9—brass; 10—Mars.

Index

Index

Index

Index

Credits

All photos clockwise from top left:
COVER: Jane Sanders (illustration); Ron
Austaing—Corbis (owl); Todd Powell
(skateboarder); Corbis (Venus); NASA (Earth);
Dinamation Int'l Corp.—TPC (dinosaur).
Inside Front Cover: Puzzle by R studio T.
Inside Back Cover: Puzzle by R studio T.
Back Cover: Joe Lertola (map); AFP—Corbis
(Mia Hamm); Brad Hamann (diagram); Jane
Sanders (puzzle); Apichart Weerawong—
AP/World Wide Photos (Chinese New Year);
Richard Olsenius/Texas A&M University—
Reuters (copy cat).

Table of Contents: 2: Ted Thai for TFK Almanac.
3: Ted Thai for TFK Almanac; 2001 Estate
Pablo Picasso/ARS NY—Corbis; Thomas
Gorman; Jane Sanders (illustration). **4:**
Courtesy 4th Dimension (3); The Field
Museum. **5:** NASA, Jane Sanders (holiday
illustration); Felipe Galindo (Einstein); Kippa
Matthews for TFK. **6:** Boris Roessler—AP;
Adobe Image Club (drums); Christie's Images—
Corbis; Peter Sibbald—TPC; Jim Cummins—
Corbis Stock Market. **7:** NASA; Stefano
Rellandini—Reuters; Joe Lertola (Texas); Chris
Hackett—Getty Images.
Who's News: 8-9: Thomas E. Franklin/Record—
Corbis Saba (firemen); Joe Tabacca—AP
(policemen); AP (Burnett); Sung Park/Austin
American Statesmen—AP (candlelight vigil);
Terence Beddis—Getty Images (background).
10-11: Steve Herbert/Observer—Getty Images
(soldier); Win McNamee—Reuters (Bush);
Rabin Mcghrabi—AFP (airplanes); Terence
Beddis—Getty Images (background). **12-13:**
Mike Powell—Getty Images/Allsport (speed
skating); Don Emmert—AFP (aerials); Mike
Hewitt—Getty Images/Allsport (bobsledding);
Lionel Cironneau—AP (figure skating). **14:**
Mark Wilson—Getty Images; Hector Mata—AP.
15: Nature Conservancy—AP; Richard
Olsenius/Texas A&M University—Reuters. **16:**
Mbari—Getty Images; Robert Beck—TPC
(O'Neal); Louis Lanzano—AP. **17:** Larry Ryan—
The Daily Tribune; Charles Platiau—Reuters.
18: Jeff Haynes—AP. **19:** Shawn Baldwin—AP.
20-21: Tim Alexander—Priority Records (Lil'
Romeo); Ho—Reuters (2). **22-23:** Ronald
Asadorin—Newscom; Reuters—TPC; Lucasfilm;
Photofest (E.T.); Grant Taylor—Getty Images
(background).
Animals: 24: Peter Charlesworth—Corbis Saba.
25: W. Perry Conway—Corbis (eagle); PD (ant);
Chip Simmons—Getty Images (hippopotamus);
Tom Brakefield—Corbis (Tasmanian devil);

Peter Johnson-Corbis (seal). **26:** Tom
Brakefield—Corbis; Tim Zurowski—Corbis; PD.
27: PD; Yann Arthus-Bertrand—Corbis.
28: G.K. & Vikki Hart—Getty Images; PD; Brian
Enting—Corbis. **29:** Stuart Westmorland—
Corbis; George Grall—Getty Images; Davies &
Starr—Getty Images; PD. **30:** Michael S.
Yamashita—Corbis; PD; Morton Beebe—Corbis;
PD. **31:** PD (ants); W. Perry Conway—Corbis.
32: PD (2); Dan Guravich—Corbis. **33:** Co
Rentmeester—Getty Images; Chris Stephens—
The Plain Dealer/AP. **34:** Jeffrey L. Rotman—
Corbis. **35:** Ted Thai for TFK Almanac; PD (2).
36: PD (lady bugs); Dan Bacon. **37:** PD (ants);
Ted Thai for TFK Almanac; Hulton Deutsch—
Corbis (Pasteur).
Art: 38: Ted Thai for TFK Almanac. **39:** Elio
Ciol—Corbis; ©2001 Estate Pablo
Picasso/ARS, NY/Corbis; Reuters NewMedia
Inc./Corbis; Geoffrey Clements—Corbis (art by
Grandma Moses). **40:** Christie's Images—Corbis
(2); Geoffrey Clements—Corbis; Francis G.
Mayer—Corbis; Archivo Iconografico/S.A.—
Corbis. **41:** Steve Skelton for TIME For Kids
(puzzle); Francis G. Mayers—Corbis;
Bettmann/Corbis (Picasso).
Books: 42: Jan Sanders (illustration); Ted Thai
for TFK Almanac. **43:** Juan Garcia. **44:** Cedar
Creek Images (Wiesner); Ted Thai for TFK
Almanac. **45:** Thomas Gorman. **46:** Jeff
Geissler—AP (Snicket). **47:** Simon Sykes—
Camera Press/Retna (Rowling); AFP (Tolkien).
Buildings & Landmarks: 48: Jacques Boissinot—
AP. **49:** Kaku Kurita—Getty Images; Larry
Lee—Corbis. **50:** The Purcell Team—Corbis;
John Heseltine—Corbis. **51:** Dallas & John
Heaton—Corbis; John Slater—Corbis; Roger
Ressmeyer—Corbis; Vladimir Pcholkin—Getty
Images (Stonehenge). **52:** Bettmann/Corbis. **53:**
Ted Thai for TFK Almanac; Bill Ross—Corbis
(Statue of Liberty); Henry Groskinsky—TPC
(Twin Towers); Bettmann/Corbis (Lazarus).
Calendars: 54, 55: Donna Disario—Corbis Stock
Market (trees); Ted Thai for TFK Almanac. **57:**
Jen Kraemer—Smith; Andy Caulfield—Image
Bank (birthstones). **58:** Encarnacion Lopez
(zodiac chart); Ted Thai for TFK Almanac. **59:**
Bettmann/Corbis (Augustus); EIT
Consortium/NASA (sun); Antonio Cidadao
(moon); NASA (Mars, Mercury, Venus);
JPL/NASA (Jupiter, Saturn).
Computers & the Internet: 60: Courtesy
AtariHistory.com; David Hardison (Activision
Pitfall); Courtesy Sony Computer Entertainment
of America (PlayStation 2); Nintendo of America
(Nintendo Game Boy Advance screen). **61:**
Felipe Galindo (2 illustrations); Ted Thai for
TFK Almanac. **62:** Jane Sanders (illustrations).
63: George Lange—TPC (Jobs).
Dance: 64: Bettmann/Corbis (dance steps);
Kent Barker—Image Bank; Chris Callis—
Courtesy Merce Cunningham Dance Co.
65: Pablo Corral—Corbis; Kevork Djansezian—
AP/Wide World Photos; Bettmann/Corbis;
Martha Swope—TPC (Hines).

Inc.—Corbis (Keys); Courtesy Ricky Martin. **186:** Adobe Image Club (6); Lynn Goldsmith—Corbis (2). **187:** Courtesy Rock and Roll Hall of Fame (3); Mosaic Images—Corbis (Davis).
Nations: 188: Charles Dharapak—Newscom. **189:** Joseph Sohm/Chromosohm—Corbis; Ted Thai for TFK Almanac; NASA (Earth). **222-236:** Joe Lertola (maps). **237:** Reuters New Media Inc.—Corbis (Blair); Felipe Galindo (puzzle).
Presidents: 238: Christie's Images—Corbis (Washington); John Trumbull/NPG/SI (Adams); Mather Brown/NPG/SI beq. of Charles Francis Adams (Jefferson); Chester Harding/NPG/SI (Madison); John Vanderlyn/NPG/SI (Monroe). **239:** George Caleb Bingham/NPG/SI (Adams); Ralph Eleaser Whiteside Earl/NPG/SI gift of Andrew W. Mellon (Jackson); Mathew B. Brady/NPG/SI (Van Buren); Albert Gallatin Hoit/NPG/SI (Harrison); LOC (Tyler); Max Westfield/NPG/SI (Polk). **240:** James Reid Lambdin/ NPG/SI gift of Barry Bingham Sr. (Taylor); NPG/SI (Fillmore); George Peter Healy/NPG/SI gift of Andrew W. Mellon (Pierce); George Peter Healy/NPG/SI gift of Andrew W. Mellon (Buchanan); William Judkins Thomson); George Peter Healy/NPG/SI (Lincoln); Washington Bogart Cooper/NPG/SI. **241:** Thomas Le Clear/NPG/SI gift of Mrs. Grant (Grant); Bettmann/Corbis (Hayes); Ole Peter Hansen Balling/NPG/SI gift of IBM; Ole Peter Hansen Balling/NPG/SI gift of Mrs. H.N. Blue; Anders Zorn/NPG/SI (Cleveland); LOC (Harrison). **242:** LOC (Cleveland); Adolfo Muller-Ury/NPG/SI (McKinley); Adrian Lamb/NPG/SI gift of T.R. Assoc. (Roosevelt); William Valentine Schevill/NPG/SI gift of W.E. Schevill (Taft); Edmund Tarbell/ NPG/SI (Wilson); Margaret Lindsay Williams/NPG/SI (Harding). **243:** Joseph E. Burgess/NPG/SI gift of Phi Gamma Delta (Coolidge); Douglas Chandor/NPG/SI (Hoover); Oscar White—Corbis (FDR); Greta Kempton/NPG/SI (Truman); Thomas Edgar Stephens/NPG/SI gift of Ailsa Mellon Bruce (Eisenhower); JFK Presidential Library (Kennedy). **244:** Peter Hurd/NPG/SI gift of the artist (Johnson); Norman Rockwell/NPG/SI gift of Nixon Foundation (Nixon); Everett R. Kinstler/NPG/SI gift of Ford Foundation (Ford); Jimmy Carter Presidential Library (Carter); Ronald Reagan Presidential Library (Reagan); Ronald N. Sherr/NPG/SI gift of Mr. & Mrs. R.E. Krueger (Bush). **245:** Bettmann/Corbis (Clinton); Eric Draper—White House (G.W. Bush). **246-247:** Steven Widoff. **248:** Dallas & John Heaton—Corbis; Felipe Galindo. **249:** Paul Morse—White House/AP/Wide World Photos; LOC; Rockwood Photo Collection— LOC; JFK Presidential Library; Diane Walker—TPC (Carter); Vermont Historical Society—AP/Wide World Photos.
Religion: 250: Bazuki Muhammad—Reuters. **251:** Peter Sibbald—TPC; Nathan Benn—Corbis; Mahfouz Abu Turk—TPC. **252, 253:** Nathan Benn—Corbis; Werner H. Miller—Corbis; Michael S. Yamashita—Corbis; Luca I. Tettoni—Corbis (2). **254:** Charles E. Rotkin—Corbis. **255:** Reuters Photo Archive.
Safety: 256: Jim Cummins—Corbis Stock Market; Ted Thai for TFK Almanac; Jacob Taposchaner—Getty Images (swimmer). **257:** Scott T. Baxter—Getty Images.

Science: 258: Tony Wharton; Frank Lane Picture Agency—Corbis; Bettmann/Corbis. **259:** NASA; Corbis; Felipe Galindo (alien germs). **261:** Ted Thai for TFK Almanac. **264:** Sean M. Dessureau—Information Please (photosynthesis); Ted Thai for TFK Almanac; Ron Watts—Corbis. **265:** Darrell Gulin—Corbis (granite); Adam Woolfitt—Corbis (limestone); Joseph Sohm/Chromosohm Inc.—Corbis (slate); Ted Thai for TFK Almanac. **267:** Bettmann/Corbis.
Space: 268: NASA. **269:** NASA; Antonio Cidadao (Moon). **270-271:** NASA (Mercury, Venus, Earth); Ted Thai for TFK Almanac; NASA (Mars); Univ. of Arizona/JPL/NASA (Jupiter); Reta Beebe, D. Gilmore, L. Bergeron and NASA (Saturn). **272:** JPL/NASA (Uranus); NASA (Neptune); Dr. Albrecht, ESA/ESO/NASA (Pluto). **273:** Ted Thai for TFK Almanac; NASA (Earth). **274-275:** Encarnacion Lopez; Jim Steck for TFK. **276:** NASA; Rykoff Collection—Corbis; Roger Ressmeyer—Corbis. **277:** Bettmann/Corbis (Newton); Corbis (2).
Sports: 278: Rich Pilling—Major League Baseball Photos; Don Smith—Major League Baseball Photos. **279:** Ted Thai for TFK Almanac; PD (baseballs); John Mabanglo (Bonds); Bettmann/Corbis (Robinson). **280:** AFP—Corbis (O'Neal); Reuters New Media Inc.—Corbis (Jordan); Chris Pizzello—AP World Wide Photos. **281:** Reuters New Media Inc.—Corbis (2). **282:** PD; Bill Vaughan/Icon SMI—Newscom (Blue Devil); Don. J. Belisle/Icon SMI—Newscom (Buckeye); Tony Donaldson/Icon SMI—Newscom. **283:** PD; Mike Blake—Newscom; Jeff Christensen—Newscom (Crouch); Jane Sanders (illustration). **284:** PD (3); Bettmann/Corbis. **285:** Peter Cosgrove—AP Wide World Photos; PD (golf ball); Ted Thai for TFK Almanac. **286:** Reuters New Media Inc.—Corbis (2). **287:** AFP—Corbis; Steve Skelton (puzzle). **288:** Chris Cole—Corbis; Stefano Rellandini—Reuters. **289:** AFP—Corbis; Ted Thai for TFK Almanac. **290:** PD; John Bazemore—AP. **291:** PD; AFP/Corbis. **292:** Reuters New Media—Corbis. **293:** U.S. Postal Service—AP World Wide Photos; Corbis/Bettmann.
U.S.: 294: Joe Lertola. **295:** Corbis (seal), Felipe Galindo. **297:** Jeff Greenberg—Photoedit. **298:** Ted Thai TFK Almanac. **299:** Felipe Galindo. **300:** Courtesy National Park Service. **301:** Courtesy National Park Service. **302:** Bill Ross—Corbis (Times Square); Ted Thai for TFK Almanac; Jane Sanders (illustration). **303:** Felipe Galindo (4); Peter Johnson—Corbis (duck). **304—330:** Joe Lertola. **331:** Joe Lertola; Andy Caufield—Image Bank (DC). **333:** Ted Thai for TFK Almanac; Burstein Collection/Corbis—TPC (Jones).
Weather: 334: Scott T. Smith—Corbis; Tom Bean—Corbis; Bryan Pickering—Eye Ubiquitous—Corbis; Richard Hamilton Smith—Corbis; Macduff Everton—Corbis; Larry Lee—Corbis; Chris Hackett—Getty Images (umbrella). **335:** Ted Thai for TFK Almanac. **336:** Ted Thai for TFK Almanac (2); William James Warren—Corbis. **337:** Dave Martin—AP/Wide World Photos; Joe Lertola. **338:** Jim Zuckerman—Corbis; Ted Thai for TFK Almanac; Jane Sanders (puzzle). **339:** Ted Thai for TFK Almanac; Brad Hamann (Fahrenheit).